CURRENT LAW AND SOCIAL PROBLEMS

Volume II

CURRENT LAW AND SOCIAL PROBLEMS

The Universe is change
Our life is what our thoughts make it

Volume II

Editor:
R. ST. J. MACDONALD

The University of Western Ontario
Faculty of Law

Published by
University of Toronto Press

Contents

CURRENT LAW AND SOCIAL PROBLEMS

Volume II

Mental Incapacity in Criminal Law

By HELEN SILVING*

NOT TOO LONG AGO the belief prevailed that insanity was a divine punishment for more or less identifiable sin.[1] Such a belief clearly did not justify exemptions from punishment for crimes committed by mentally ill persons. With the progress of science, this belief was replaced by recognition of the fact that insanity is a scientifically cognizable phenomenon, mental disease. But the metaphysics of insanity was not simultaneously overcome. Mental disease, while no longer theologically or magically tainted, was still conceived of as an absolute ontological entity, only now possessing the immanent quality of exempting from state authority and legal punishment. In this view, mental disease must exempt from responsibility as if by force of its very nature. Legal rules do not possess the power to affect this natural law exemption.

The modern revolution in science, marked by Einsteinian physics, the economics of marginal utility, Freudian psychology, and Kelsenian jurisprudence, originated a new philosophy of science. This philosophy sheds doubt on the old ontology of mental disease and of the mental incapacity exemption. The world of fixed things and exclusively conscious static psychological realities collapsed. The universe was de-substantialized. Physical things were shown to be constructs formed from phenomena observed from various physical standpoints; economic value was recognized to be the constructive

*Helen Silving, Jur.D., Pol.Sc.D., LL.B., Professor of Law, University of Puerto Rico; Adviser to the Legislative Penal Reform Commission of the Commonwealth of Puerto Rico. This is an enlarged text of a lecture delivered in the Criminal Law Week of the Law Faculty of the University of Puerto Rico on Friday, June 23, 1961. The views expressed in this article are exclusively those of the author. They do not reflect the opinions of the Penal Reform Commission, or of any Department of the Government of the Commonwealth.

[1]For remnants of this view see *State* v. *Harrison* (1892), 36 W. Va. 729, 15 S.E. 982, 18 L.R.A. 224, on origins of melancholia.

result of various market valuations; mental life was shown to be a dynamic process, integrating immediately experienced phenomena of the Conscious and indirectly experienced or reflected phenomena of the constructive Unconscious. Similarly, Kelsenian thought questioned the metaphysics of traditional legal concepts. Kelsen taught that the key concepts in law do not denote pre-existing realities of nature but rather symbolize functional constructs, which are creatures of law. Thus crime and responsibility, guilt and innocence, ceased to be given "natural" theological realities and became constructive results of legal imputation or its negation. Guilt in this new light is imputed to man, ascribed to him by law; it is not inherent in him or in his conduct. Guiltlessness or exemption does not mean natural innocence or virtue but is denial of imputation. Obviously the question arose: why in certain situations do we impute guilt to a man and why do we in other situations deny guilt or exempt? Thus there was reached the Copernican turn in criminal law thought: that ascription or non-ascription of guilt, constituting the concepts of crime and responsibility, and of denial of crime and exemption from responsibility, is not derived from immanent ontological states of pre-existing natural crime and immanent responsibility or their absence, but from policy considerations, on the basis of which law does or does not ascribe guilt.

A change parallel to that which occurred in the sciences, from an ontological to a functional constructive approach is noticeable in the philosophy of language. Originally, name-giving was the discovery of the nature of things. There comes to mind the biblical statement that God brought all things to Adam "to see what he would call them; and whatsoever Adam called every . . . creature, that *was* the name thereof."[2] The name *was* the thing; it reflected its nature and reality and lived in it. Naming or defining, was an act of cognitive and logical necessity. In this truly biblical sense, the name "mental disease" was, until quite recently, considered to represent an ontologically given state of mind, to be discovered simply by medical observation. Is dipsomania a mental disease? Whether it is or not was thought to be quite independent of

[2]Gen. 2:19.

medical judgment recognizing or not recognizing it as such. There was thought to be no element of arbitrariness in including it in, or excluding it from, the definition of mental disease. Doctors could "discover," as one discovers an oil-well, by observing the phenomenon dipsomania, whether it is or is not a mental disease. The law, of course, had no part in such inclusion or exclusion.

In the light of the modern philosophy of language, names or definitions are not immanent qualities of things but conventions. We agree to give to certain phenomena certain names, and we do so for a purpose, namely, that of communicating conveniently. We may very well call certain phenomena by a certain name for one purpose but not for another purpose. In the sciences we give names to phenomena for the special purpose of communication among men of a particular science. There is, of course, a policy in combining a number of phenomena under one name within a science: to enable men of that science to exchange meaningful information and instruction—meaningful in the sense of denoting features that are relevant from the standpoint of that science and enabling the dispensation of relevant professional judgments. Thus in psychiatry a doctor may tell another doctor that a patient is a schizophrenic, and by this means he tells his colleague that this patient is classifiable within a given psychiatric category and should be treated in a certain way. Doctors do not as a rule use the term "mental disease," but in the rare instances in which they do, they merely mean to tell each other that persons described by that term are in need of psychiatric treatment or hospitalization. What significance does a medical communication of this type have in the area of criminal law? *Prima facie*, none whatever. Lawyers are not parties to the communication convention of doctors. To us this communicative scheme of doctors is as Chinese is to people who do not speak Chinese. Our policy is distinctive; our frames of reference and standards of relevance are different, and it is to legal policy, legal frames of reference, and legal standards of relevance that our means of communication, our language, and our names and definitions are geared.

Of course, law is a more "social" discipline than is medicine. It must communicate meaning not only within the circle of lawyers but also to laymen. Moreover, it must consider knowledge afforded by the sciences, particularly by psychology and psychiatry. To be able meaningfully to address itself to men, law must take into account the ways in which the human mind operates. To pierce the veil of psychological and psychiatric knowledge, it is imperative for lawyers to establish some means of communicating with psychiatrists and psychologists. This can be done in one of two ways: either by creating a special language of forensic psychology and psychiatry, based upon conventions between lawyers and psychiatrists, or by law's adopting psychological and psychiatric terminology of widest and least controversial use, provided that that which such terminology stands for is found to be legally relevant. However, it is important to stress—since this has often been misunderstood—that the difficulty of communicating between law and psychiatry lies not in the fact that psychiatrists disagree with each other or frequently reverse themselves—lawyers do that also—but in the fact that they do so on legally irrelevant grounds[3] or on grounds whose relevance to law has not been demonstrated.[4]

The ontological approach to language is being successfully overcome in the area of legal language generally. Thus, we have witnessed the failure of the one-time belief that the nature of an

[3]See, e.g., Judge Burger's opinion (concurring in result only) in *Blocker* v. *United States* (1961), 288 F.2d 853, 857, at pp. 860–1 (App. D.C.).

[4]Dr. Philip Q. Roche, *The Criminal Mind* (Isaac Ray Award Book, 1958), p. 15, suggests: "If lawyers and psychiatrists will agree to regard 'mental illness' and 'insanity' less as they are verbally defined and more as what we do to people to whom we attach such terms, we will be nearer the sharing of behavioral reality not only that of others but of ourselves." For this Dr. Roche cites Bridgman's statement, "The true meaning of a term is to be found by observing what a man *does* with it, not by what he *says* about it." There are two difficulties which render this suggestion impracticable in the field of law–psychiatry intercommunication. Observations of psychiatrists' "doing" can be useful in law only if such observations can be conceptualized and verbalized, for law must generalize and must express its generalizations. Bridgman's suggestion admits verbalization of observations regarding what is done. If what the psychiatrists are doing is susceptible of verbalization, there should be no problem, for it would hardly matter whether the verbalization is done by psychiatrists or by lawyers. But the fact is that psychiatrists claim that such verbalization is often impossible. Secondly, psychiatrists' "doing" presents a distinctive problem. In contrast to physicists, psychiatrists operate predominantly verbally; they communicate with patients linguistically, but the language of this communication is distinctive and not communicable to persons not possessing an intricate knowledge of psychiatry.

issue as being one of law or fact is an immanent quality of such issue, so that the question of whether an issue X presents a question of fact or a question of law, may be resolved simply by observation of X and itself answered as a question of fact. The distinction between law and fact has now been shown to be relative and functional, and the question whether issue X presents a question of fact or a question of law is today known to be a question of law and not a question of fact. Yet the old metaphysical view of fact or question of fact is maintained tenaciously in the area of exemption for mental incapacity. The inconsistency of this view with the now generally prevailing jurisprudence of law and fact calls for a closer examination of certain assertions, such as, whether psychopathy is a "mental disease" is a "question of fact," which the jury must answer.

If we want to build a rational structure of criminal law we must start with fundamentals. In order to formulate a sound exemption for mental incapacity we must view the task before us as posing this basic question: what is the purpose of the exemption? An exemption is assumed to be an exception from responsibility for the commission of crime which normally takes the form of punishment. An inquiry into the purpose of the exemption must hence proceed from a notion of the nature and function of that from which the exemption is to be granted, namely, punishment. We must ascertain the purpose of punishment and then seek the conditions in which that purpose is inapplicable. The quality or condition that is incompatible with the policy objective of punishment should afford a definition of the exemption. The problem of exemption ought to be cast in terms of the questions: what is the meaning and function of that from which we exempt? and, what quality is it that does not respond to this meaning and function? rather than in terms of an *a priori* notion that mental disease possesses an inherently exempting power, the sole problem being to discover the exact meaning of such disease.

Today, the meaning and function of punishment ought to be considered in conjunction with another type of state intervention in criminal law, namely, the measure. The division into punishment, on the one hand, and "measures of security and cure," on the other, corresponds to the duality of purpose pursued by criminal law: the punitive or retributive end and the protective and curative end. An exemption from punishment, accordingly, does not mean exemption from all state intervention; a person who, because of his mental state, is found to be exempt from punishment, may very well be subject to the second type of sanction, the measure. However, in this paper I shall deal only with exemption from the punitive scheme. The discussion of measures to be applied within the protective scheme to persons exempt from punishment by reason of mental incapacity I shall take up in another publication. In this paper I shall discuss the purpose of punishment and the area to which it is inapplicable; critically review the available tests of exemption; and present a new test of the mental incapacity exemption.

I. THE PURPOSE OF PUNISHMENT AND THE AREA TO WHICH IT IS INAPPLICABLE

IT WOULD far exceed the scope of this paper were I to undertake an exhaustive study of the various views on the policy or function of punishment expressed throughout history. Moses, Mordecai, Christ and Mohamed, Confucius and Buddha, Plato, Aristotle, Draco, Solon, Cicero, St. Augustine and St. Thomas, Pufendorf and Spinoza, Bentham, Beccaria, Montesquieu and Rousseau, Kant, Hegel and Fichte, Hobbes and Feuerbach, to mention but a few of those whose thought has shaped notions of legal morality, would have to be consulted. I shall select four views that seem to me to be particularly pertinent to a contemporary discussion, since they fit into the schemes of ideas expressed in laws which are now in force, and in drafts and reform projects of civil and common law countries. The first view is that punishment is a response to guilt or culpability; the second is that it is a functional means of deterrence; the third is that it is a reformation device; and the fourth is that it is a social-political means of asserting and maintaining legal prohibitions of relative gravity.[5] If we assume the first view to be correct—this, in fact, is the view most frequently encountered in our decisional law—we ought to conclude that a person must not be punished if he is not guilty; if we accept the second view, we should decide that a person must not be punished unless he is deterrable or unless other persons can be deterred by his being punished; if we assume the third view to be correct, it follows that a person who is not reformable ought not to be punished; and if the fourth view is taken to apply, the inference is that a person must not be punished if this does not serve law's assertion. In this scheme the definition of incapacity appears to be determined by the policy of punishment. Assumption of a converse relationship also implies a policy disposition, but the true policy considerations motivating such disposition may not be conscious.

As the above mentioned meanings and purposes of punishment often overlap, so do the views on incapacity. Nor are these purposes necessarily exclusive of each other; rather, they may be combined in various schemes. Indeed, it is possible to derive partial solutions to the problem of incapacity from each of these purposes, provided that we assume them to be valid at least in certain areas. When punishment is assumed to serve more than one purpose, caution should be exercised to avoid confusion of the several purposes and particularly indiscriminate or unconscious substitution of one purpose for another. For this reason each potential purpose should be viewed in isolation. This method of analysis also helps clear elaboration of the distinctive significance of each such purpose for the formulation of exemption on the ground of incapacity.

A. *Guilt as Directive in Punishment: Mental Incapacity Exemption Conceived as a Quality Excluding Guilt*

Guilt is one of the most elusive concepts in ethics, religion, and law. In Anglo-American law, there has recently been little concern with the meaning of guilt or culpability. As may be seen from the manner in which the term culpability has been used in the Ameri-

[5]For a more elaborate treatment of this position of the writer see Helen Silving, " 'Rule of Law' in Criminal Justice," in G. O. W. Mueller (ed.), *Essays in Criminal Science* (1961), p. 77, at pp. 85–9.

can Law Institute's Model Penal Code,[6] it is taken to mean interchangeably two things: (i) the mental element in crime: intent, recklessness, or negligence; (ii) a type of blameworthiness, at times identified with the attribution of responsibility for failing to observe a proper standard of conduct,[7] at other times taken to refer to social censure generally. By contrast, in civil law countries the meaning and function of guilt has been the subject of vigorous controversy and voluminous legal literature.[8] But the theory that may provide the most valuable contribution to clarification of the issue is of pre-war vintage: the phenomenological theory of guilt. In the following paragraphs I shall discuss (1) guilt as identified with intent; (2) guilt conceived of as blameworthiness; (3) guilt in the light of phenomenological thought; (4) guilt as interpreted by the present writer.

(1) GUILT AS INTENT

If we proceed from the concept of guilt or culpability in its widest sense, as accepted by usage, its simple equation with, for example, intent is questionable, provided that by "intent" we mean a descriptive category and not, as is often implied, a sort of objective culpability, such as the attribution of intent notwithstanding the absence of knowledge of what one ought to know, on the basis of other men's knowledge. For guilt is a normative concept, invoking the idea that the conduct of which one is said to be guilty is bad. Even if we prefer to discourse in the descriptive psychologizing fashion of the philosophical positivistic method, in which values are con-

[6]American Law Institute Model Penal Code, Tentative Draft No. 4 (1955), §2.02, entitled "General Requirements of Culpability," deals with the mental element, labelling it as "minimum requirements of culpability" (§2.02(1)). In subdivision (2)(c) of the same section, the risk which it is "reckless" to take is qualified as one of such nature and degree that "its disregard involves culpability of high degree." In subdivision (2) (*d*), "negligently" is circumscribed in terms of "substantial culpability."

[7]Alternatives to "culpability" qualifications in the definitions of "recklessness" and "negligence" (see *ibid.*) are: "its disregard involves a gross deviation from proper standards of conduct" (s. 2.02 (2)(c)); substantial deviation from the standard of care that would be exercised by a reasonable man in his situation" (s. 2.02 (2)(*d*)).

[8]On some aspects of this controversey see Paul K. Ryu and Helen Silving, "Error Juris: A Comparative Study" (1957), 24 *U. Chi. L. Rev.* 421, at pp. 440–58.

sidered in terms of factual reactions to concepts viewed as values, that is, in terms of the beliefs or feelings which people entertain that things are good or bad, we must still concede the good or bad to be distinctive reaction contents, namely, normative contents. Hence, guilt cannot be simply defined as intent or negligence *per se*. Some link is missing that would indicate that to have a certain type of intent is or is felt to be bad. Thus guilt must be assumed to imply at least some element or qualification other than intent.

When we apply the doctrine which equiparates guilt with intent to the area of exemption, the need for a qualification becomes obvious. A person suffering from melancholia or from paranoia undoubtedly intends to commit the acts he in fact commits.[9] As Roche points out, "mental illness does not abolish intent but *releases it*."[10] Indeed, the intent of a mentally ill person is usually more intensive than that of a healthy one. Yet, according to the overwhelming weight of opinion, a person suffering from melancholia or from paranoia ought to be exempt from punishment. Scholars in common and civil law countries alike have suggested that to intend must mean to intend rationally or to intend with rational motivation, and that to know must mean to know with feeling or to know profoundly and not merely on a verbal level.[11] But, strangely enough, neither rational motivation nor profound knowledge is required in cases where mental incapacity is not in issue. This means that if we are to follow these suggestions, we must assume that a normal individual may very well be guilty if he intends irrationally or knows superficially, but that an individual suffering from mental incapacity is exempted when his knowledge or intention is so characterized. This brings us back to the initial question of what constitutes the mental incapacity that produces this effect.[12]

[9]See Royal Commission on Capital Punishment, 1949–53, *Report* 1953 (Cmd. 8932), p. 110 (hereinafter cited as *Royal Comm. Report*).

[10]*Supra* note 4, at p. 88.

[11]See Jerome Hall, "Psychiatry and Criminal Responsibility" (1956), 65 *Yale L.J.* 761, 774–5; Ernst Seelig, "Zum Problem der Neufassung des § 51," in *Festschrift für Edmund Mezger* (1954), p. 213, at pp. 223–6.

[12]If we prefer to put the issue in terms of "intent," then the question is: at what degree of loss of "ego control" is a person to be deemed no longer free enough to have a "*relevant* intent"? This raises the problem of "freedom" as formulated by Rheinhard Frank.

Although no one today believes that mental illness necessarily excludes intent, the pertinent exemption is often referred to as mental incapacity to commit crime, as though the disease necessarily removed the mental element of crime. Nor is this but an anachronistic manner of speech. Mr. Justice Frankfurter, for example, has expressed the view that, since proof of the accused's insanity is equivalent to proof that "he had not the mind capable of committing murder," to impose upon him the burden of proving insanity beyond a reasonable doubt is inconsistent with the constitutional requirement that the prosecution must prove the mental element of intent, premeditation, and deliberation as part of guilt.[13] In what sense is a mentally ill person incapable of committing a crime? Since he is often capable of forming an actual psychological intent as well as of deliberating and premeditating, obviously "incapacity to form an intent" implies something other than actual inability to form the psychological state of mind which is usually assumed to constitute the mental element in crime. That qualifying factor, which renders the conduct and the mental state of the mentally ill person, as distinguished from similar conduct and mental state of a healthy one, not guilty is the object of our search.

Since the notion of the mental element, as understood today, cannot provide the answer to our query for the proper test of the so-called mental incapacity exemption, we must look to other potential solutions. We may recall that traditional law refers to intent as malice, wicked will or vicious will, or evil intent. This implies a type of qualification such as has been suggested already, namely, a normative one. The quality that precludes guilt is one which renders the conduct of the person concerned not blameworthy. Thus the doctrine which defines guilt as the psychological factor in crime—a doctrine that might be expected to yield an answer to the question of what psychological qualities should exempt from punishment—does not afford a solution. We must still inquire wherein exactly lies the element of blameworthiness in guilt.

[13]See Mr. Justice Frankfurter's dissent in *Leland* v. *Oregon* (1952), 343 U.S. 790 (holding Oregon's requirement that the accused prove insanity beyond a reasonable doubt constitutional, the Supreme Court majority finding that the prosecution's burden of proving all elements of crime, including wherever pertinent "purpose and malice, premeditation and deliberation," satisfies the requirement that the prosecution prove "guilt"), at p. 802.

(2) GUILT AS BLAMEWORTHINESS

Assuming guilt to include or, indeed, to be blameworthiness, the problem is to determine the standard of the judgment of blame. It may be religious, ethical, or social-political. In a legal system which adopts the principle of separation of church and state, a religious standard is excluded except where it assumes the guise of a general cultural or community standard. In the last analysis, the same is true of a secular ethical standard. In common law countries the relevant standard is usually assumed to be a social one, since even those who insist that it must be moral actually think of morality as a system of moral norms that are culturally accepted.[14] Blameworthiness is thus predominantly believed to be rooted in a community judgment. It reduces itself to those qualities of conduct or of being which the community considers to be bad. One might expect exemption from blameworthiness to be definable in terms of the factors that eliminate these qualities. But the fact is that the exempting qualities are not deemed to be fully inferable in this negative manner from the guilt-constituent factors; they are rather derived from an independent community judgment. Indeed, leading German jurists have taken the converse position, namely, that the meaning of guilt must be inferred from the principal exemption from guilt, the exemption of legal error, and that there ought to be no other definition of guilt in a code.[15]

From the standpoint of a system of rule of law, everything which is considered to be legally blameworthy is contained in the patterns of conduct and of mental state described by statutes. By the same token, if any element of blameworthiness as thus required is missing, there is, within a system of *nullum crimen sine lege*, no need for an exemption. Were the assertion that insanity excludes intent taken seriously, no plea of insanity would be necessary. Yet it is required in our law.

Whatever the essence of blameworthiness in the judgment of the community, it may not afford a basis for defining what is not

[14]See, e.g., Sir Patrick Devlin (Lord Justice Devlin), *The Enforcement of Morals* (Maccabaean Lecture in Jurisprudence of the British Academy, 1959).

[15]M. E. Mayer, *Der allgemeine Teil des Deutschen Strafrechts* (1923), p. 316, states: "The doctrine of error is . . . not but a consequence to be derived from the doctrine of guilt; it is the doctrine of guilt itself. . . ."

blameworthy, for community judgment does not necessarily operate in terms of simple logic. Exemption from guilt in the judgment of communities need not be equated with absence of that which constitutes guilt, but may well be rooted in an independent consideration. I shall not dwell upon the scope of admissibility of such inconsistent approach. For this is but a partial issue of a comprehensive problem which cannot be discussed in this paper—that of the limitations which the idea of democratic law imposes upon rule by community judgment. But two questions require special treatment in any contemporary discussion of mental incapacity, because their resolutions implied in recent leading decisions and policy suggestions are based on inadequate jurisprudential analyses. These questions are: (a) what is the proper form of manifestation, and (b) what is the proper basis of formation, of community judgment?

(*a*) *Manifestation of community judgment.* The community, as a body of individuals, must act through an agent. The question is: what community organ should be authorized to express community judgment on blameworthiness or on exemption from it? Is it the legislature, the courts, or the juries? That the decisive role in defining blameworthiness, whether it be expressed in descriptions of crime or in personal qualifications of offenders, must be attributed to legislatures is treated as a truism in civil law countries. In the United States, *per contra*, the view has been advanced that a determination of blameworthiness is a judgment upon a moral issue which must be rendered by the jury, since this issue is one of fact. One might wonder how this fits the definition of the term "fact" as conceived in the ancient rule, *ad quaestionem facti non respondent judices, ad quaestionem juris non respondent juratores*. Traditionally, judges were required to be just, whereas jurors have been described as men good and true, although of course in the very early days of legal development truth and justice were not clearly separated. In our times, to be sure, juries have been expected to manipulate justice, even *contra legem*. That they must answer senseless questions, however, is an innovation introduced by Judge Thurman Arnold, who advocated treatment of such questions as "moral issues."[16] Judge Arnold justified assignment of moral issues to juries not on the assumption that a moral question is one of fact[17] but rather on his anthropological approach to social ideals. In the light of the latter, scientific truth, morality, justice to the accused, rule of law, are all symbols of irrelevant content which have no direct impact upon legal reality, since law develops, "as language develops, in spite of, and not because of, the grammarians."[18] The function of these symbols is to dramatize legal processes, which are rituals that impress the public and thus enhance the prestige of law. Trial by jury is such a ritual, and hence to uphold a jury's authority in passing judgment on blameworthiness is more significant than either consideration of scientific truth or meting out justice to the accused. Thus, in the much cited *Holloway Case,*[19] the District of Columbia Court of Appeals approved submission to the jury of scientific evidence which the court itself stated to be false, even though it considered such evidence decisive of the issue of exemption on the grounds of mental incapacity. The policy ideal incorporated in this case is government by illusion, indeed, by deception of the public, serving an imaginary public good, to which

16*Holloway* v. *United States* (1945), 148 F.2d 662, at pp. 666–7 (App. D.C.).

17He stated that "the issue of the criminal responsibility of a defendant suffering from mental disease is not an issue of fact in the same sense as the commission of the offense." *Ibid.*, at p. 666.

18Thurman W. Arnold, *The Symbols of Government* (1935), p. 34.

19*Supra* note 16, at p. 667, where Judge Arnold said that "to command respect criminal law must not offend against the common belief that men who talk rationally are in most cases morally responsible for what they do." At the same time, he pointed out that this common belief is scientifically wrong, for it is based on the incorrect assumption that "there is a faculty called reason which is separate and apart from instinct, emotion, and impulse, that enables an individual to distinguish between right and wrong and endows him with moral responsibility for his acts" (at p. 666). Compare with this position the enlightened statement of Mr. Chief Justice Warren in *Blackburn* v. *Alabama* (1960), 361 U.S. 199, at p. 209: "Nor have we overlooked the testimony of the Chief Deputy that Blackburn 'talked sensible,' was clear-eyed, and did not appear nervous. But without any evidence in the record indicating that these observed facts bore any relation to Blackburn's disease or were symptoms of a remission of his illness, we are quite unable to conclude that such an inference can be drawn." Modern psychiatry teaches that composure and calmness after the commission of a crime does not indicate mental health. In a Puerto Rican case, evidence of calmness and reasoning ability after commission of the crime was given almost decisive weight as against overwhelming proof of schizophrenia. *Pueblo* v. *Sánchez Maldonado* (1956), 79 D.P.R. 116, at pp. 121–2.

the man Holloway may just as well be sacrificed. The psychiatrist Dr. Roche, in turn, apparently believing Judge Arnold's views to reflect prevailing legal ideas, declared that since the question raised by the ruling in the *Durham Case*,[20] whether an act is "the product of mental disease or defect," is not scientifically answerable—being scientifically senseless—it is a moral question which the jury must answer.[21] Judge Bazelon in the *Durham Case*[22] managed to escape the jurisprudential nihilism of Judge Arnold by declaring that the issue of mental incapacity must be answered by the jury since it raises a moral problem and thus an issue of fact. Because of the great importance which the *Durham Case* has assumed in recent legal disputes, it is necessary to discuss the methodological basis of its assignment to the jury of the questions of defining the general terms "mental disease" and "product of mental disease," on the ground that these are "questions of fact."

When stating that definition of key concepts in the mental incapacity exemption is a question of fact, Judge Bazelon merely repeated a theme elaborated by the New Hampshire judges in 1869–71.[23] In doing so, he seems to have overlooked the fact that words are means of communicating ideas and that identical words may communicate entirely different ideas in 1870 and in 1954, indeed, may be meaningful in 1870 but meaningless in 1954.[24] Actually, both the phrase "issue of fact" and the phrase "mental disease" have an entirely different meaning today from that attributed to them in 1870, and the phrase "product of mental disease" was believed to be meaningful in 1870 but is deemed without meaning today.

When the New Hampshire judges, in formulating their famous mental incapacity test, expressed the view that what constitutes

[20]*Durham* v. *United States* (1954), 94 U.S. App. D.C. 228, 214 F.2d 862.

[21]Roche, *supra* note 4, at pp. 259–68.

[22]*Supra* note 20, at pp. 875–6.

[23]*State* v. *Pike* (1870), 49 N.H. 399; *State* v. *Jones* (1871), 50 N.H. 369, The New Hampshire judges, however, did not describe this issue as a moral one. They rather thought the questions of whether a man possesses a mental disease and whether his act is a product of such disease are questions of the same nature as the question of whether he has fever. So is the question of what a mental disease is.

[24]Notice the developments in the philosophy of language, marked by names such as Rudolph Carnap, Ludwig Wittgenstein, and John Wisdom.

mental disease and what is a product of such disease are questions of fact to be answered by juries, they proceeded from the assumption prevailing at the time that the quality of a question, as one of fact or law, is an inherent ontological attribute.[25] In recent decades, however, as suggested above, the one-time belief in the absoluteness of the distinction between law and fact has been abandoned. Today it is general law-school knowledge that "law" and "fact" in the statements "this is a question of fact" or "this is a question of law" indicate normative determinations reached by decision-makers on policy grounds rather than immanent attributes of the given questions.[26] Whether a question is one of law or one of fact is a question of law and not a question of fact. When it is thought desirable on policy grounds to assign a question to the jury, it is characterized as a question of fact; the reverse procedure of characterizing a question as one of fact by merely observing its nature is no longer deemed valid. However, the policy of assigning a question to the jury as one of fact is not entirely unrelated to certain features of the question that is in issue—features that must be evaluated in the context in which that question appears. One of the relevant features is the degree of generality of the potential answer to the question.

As suggested by Mezger,[27] the distinction between law and fact is one between the general and the particular. The problem is: at what level of generality should we assume a question to be general enough to be deemed a question of law? Levels of generality of questions of diverse content can be compared, and it is thus possible to decide whether a question is one of such generality as is usually—meaning, so far as issues other than the one being discussed are concerned—thought to qualify a question as one of law. But, of

[25]On Judge Doe's insistence upon the immanent quality of a question, as one of "fact" see John Reid, "Understanding the New Hampshire Doctrine of Criminal Insanity" (1960), 69 *Yale L. J.* 367.

[26] See Helen Silving, "Law and Fact in the Light of the Pure Theory of Law," in Paul Sayre (ed.), *Interpretations of Modern Legal Philosophies* (1947), p. 642.

[27]"The decisive demarcation line runs not between the 'factual' and the 'legal' but between the 'individual circumstance' and the illegality of the 'total act.'" Edmund Mezger, in "Strafgesetzbuch nach dem neuesten Stand der Gesetzgebung," *Leipziger Kommentar* (founded by Ebermayer, Lobe, Rosenberger) (1953), Vol. I, at p. 449.

course, as a matter of sound policy, the analogies ought to be drawn from identical fields of law, for a determination of a question as one of law or of fact implies a jurisdictional disposition; and one may very well wish to declare a question of identical level of generality to be one of fact in civil cases but not in criminal cases. In drawing analogies of this nature it is also important to consider whether the jury possesses the necessary relative qualifications for determining the questions which are being compared.

In the *Durham Case* Judge Bazelon drew an analogy, such as has been suggested, when he said that the questions of fact under the test laid down in the case, namely, whether the accused suffered from a mental disease and whether his act was the product of the disease, "are as capable of determination by the jury as, for example, the questions juries must determine upon a claim of total disability under a policy of insurance where the state of medical knowledge concerning the disease involved and its effects, is obscure or in conflict."[28] Even if the analogy applied in this instance could be said to be methodologically unobjectionable, it would be improper to invoke such a private law analogy in criminal law, since the requirements of legality are much more stringent in the latter branch of law than in the former. Apart from this, is the level of abstraction or generality similar in the two situations? Clearly, "total disability" is a more determinate concept than "mental disease": that for which a person must be disabled is known whereas responsibility, of which the mentally diseased is supposed to be incapable, is precisely that which we are expected to determine by the term "mental disease." Disability in insurance is an earning disability that can be expressed in dollars and cents by comparing pre-injury average wages and post-injury earning potential or actual earnings.[29] Also, as regards a lay jury's qualifications for answering

[28]*Supra* note 20, at p. 875.

[29]"Total disability" is not "absolute helplessness" but "total earning unfitness." William R. Vance, *Handbook on the Law of Insurance* (3d ed.; 1951), p. 1050. In workmen's compensation statutes "total disability" imports payments of certain percentages of total wages, whereas "partial disability" imports payments of percentages of the difference between prior pay and post-injury earning capacity or actual wages. See William R. Schneider's *Workmen's Compensation* (Permanent Edition, 1940), Vol. IV, for the respective provisions.

the questions, expecting a jury to decide whether a claimant has lost his earning ability is obviously more rational than requiring it to determine whether an accused was responsible. What is the source of this peculiar equiparation of the issue of "disability" and that of "irresponsibility"?

Any student of the New Hampshire cases who notices their persistent concern with whether a legal test is or is not necessary, is bound to ask: a test of what? In some passages the judges speak of a test without indicating what is being tested; in others, of insanity as object of the test; in still others, they seem to use the term "lack of responsibility" as equivalent to insanity. One gains the impression that they are using the concept of insanity or mental disease or irresponsibility as if that concept itself were an existentially given entity. To define such concept, in the opinion of the New Hampshire judges, requires discovery of the inherent attributes of such an entity rather than agreement or convention over a functional use of a term. While insanity is a subject of medical study and hence a medical matter, it is a reality which medical men may discover but whose scope they cannot determine for any purpose. Thus, whether dipsomania is a kind of insanity is not a matter of medical conventional definition but a question of fact. One doctor may make the correct discovery about this question, while another doctor may err. But there has since occurred a total desubstantialization of scientific concepts. Scientific definitions are reached by convention aimed at facilitating communication. Medical men may properly agree to define mental disease in such a manner as to include psychopathy or neuroses; they may equally properly agree to define the term so as to exclude these states. The agreement to choose the former or the latter alternative is guided by considerations of medical intercommunication with a view to medical dispositions. The assumption that the definition implies a "discovery" of any attributes that are inherent in the notion of mental disease or, indeed, of any attributes that are also relevant in law, is not warranted. In fact, Judge Bazelon now asserts that the medical label given to a subject's condition is not decisive and that "(l)egal consequences depend rather upon the jury's determination, from all the facts, as to the individual's mental health or illness."[30] This complicates the issue, adding the problem of finding the discipline to which mental disease, as used in the Durham test, belongs. For, obviously, within that test, in order to ascertain whether, for example, a psychopath is exempt, the jury must establish whether at the time of the act he suffered from a "mental disease" or "illness."

In its famous "moral judgment" conclusion, the *Durham Case* states that whether a person is to be classified as suffering from a mental disease depends on the moral judgment of the jury.[31] This is a peculiar and misleading usage of language, reducible to the assertion that mental disease is a moral quality. The nature of this moral quality is not disclosed except to the extent of implying that it is predicated upon "all the facts." This, then, is apparently the meaning of the phrase that mental disease is a question of fact. Analytically it amounts to delegating to juries the function of determining general issues, such as whether kleptomaniacs, pyromaniacs, psychopaths, as classes, ought to be exempt from punishment. Determining whether such broad classes should or should not be exempt is as much a legislative task as is the question whether persons engaged in error regarding an essential fact ought to be exempt. The dubiousness of this delegation of power to juries is magnified by the fact that juries are at the same time misled by being told that they must find whether the person concerned suffered from a mental disease,[32] which term, within modern linguistic usage, conveys the idea of a psychiatric category. The Durham position is indefensible within a system governed by the rule of law, both on the ground that it delegates essential legislative power to juries and on the ground that it misleads the jury, the accused, and the public. It is by no means coincidental that this position has been

[30]See Judge Bazelon's dissenting opinion in *Lyles* v. *United States* (1957), 254 F.2d 725, 734, at 735–6 (App. D.C.), *cert. den.*, 356 U.S. 961, 78 S. Ct. 997 (1958). "Testimony that the individual suffers from a named condition," Judge Bazelon said, is of aid to the jury "only to the extent that the jury is otherwise informed of the nature of the condition."

[31]For text of the passage see *infra*, note 156.

[32]See Judge Burger's opinion in *Blocker* v. *United States*, *supra* note 3, at p. 869.

reached by methods which defy the contemporary philosophy of language, new insights into psychological reality, and the modern jurisprudential conception of law and fact.

The legality principle, of course, has a narrower rationale in the area of the mental incapacity exemption than in that of specific legal prohibitions. In the latter area, the principle requires that man know or be able to know what he must not do to avoid punishment and that this knowledge or knowability be present in advance of the commission of crime. But it is not important that he know in advance of crime under what terms he will be held to have possessed or not to have possessed mental capacity, for that knowledge does not and should not affect his decision to act or to forego acting. However, legality in the sense of protection against arbitrariness and inequality of law administration also applies to the mental incapacity exemption. On this ground, to use another example, it is as improper to leave the scope of the term "mental disease" (as a test of exemption) to the jury's definition as it would be to give the jury authority to determine what constitutes self-defence under a rule providing exemption for anyone acting in self-defence, without further specification.

(*b*) *Formation of community judgment*. On what basis should community judgment be reached? The principal question is: what role should the psychiatric expert play in arriving at such judgment? At the legislative level, in order to formulate a sound mental incapacity exemption, legislators ought to know how the human mind operates, for today this is much less a matter of common knowledge than it was once assumed to be. Psychiatrists and psychologists must tell them what generalizations can be made. If no functional generalizations can be made, the implication is that the exemption cannot be cast or cannot be fully defined in terms of psychiatric categories; in this event legislators must derive its operational categories from disciplines other than psychology, for example, from sociology. In no event should they leave the matter of determining mental incapacity on a case-to-case basis to the jury under psychiatric guidance, without specification of the nature or scope of such guidance. In assessing the usefulness to law of different kinds of scientific insight, a distinction should be observed between those that can be put in general categories and those that cannot. One might even doubt that a discipline that cannot generalize meaningfully may be classified as a science, as normally understood.

At the trial level, psychiatric experts are needed as witnesses testifying to observations of operations of the mind of the accused. Whether or not the psychiatrist should be permitted to testify in terms of conclusions, such as whether or not the accused comes within the exemption as defined, depends on whether or not the psychiatrist can support opinions he expresses on rational grounds. If such grounds cannot be verbalized, his opinions should not be admissible. An accused may be rational or irrational, but the administration of justice—of which expert testimony forms a part—must be rational. No expert opinion should be allowed to stand if it is based merely on feeling and intuition.

(3) GUILT IN THE LIGHT OF PHENOMENOLOGICAL THOUGHT

According to the phenomenological theory of guilt developed by Felix Kaufmann on the basis of the Kelsenian notion of imputation, guilt does not exist *per se*, but rather consists in ascription of guilt by virtue of certain postulates addressed to law; indeed, guilt is these postulates. It is a symbol summarizing certain social-political policies; it means the totality of functions which that concept is supposed to perform.[33] Applying this approach to our own policies, guilt would mean or represent the demands, among others, that no one must be deemed guilty unless he possessed the required intent

[33]Felix Kaufmann, *Die philosophischen Grundprobleme der Lehre von der Strafrechtsschuld* (1929). The author states at pp. 72–6:

"The concept of guilt is closely connected with that of the purpose of punishment. As a rule, one assumes the presence of guilt when he regards punishment to be proper and one assumes the presence of grave guilt when he regards severe punishment to be proper. . . .

". . . [L]et us consider what are in general the aims of a theoretical analysis of the concept of guilt. The aim is often expressed by proclaiming what 'function' the concept of guilt is to 'perform'. Thereby, the following ends are postulated: Firstly, it should be defined in such manner as to make it possible to distinguish with precision guilt from non-guilt; secondly, it should permit gradation that might make it possible to speak of a greater or lesser 'graveness' of guilt; thirdly, it should be possible to deduct from it the logical relation of the 'types of guilt', intent and negligence, to it [guilt] as overall concept; fourthly, it should be clear that the grounds which exclude guilt, in a narrower sense (state of necessity,

or recklessness; that no one should be punished severely if he committed a minor act, meaning an act of small social harmfulness; that no one should be punished unless all elements of crime are properly proven; and so forth. We could equally well say that unless all the demands we thus address to law are fulfilled, it would be unjust to punish a man or to hold him responsible or to blame him, blame meaning social censure rather than a particular moral, religious, or ethical blame. Though Kaufmann believed in a utilitarian notion of guilt, his theory, in its philosophical implications, lends itself to enlargement into a general theory of guilt. Guilt as a general sociological concept may assume any content, depending on the preferred approach, whether it be theological, metaphysical, utilitarian, existentialist, and so on.

(4) GUILT AS INTERPRETED BY THE WRITER

Guilt in law is always an expression of legal or policy demands. In a theocracy or in a state in union with a church, these demands are theological; in a state governed by some other philosophy, they are the demands of that philosophy. In a democratic state—I believe democracy to be a *sui generis* philosophy—these demands are democratic.[34] Subject to certain limitations implied in the concept of democracy—for example, those imposed by civil liberties—the community determines the contents of legal rules; but just as the community does not define the meaning of democracy, its philosophical judgment on the nature of guilt, as contrasted with its social judgment on legal contents, cannot afford a proper basis for defining guilt. Rather, adoption of a "democratic concept of guilt" may be demanded of legislators just as adoption of a democratic law of election may be demanded of them.

duress, substantial error) actually obliterate the guilt element; and fifthly, there should appear the relation of guilt to mental capacity or incapacity.

"Actually, the task involved [in formulating the guilt concept] is to carry out an *abstraction* of a certain type. One is conscious of the fact that each of the five mentioned relationships contains the same element and the task is to *isolate* it."

[34]On the *sui generis* nature of the philosophy of democracy see Helen Silving, "The Conflict of Liberty and Equality" (1950), 35 *Iowa L. Rev.* 357. To What extent the tenets of such philosophy permit incorporation by law of particular theological or secularly philosophical views, is an intricate problem which cannot be discussed in this paper.

Wherein does the democratic concept of guilt consist? In a democracy, obedience to demands of the community, formalized in duly enacted law, is a duty of citizenship. Guilt consists in violating the basic political postulate of substantial conformity to community rules. Dean Paul K. Ryu and the writer expressed this idea in the following terms: "We believe that in a free society the sanction of the community is imposed neither for 'rebellion' nor for 'disobedience' but simply for violation of a duty toward the community —the actor's duty, as a member of the community, to abide by its rules."[35] This definition led us to postulate admission of error of law as a general defence open to any man without requirement that the error be based on a mental incapacity. The mental incapacity exemption is distinguishable from the error of law exemption in that it is concerned with the general fitness of the individual as a law-participant, representative of the community, rather than with the single issue, "Did he know the law? Did he know that the specific act he was committing was legally 'wrong'?" However, there should be a certain correlation between the rule on legal error and the definition of the mental incapacity exemption. The assumption is made that an important part of the process whereby a group becomes a legal community is that its members share in the making and maintenance of law, whether in the form of enforcement or obedience. Such sharing of law presupposes a certain standard of normality in cultural patterns and personality make-up, a standard that may vary from one community to another. Application of punitive law presupposes awareness of the law; it also presupposes subjects who are normal, average members of the community to whom laws are addressed. A person who does not meet the minimum standard of balance in personality organization that qualifies him as "representative of his community" ought not to be held guilty of crime against that community. Since he is not an average law participant, law cannot be meaningfully asserted against him. This norm is based on a political and not on a scientific principle. Guilt in a democratic society is a social-political concept.

[35]Ryu and Silving, *supra* note 8, at p. 468.

B. *Punishment as a Functional Means of Deterrence: Mental Incapacity as "Non-deterrability" or Unfitness to Serve as Means of Deterring Others*

As stated above, if punishment is assigned the function of deterring the actor, then we must assume that persons whose state of mind is such that they are not susceptible to deterrence by punishment ought not to be punished. If, on the other hand, punishment is expected to function as a deterrent to others, then those whose punishment would not deter others ought not to be punished. One might, of course, generally define mental incapacity for legal purposes as "non-deterrability," and leave it to psychiatrists to advise in each case whether or not the accused is deterrable. But that non-deterrability cannot be assumed as the exclusive standard of exemption from punishment follows from the fact that such assumption would lead to exclusion in the first place of the most controversial group, namely, psychopaths. Moreover, non-deterrability by punishment is not the most outstanding characteristic of psychotics—the group which undoubtedly should be exempt from punishment;[36] nor is deterrability by legal punishment a special feature of the average individual. The Danish Penal Code which adopts the non-deterrability test, formulates it as a merely supplementary category.[37]

Michael and Wechsler expressed the view that punishment's failure to deter a mentally ill person applies to others also; normal persons are not deterred by the sight of an insane person's being punished because they do not identify themselves with him and do not expect to share his fate.[38] For this the authors cite no psychological authority. That identification with the accused works on such rational level may well be doubted in the light of the studies

[36]See Angus MacNiven, "Psychoses and Criminal Responsibility," in L. Radzinowicz and Turner (eds.), *English Studies in Criminal Science* (1949), Vol. II (entitled *Mental Abnormality and Crime*), p. 8, at pp. 52–3. Henry A. Davidson, "Criminal Responsibility: The Quest for a Formula," in P. Hoch and J. Zubin (eds.), *Psychiatry and the Law* (1955), p. 61, at pp. 63–4.

[37]Danish Criminal Code of 1930, as amended (transl. by E. Giersing and M. Grünhut; Copenhagen: G.E.C. Gad–Publishers, 1958), ss. 16, 17.

[38]Jerome Michael and Herbert Wechsler, "A Rationale of the Law of Homicide" (1937), 37 *Colum. L. Rev.* 701, at pp. 752–7.

made by representatives of dynamic psychology.[39] In any event, the doctrine of deterrence, formulated classically in the high days of belief in man's rationality and in his ability always to calculate in business-like fashion the balance of pleasure and pain, has lost its scientific foundation: we have acquired some knowledge of the Unconscious, which follows its own scheme of pleasure. But we have not yet acquired sufficient insight into the impact of punishment upon the Unconscious to be able to say generally whether or not punishment of a mentally ill person deters others. Even proceeding from a conventional view of deterrence, one might well doubt that so-called normal persons do not identify themselves with those mentally ill persons who do not manifest outward signs of madness and who, nevertheless, ought to be exempt from punishment, according to a consensus of opinion. In sum, we do not have sufficient knowledge of the operation of deterrence generally to be able to accept it as a principal basis of punishment; by the same token, no foundation has been laid for defining the mental incapacity exemption simply in terms of non-deterrability. One might suggest non-deterrability as a separate, supplementary ground of exemption, but this is unnecessary, given a comprehensive test, as will be recommended below.

However, in the law of measures, the doctrine of deterrence may serve a useful function. In the case of the so-called psychopaths or sociopaths, whose most characteristic feature is their individual non-deterrability, there is good reason for adopting special devices, as are suggested by Danish experiences with special treatment centres for such persons.[40]

C. *Punishment as a Means of Reformation: Mental Incapacity as an Inability to Be Reformed*

Constitutions, statutes, and judicial decisions often proclaim reformation to be the principal, indeed, even the sole, aim of criminal

[39]The "scapegoat ideology," described by Reik, Wittels, Alexander and Staub, Reiwald, and others and believed to be based on "identification with the accused," is not predicated upon mental health of the latter. Notice that the prototype of all scapegoats was an animal.

[40]Compare *supra* note 37. The pertinent measures will be discussed in a separate paper.

law state intervention. I have submitted in another context[41] that though reformation may be a proper aim of state intervention by methods other than those of the criminal law, the latter is not a fit province for reforming the offender. Certainly, punishment by the state is hardly an appropriate means of achieving reformation. As a direct reformative device, punishment is expected to function via its deterrent effect; but, as has been shown, the effectiveness of deterrence is doubtful. At best one could assert that punitive intervention provides an opportunity for reformative treatment. The primary obstacle to a consistent use of treatment during the course of punishment is that the latter must ultimately be limited by the scope of the crime committed, whereas the extent of intervention required by the need for treatment is not proportionate to the graveness of the precipitating crime.

However, assuming reformation to be a proper end of punishment, exemption should be accorded to the unreformable. In a dual system this result is less absurd than in a monistic one, for acquittal of a person found to be unreformable on the ground of insanity would automatically open the possibility of applying protective measures. Nor would it be necessary to cast the test in terms of absolute unreformability. It would suffice to formulate the mental incapacity exemption as "incapacity to be reformed by punitive means or in the course of punishment." This, however, would place within the exemption's scope a large number of persons whom the public would hardly consider fit grantees of exemptions from "blame." Psychiatrists, many of whom oppose punishment in principle, are likely to extend the classification "unreformable" to an unduly large group of offenders. Also to be considered is the difficulty of diagnosis.[42] Again, as in the case of deterrence, the

[41]On this see H. Silving, "Rule of Law in Criminal Justice," *supra* note 5, at pp. 138–40.

[42]Johs. Andanaes, Review of v. Eyben, *Strafudmaling* (1955–6), 6 *Brit. J. Delinq.* 152, at p. 155, notes how little we understand "about reformation of the individual offender. We know little of what positive or negative significance punishment has for the criminal; still less ground do we have for judging the probable influence of a penalty of 30 days, for example, instead of 3 or 6 months."

It may be interesting to note that the Supreme Court of Poland held the notion of the "unreformable" (art. 84, Polish Penal Code of 1932) to be "contrary to the principles of socialist legality and to the paramount tenet that, under the condi-

reformative potential of an individual may be an important consideration within the law of measures.

Of greatest practical significance is the positive harm which punishment may cause certain subjects. There are persons who, far from being deterrable or reformable by punishment, are likely to deteriorate as a result of punitive intervention. Could the likelihood of deterioration be accepted as a workable basis for exemption? The Danish test makes allowance for it. But the usefulness of the harm feature as a special ground for exemption is dubious. If the general test of mental incapacity is wide enough, it will embrace individuals with this feature. In the event that such an individual does not come within the exemption, he might in appropriate cases be accorded probation, provided that he is not dangerous.

D. *Punishment as Law Assertion: Mental Incapacity Exemption Where Punishment Is Not Law Assertive*

When assumed to have the function of manifesting law's prohibition of socially undesirable conduct, punishment is necessary to document the prohibition rather than as a means of inflicting suffering upon the actor. Inflicting suffering should never be the purpose of legal operation, though it may be an unavoidable incident of another proper aim, as is that of law documentation. Punishment is necessary simply because no other device has yet been invented to serve such documentation. Treatment cannot function as its substitute, since it must be geared to the offender and not to his crime and is thus inapt to reflect the relative gravity of the

tions of a popular State, there can be no question of unreformable crimes, for a popular State affords full opportunity of integrating every criminal—after completion of his punishment—in the creative effort of the nation, contributing to the education of the criminal." Decision rendered on April 8, 1952 (IV, K. 19/51), Collection of Supreme Court Decisions 1952, Item 67, at p. 228. This decision obviously proceeds from the assumption that the exclusive sources of crime or of unreformability of the offender are economic conditions. Dynamic psychology refutes this assumption by pointing to the deeper psychological roots of criminality. However, within the political ideology and constitutional doctrine of the western world, the notion of the "unreformable offender" is repugnant to the basic postulate of "man's dignity."

prohibition that has been violated; even in the law of measures, which is focussed on the offender, the relative gravity of the criminal act should be a highly relevant consideration.

An important implication of interpreting punishment as a means of law assertion is the insistence on equality of treatment. Non-discriminatory punishment of those who commit the same category of act in similar circumstances is a condition of the state's right to punish as a means of asserting its prohibitions.

Implicit in the concept of similarity of circumstances is that of an average personality make-up. It follows that a "non-average" individual should not be subject to the punitive treatment devised for average community members. Measures are the appropriate devices applicable to the "non-average." Measures, of course, must also be administered on an egalitarian basis, but equality in measures is judged from the standpoint of their distinctive aim: protection of the community. As the protective need varies, so do the types of indicated measures, due consideration being given even in the context of measures to the seriousness of the criminal act that has been committed.

Summary

Assertion of legal prohibition is the proper end of punishment. Such assertion, however, is not admissible except as a reaction to "guilt." Mental incapacity is that mental make-up which renders these postulates inappropriate for certain types of persons. As guilt is violation of the basic political demand of abiding by the law addressed to the average community member, non-average personality make-up, which makes it extraordinarily difficult for an individual to conform to the community's norms, excludes guilt. Law assertion applied to the "non-average" person, who is not properly representative of the group mind, is socially inadequate. This view of the policy of punishment will guide the writer's formulation of the mental incapacity exemption. Before suggesting a new definition of mental incapacity, however, it is necessary to outline the definitions that are now available in laws and reform drafts and projects.

II. AVAILABLE MENTAL INCAPACITY TESTS

THE AVAILABLE mental incapacity tests must be presented in historical perspective because in many of them ancient policy reasons and scientific or philosophical background have become obscured; the principle of legal inertia helps to maintain atavistic legal rules by repressing their true historical rationales. As so often happens in law, the original reason for a rule is long forgotten though the rule itself lingers on by the sheer weight of its age, while desperate attempts are made to find a new rationale for it.

This part of the paper is divided into two sections, the first dealing with total and the second with partial exemption tests. The tests will be considered according to principles of similarity rather than chronologically. Anglo-American law will be discussed first, and civil law tests will be presented for purposes of comparison. In the former, the prevailing total exemption rules are the M'Naghten Rules, either alone or as supplemented by the Irresistible Impulse test, on the one hand, and the New Hampshire–Durham Rule, on the other hand. Revised versions of the combination of M'Naghten and Irresistible Impulse are the tests of the Model Penal Code. Comparable tests in civil law countries are those of the German and Swiss federal law, whereas the Spanish test resembles Durham. I shall discuss M'Naghten's, the Model Code's, and the German test in one sub-section, and the New Hampshire, Durham, and Spanish test in another.

A. Total Exemption Tests

Group 1. M'Naghten's Case; Irresistible Impulse; Model Code Tests; German Test

(1) M'NAGHTEN

M'Naghten's Case[43] furnishes a background that is allegedly inconsistent with the rules that bear the accused's name. M'Naghten was a paranoiac who believed himself to be persecuted by

[43](1843) 10 C. & F. 200 (H.L.).

Tories and to have been compelled by them to commit the murder for which he was indicted.[44] Even in the very act of diseased killing he committed a truly Freudian slip: he wanted to kill Sir Robert Peel, but mistook Peel's secretary, Drummond, for him and killed Drummond. M'Naghten was acquitted on the ground of insanity, although he undoubtedly knew that he was doing something "he ought not to do" according to the law of the land. Since the crime was political, a debate ensued in the House of Lords, and the Lords addressed to the judges of England an inquiry about the proper tests for acquittal on the basis of mental incapacity. The judges' answers constitute the famous M'Naghten rules, formulated in an advisory opinion of uncertain scope: it is possible that the judges only purported to define the mental incapacity exemption applicable to persons suffering from delusions.[45] The fact that rules of this nature are persistently followed in many parts of the common law world should make us pause to reflect on the true historical meaning of these rules and the nature of their impact on contemporary thought.

The judges' answer that has played the most significant role in Anglo-American law is known as the right-wrong test, reading thus: ". . . to establish a defence on the ground of insanity, it must be clearly proved that, at the time of the committing of the act, the party accused was labouring under such a defect of reason, from disease of the mind, as not to know the nature and quality of the act he was doing; or, if he did know it, that he did not know he was doing what was wrong." Our first task is to establish the historical rationale of the test. Undoubtedly, the decisive part of the test—the

[44]M'Naghten said: "The Tories in my native city have compelled me to do this. They follow and persecute me wherever I go, and have entirely destroyed my peace of mind. . . . They have accused me of crimes of which I am not guilty; they do everything in their power to harass and persecute me; in fact they wish to murder me. It can be proved by evidence." Ellison and Haas, "A Recent Judicial Interpretation of the M'Naghten Rule" (1953), 4 *Brit. J. Delinq.* 129.

[45]This interpretation is obviously suggested by one of the questions to which the so-called right-wrong rule is the answer: "What are the proper questions to be submitted to the jury, where a person alleged to be afflicted with insane delusion respecting one or more particular subjects or persons is charged with the commission of a crime (murder, for example), and insanity is set up as a defence?" If the answer given by the judges is responsive to this question, then it is clearly limited to a situation where delusion is present.

part which has provided the basic incapacity definition throughout the common law world for over a century—is the "knowledge" portion, knowledge of the nature and quality of the act and knowledge that it was wrong. Lack of knowledge apparently was that which in the judges' opinion absolved the defendant from responsibility. For certainly no firm opinion had yet developed that mental disease *per se* justifies impunity. Let us not forget Ferri's remark that "(l)ess than one hundred years" before his time "the insane were punished as guilty and were objects of public execration, because the effect of a diseased organism was imputed to their malevolent will."[46]

Professor Ryu and I have found two clues to the historical meaning of the M'Naghten test.[47] We traced the test to two remote sources—sources which so often supply the historical solution for contemporary legal rules—the Bible and Roman law. The right-wrong test goes back to the good and evil test,[48] and the latter constitutes both the rationality standard of the Bible[49] and the biblical condition and origin of sin.[50] Sin began with acquisition of knowledge of good and evil, and remained predicated upon such knowledge. The Bible exempts from punishment persons acting in ignorance of the prohibition. Both the Talmud and the canon law consider guilt to be predicated upon the actor's knowledge of the law that is being violated because, according to these sources, guilt is defiance of the law, disrespect for the laws of God, or disobedience to the Lord.[51] In early foreign legal sources we also find the mental incapacity exemption based on a doctrine of legal error which is undoubtedly referable to the Bible via canon law. Thus,

[46]Enrico Ferri, *Criminal Sociology*, in *Modern Criminal Science Series* (1917), at pp. 356–7.

[47]Ryu and Silving, *supra* note 8, at p. 430.

[48]*Arnold's Case* (1724), 16 St. Tr. 695, at p. 765; cf. prosecution's contention in *Earl Ferrers Case* (1760), 19 St. Tr. 866, at p. 947. For discussion of these cases see Turner (ed.), *Russell on Crime* (10th ed.; 1950), Vol. I, pp. 48–9.

[49]Gen. 2:9, 17; 3:22.

[50]The knowledge acquired by original sin, the knowledge of "good and evil," was knowledge of sex taboos, which was apparently deemed the prototype of knowledge of prohibition generally. Gen. 2:25; 3:7, 10, 11, 22.

[51]On this see Ryu and Silving, *supra* note 8, at pp. 424–5, 427–9.

the Siete Partidas[52] declare that the *"loco o desmemoriado"* (lunatic or person without memory) is not subject to punishment because "he neither knows nor understands the error he makes."

Surely the stated features of biblical law could hardly have failed to influence decisions at a time when judges believed that the knowledge precluded by insanity was awareness that a crime was a violation of "the laws of God and nature,"[53] of which the phrase "the laws both of God and man," appearing in the M'Naghten instructions,[54] is but a slight variation. The law of error dominates not only the right-wrong portion of the judges' answers but all the other answers as well. The answer to the first question submitted by the Lords asserts that a person who knew that "he was acting contrary to law" is responsible, even though he suffered from a delusion that he was "redressing or revenging some supposed grievance or injury, or producing some public benefit." This answer perfectly reflects the historical and contemporary rule of the "law of error of law."[55] The answer to the fourth question states that if "a person, under an insane delusion as to existing facts, commits an offence in consequence thereof . . . he must be considered in the same situation as to responsibility as if the facts with respect to which the delusion exists were real." This is precisely the rule obtaining in the law of error of fact.[56] The duality of "error of fact" and "error of law" is considered in the crucial knowledge test, contained in the answer to the second and third question, which deals with knowledge of the nature and quality of the act (knowledge of fact) and knowledge of wrong (knowledge of law). The phrase "nature and quality of the act" is likewise derived from the

[52]VII, lib. III, titulo 8°, quoted in A. Quintano Ripollés, *Comentarios al Codigo Penal* (1946), Vol. I, at p. 64: *"Otrosi decimos, que si algun home que fuese loco o desmemoriado, matase a otro, que no cae por ende en pena alguna, porque no sabe ni entiende el yerro que face."*

[53]*Bellingham's Case* (1812), Collinson, *Lunacy* Vol. I, p. 673 n., cited in Russell, *supra* note 48, at p. 50.

[54]Lord Chief Justice Tindal's charge to the jury in the *M'Naghten Case, supra.*

[55]On this see Ryu and Silving, *supra* note 8, at pp. 455–6. A person who knows the legal provision but disagrees with it will not be excused.

[56]As stated by Rollin M. Perkins, in *Perkins on Criminal Law* (1957), p. 826, an error of fact will excuse only if it is "of such a nature that the conduct would have been lawful had the facts been as they were mistakenly supposed to be."

law of error, namely, the Roman-canon law notion that, to be relevant, an error cannot be simply an *error qualitatis* but must affect the "nature" of the thing, its "substance"; it must be an error as to its *materia* and *qualitas*.[57]

One might argue, of course, that the crucial M'Naghten rule appears to test rationality rather than error, the relevant passage reading: "labouring under such a defect of reason, from disease of the mind, as not to know. . . ." But remarkably little concern has been shown throughout the century about the M'Naghten stress on disease of the mind or defect of reason.[58] What matters in M'Naghten, as in the Bible, is lack of knowledge and not insanity, which in the Bible—far from constituting an excuse—was believed to be a source of divine inspiration.[59]

There is one feature of the right-wrong rule which does not appear in the other M'Naghten answers and which deserves special consideration: the phrase that the defendant, to be exempt, must not have known that he was doing what was "wrong." In contrast to this formulation, the answer to the first question states that the defendant acting under a delusion is responsible if he knew that he was acting "contrary to law," meaning thereby "the law of the land." The meaning of the term "wrong" in the right-wrong test has been a most controversial subject, and it would seem that its use, in contrast to the immediately preceding use of the term "contrary to the law of the land," suggests that the purported meaning is moral rather than legal wrong. Yet in England, as well as in many other jurisdictions, including Puerto Rico, it has been held that wrong means contrary to the law of the land.[60] Much has been said about this subject, but the law of error alone can afford the proper solution as intended by the M'Naghten judges. In the situation obtaining in the first answer the defendant has admitted

[57]Digest 18. 1. 9. 2; *ibid.* 18. 1. 14.

[58]See on this Norval Morris, "The Defences of Insanity in Australia," in Mueller, *supra* note 5, p. 273, at p. 278.

[59]For citations see Silving, "Psychoanalysis and the Criminal Law" (1960), 51 *J. Crim. L., Criminology & Pol. Sc.* Notice also Saul's change from prophetic inspiration (I Sam. 10:6, 10–12) to mental disease (I Sam. 16:14, 15–23; 18:10–12).

[60]On the state of the rule in England see Morris, *supra* note 58 at pp. 284–5; in Puerto Rico see *Pueblo* v. *Alsina* (1956), 79 D.P.R. 46, at pp. 66–8.

that he knew the law of the land; with this the issue of error of law is foreclosed. In the situation obtaining in the right-wrong answer, the defendant puts his error of law in issue. But how can he do that? The judges' obvious answer is that "the law is administered upon the principle that every one must be taken conclusively to know it, without proof that he does know it." Yet the judges seem to be in a dilemma, there apparently being some relevance in the defendant's contention that he did not know that what he was doing was wrong. One might hence expect that such wrong in the judges' view must be either, not the wrongfulness of the particular act, but a general abstract wrong or a moral wrong. But the first alternative was specifically rejected by the judges, who insisted that the knowledge in issue must be "the party's knowledge of right and wrong in respect to the very act with which he is charged." As regards the second alternative, England, the country closest to the rule, interprets wrong as legal and not a moral wrong.

The judges' answer seems to suggest that the decisive concept is an intermediate one. They apparently encountered the basic difficulty facing all those who insist on legal knowledge as a condition of responsibility: can laymen be expected to know the law of the land? And they seem to have solved this problem in exactly the same manner it was solved by modern advocates of the defence of *error iuris*. To be responsible, a layman cannot be expected to know the words of the law or the pertinent legal rule itself; but he must have made an "evaluation in the lay sphere, parallel" to the evaluation expressed in the law.[61] He need not have actual knowledge of the law of the land, but he must know "that the act was one which he ought not to do," and the norm contained in his understanding of that which he ought not to do must correspond to that expressed in the legal prohibition.[62] There must be a parallelism, not an identity, between that which the law prohibits and that which in the actor's view is a legal wrong. The actor's knowledge must be a knowledge of law, but not a technical knowledge of the

[61]On this see Ryu and Silving, *supra* note 8, at p. 463.

[62]The actor must have a layman's understanding of the law—an understanding that reflects the essence of the legal prohibition without amounting to the technical comprehension expected of lawyers.

precise wording or meaning of the legal rule. It is rather a knowledge of the norm expressed in the legal prohibition. For example, concerning the law of homicide, he must know that killing is a crime. The question remains of how this interpretation can be reconciled with the conclusive presumption of legal knowledge expressly mentioned by the judges. That presumption apparently applies only to knowledge of the law of the land, but not to knowledge of the norm expressed in law. Only if the actor knows, in his lay fashion, that what he is doing is legally wrong, and not otherwise, is he conclusively presumed to know the full scope of the law of the land. Except as thus interpreted, the words of the M'Naghten opinion seem to make no sense.

Thus, all the M'Naghten answers are ultimately reducible to rules on "error."[63] Their rationale is derived from the law of error. In no event do these rules attempt to define insanity or to set forth an exemption deriving its justification from an immunizing quality of insanity. They do not aim at exempting the mentally ill, but purport to exempt a defendant engaged in error, whether of law or fact. In the M'Naghten era apparently the law was in a stage of transition regarding both the defence of legal error and the place of mental disease in criminal responsibility. Thus these two puzzling legal notions came to be confused in one answer that has since confused generations of lawyers.

In evaluating the M'Naghten right-wrong rule, we must keep in mind that historically it is a rule closely connected with the defence of error of law and of fact. It is part of a comprehensive system of law based upon a philosophy that conceives of punishment as a sanction imposed upon disobedience to law, contempt of the law, or of the authority which issues it. Disobedience, of course, is predicated upon knowledge of the prohibition. In a sense, this rule is a corollary of the legality principle which makes it a condition of punishment that the law upon the violation of which it is imposed be knowable to the offender. The latter principle is a postulate focussing on the objective quality of the law's being knowable in

[63]The history and justifications of the law of legal error are discussed in Ryu and Silving, *supra* note 8, at pp. 423–39.

advance of the offence, whereas the mental capacity rule focusses on the subjective factor of personal capacity to know or actual knowledge of the pertinent law. Accessibility of law is stressed in the Bible.[64]

M'Naghten's root in the law of error affords a clue to its persistent appeal to lawyers. Rejection of the defence of legal error is a solution based on convenience, not on requirements of justice. One of the several instances in which a tendency to revert to the ancient defence of error is noticeable is the defence of insanity.

The challenges of the M'Naghten right-wrong test may be divided into several conceptual phases: (i) the phase concerned with the propriety of the moral discernment test; (ii) the phase in which doubt was cast on irrationality being a proof of mental illness; and (iii) the phase in which the contention was advanced that the mental incapacity definition should not be couched in terms of any particular symptom.

In the first phase much criticism was based on the alleged inability of psychiatrists to testify regarding moral values. Zilboorg particularly, but others as well, have asserted that psychiatrists cannot honestly testify to an accused's knowledge of right and wrong, since the latter concepts present no scientifically cognizable categories.[65] This criticism is based on a methodological fallacy. There is an essential difference between approving of or accepting social or legal postulates as valid or as values in a normative sense, that is, recognizing their obligatory force, and admitting their existence as contents of thought or of the conscience of the community. The latter existence is a scientifically provable reality. The sciences which deal with this reality are anthropology, sociology, and social psychology. Dynamic psychology, of which Zilboorg purports to be a spokesman, itself describes man's "modifying his wishful thinking to conform to the realities of existence," a change "from thinking on the basis of the *pleasure principle* to thinking on

[64]Deut. 30:11–14.

[65]"The psychiatrist [in court] is asked whether a given person knew the difference between right and wrong; this is not a psychiatric question." Gregory Zilboorg, *The Psychology of the Criminal Act and Punishment* (Isaac Ray Award Book, 1954), p. 112. See also Roche, *supra* note 4, at p. 107.

the basis of the *reality principle*,"[66] as a phenomenon of normal human development. As he grows, the infant learns to sacrifice or postpone gratification in order to earn parental love; the mature person must do so to earn social approval or at least to incur no social disapproval, of which the community censure expressed in legal punishment is but a particular form. An average conscience, a normal superego is essential to mental health.[67] Perhaps the psychiatrists' complaints over testifying on a matter alien to their science when answering the question of whether the accused knew that he was doing what was wrong could be avoided if the term "knew" were replaced by "believed."

As the alleged metaphysics of the right-wrong notion, so has also the "transcendental meaning" of the "nature and the quality of the act" been subjected to vigorous criticism.[68] This criticism is entirely unwarranted in the light of the historical meaning of the phrase "nature and quality." As shown above, in the Roman-canon law,

[66]Karl A. Menninger, *The Human Mind* (3d ed.; 1955), p. 323.

[67]Said Zilboorg, the foremost critic of the law's alleged demand that psychiatrists recognize the reality of social "right and wrong":

"It so happens that psychoanalysts consider criminals anti-social people, and also psychologically sick people. We do not consider *criminality* but the *criminal*, and while we call his criminal acts anti-social we do not consider them psychopathological because they are anti-social, but because psychologically they are not normal regardless of whether the acts are anti-social or not. When a man rapes and kills a woman, or when a woman kills her child, we consider them psychologically abnormal not because the law calls them criminals, but because the capacity to love in such individuals is perverted: it is associated with death instead of life; it is not genital but anal-sadistic, primitive, archaic, infantile." Zilboorg, "Social Responsibility," in K. R. Eissler (ed.), *Searchlights on Delinquency* (1949), p. 329, at p. 335. Since the social aspects of rape and child-killing are apparently irrelevant to this psychiatrist, one might expect him to answer the obvious question of how he reaches the conclusion that it is undesirable to have a sexuality that is "not genital but anal-sadistic, primitive, archaic, infantile." Is this undesirability evinced in science? In *The Psychology of the Criminal Act and Punishment*, *supra* note 65, at p. 122, Zilboorg concedes that the demands of psychiatrists that their views be admitted into open court are, "be it underscored again and again, . . . of a moral nature." In "Social Responsibility," *ibid.*, Zilboorg also admits (at p. 337) that psychoanalysis "is based primarily on humanistic individualism" which is a moral position. One might then wonder why the same author rejects the imputation that psychoanalysis should help to fight such obviously anti-individualistic political movements as fascism on the ground that this would imply abandonment of the "scientific" stand. Confusion of the scientific and the therapeutic functions of the psychiatrist is often combined with a lack of appreciation of the distinctiveness of the social responsibility of the psychiatric profession. For a rational approach to the problem of values in psychiatry see Heinz Hartmann, *Psychonalysis and Moral Values* (1960).

[68]Zilboorg, *supra* note 65, at pp. 3–26.

which profoundly influenced the development of English criminal law, that phrase denotes those qualities of the act which constitute its very nature, that is, those of its attributes which give it its distinctive relevance in the given context. Translated into contemporary language, "nature and quality" means that quality which corresponds to the legal or statutory description of the crime charged, or putting it differently, that quality which makes the act criminal.

In the second phase of the critique of M'Naghten the attack focussed on its taking rationality to be a test of capacity when dynamic psychology had shown that unconscious, irrational motivations influence actions of all normal individuals. Of course, there is a difference between an irrational conduct of an otherwise normal person and such conduct of a mentally ill person. Perhaps the difference may be found to lie in the amenability of the former to be persuaded by rational reasoning that his own conduct was irrational or, generally, to be rationally motivated. But acting upon irrational beliefs—even failure to be persuaded by rational arguments—alone cannot be taken as a test of mental incapacity, for this would place all those holding peculiar religious beliefs within the category of the mentally incapacitated.

The third phase of the challenge of M'Naghten is marked by its critique in the *Durham Case*. There Judge Bazelon said: "The fundamental objection to the right-wrong test . . . is not that criminal irresponsibility is made to rest upon an inadequate, invalid or indeterminable symptom or manifestation, but that it is made to rest upon *any* particular symptom. In attempting to define insanity in terms of a symptom, the courts have assumed an impossible role, not merely one for which they have no special competence."[69]

Of course, psychiatrists judge whether a person is mentally ill or in need of treatment on the basis of observable symptoms, whether these be physical or behavioural. How else can we reach other men's minds?[70] In fact, in the light of contemporary critical philo-

[69] *Durham* v. *United States*, *supra* note 20, at p. 872.

[70] Of course, one might well doubt that we can ever know other men's minds, but if we can do so, there is no doubt that the vehicle of such cognition is symptomatic behaviour. See John Wisdom, *Other Minds* (1952).

sophy, reality consists only in symptoms, in the sense of the observable and meaningfully expressible by language; use of language that seems to suggest reference to a reality behind symptoms is only an abbreviated manner of connecting a plurality or selectivity of symptoms for purposes of convenience. Descriptions of so-called psychological realities are always denotations of symptom groups. Etiological explanations are likewise expressions of symptoms of etiology. To be meaningful, any psychological concept must be reducible to symptoms. Indeed, symptoms are not representatives of something; they are the thing itself. The mind, the Conscious, the Unconscious, and so on, are constructs ultimately expressive of groups of symptoms,[71] just as the object of modern physics is a construct built from data (symptoms) obtained from different physical points of observation. None of these concepts represents a separate ontological entity.

However, Judge Bazelon's rejection of symptoms seems to refer to a specific "symptomatology." It reflects psychoanalytical stress on etiological factors rather than on symptoms in terms of presently observable deviations of behaviour or failures of functioning. To explain why this essentially correct psychoanalytical position cannot be adequately incorporated in law, it is necessary to explain the difference between psychoanalytical and conventional symbolism.

When a psychoanalytical patient communicates with his psychiatrist, the contents of his speech assume a meaning which does not correspond to the conventional social understanding of terms such as are used. The words are set within a new frame of reference established by analytical science and relating present experience to one long past. Identity or disparity of meaning is not the same in conventional symbolism and in analytical symbolism. What has been said of words is also true of other personality expressions. The total behaviour complex of the patient means something different in psychoanalysis from what it means in general

[71]Freud "discovered" the Unconscious by listening to what patients said and by observing what they did. All these statements and conduct patterns were to him symptoms of the Unconscious. In realistic terms, these "symptoms" *are* the Unconscious, for certainly no one has experienced it directly. When the "Unconscious" becomes conscious, the now conscious is again a "symptom" of the formerly Unconscious.

social life. Also, the relevance and significance of behaviour are judged by its relation to past experience, its etiology, rather than by its present social import. Mental illness as a pattern of behaviour is thus evaluated in terms of etiology rather than in terms of a present significance. For example, failure to distinguish right from wrong, in the light of psychoanalytical interpretation, may have several meanings, depending on the etiology of such failure, while it has a constant meaning in other social contexts.

But there is a significant difference between the social import of this psychoanalytical insight in psychiatry and in law. Psychiatry does not require a final discrete definition of those mental phenomena which are to be relevant for its purpose. It may proceed tentatively and experimentally. But the law must operate on the basis of discrete definitions that might serve as standards of final determinations. Psychoanalysis does not provide the law with workable tools of such determinations. It can supply only a very broad definitional frame for the mental incapacity test, as, for example, ego impairment. Resort to symptoms is thus imperative, though the symptoms need not consist of such narrow and inflexible features of specific faculty failure as the M'Naghten knowledge defect.

Inability to testify in terms of symptoms has been also a favourite argument of psychiatrists opposed to the M'Naghten test. They indeed assert that their diagnoses are made longitudinally,[72] and that how they are reached cannot wholly be verbalized.[73] I assume that those methods that cannot be verbalized are intuitive. This means that such diagnoses are referable to symptoms in the mind of the psychiatrist that cannot in turn be related or unequivocally related to symptoms exhibited by the subject of observation. What these psychiatrists, then, assert is that they ought to be permitted to testify not to their opinions supported by rational evidence but to their own intuitive reactions to unspecifiable experiences. It is

[72]Winfred Overholser, *The Psychiatrist and the Law* (Isaac Ray Award Book, 1953), p. 25.

[73]John C. Whitehorn, "Report to the Governor's Commission on Legal Psychiatry, Maryland," quoted in John M. Macdonald, *Psychiatry and the Criminal* (1958), p. 65.

submitted that if the law is to accept the psychiatrists' intuitive judgments of mental incapacity as bases of exemption, much more would have to be done than reformulating the incapacity test, as has been done in the *Durham Case*. Intuitive judgment, charismatic dispensation of justice has been alleged in civil law countries to be a peculiar function of the lay jury. Where the limits of reason are crossed, a juror is expected to feel what the true facts are. Because feeling is the source of their ultimate judgment, jurors are not expected to state any reasons for their findings. But to permit a witness—the expert is in the last analysis one—to testify to his feelings, as contrasted with his rational observations and opinions, would constitute such departure from established rules of proof of the common law as to call perhaps for a constitutional amendment. Whatever the shortcomings of M'Naghten, its inadequacy does not lie in forcing psychiatrists to state the bases of their opinions.

The most significant criticism of M'Naghten is addressed to the narrowness of the test. The latter does not exempt all those who, in the light of sound policy, merit exemption. In trying to fit M'Naghten into a broader exemption policy, the adherents of the test claim that it stands for more than it verbally expresses. Invoking the unitary conception of the human personality, prevailing in modern psychology, Jerome Hall, for instance, alleges that since such a conception implies a necessary affecting of reasoning by mental illness, an impairment of reasoning may be taken as a test of such illness.[74] The opponents of M'Naghten rejoin that "the various functions of mentation are disparately affected in various diseases and different individuals,"[75] so that it is possible for a person suffering from a serious disease not or not yet to show any signs of defective reasoning or knowledge capacity. There are states of mind which, in the light of sound policy, ought to be included in the exemption, but in which there is a marked failure in feeling or volition though no apparent cognitive failure. The M'Naghtenites, in turn, advance the proposition that knowledge means more

[74]Hall, *supra* note 11, at pp. 774–5.

[75]Manfred S. Guttmacher, *Principal Difficulties with the Present Criteria of Responsibility and Possible Alternatives*, Appendix B, §4.01, Model Penal Code, Tent. Draft No. 4 (1956), p. 170, at p. 175.

than mere knowledge or verbal knowledge. According to them, it means profound or sound knowledge, the knowledge of a rational individual, in which feeling and volition participate.[76] This is sheer semantics. The opponents might as well accept the challenge and merely ask that the meaning of knowledge as interpreted by the modern M'Naghtenites be verbalized or specified in the statutory or other legal definition of the incapacity test. For this would obviously require introduction into the test of both volition and feeling.

However, the defect of the knowledge test is not only that it is too narrow but also that it is at times too wide, from the standpoint of sound policy. Not only is a failure of cognition not the sole test of mental incapacity, but flagrant, absurd cognitive failures do not necessarily point to such incapacity.[77] Some other or additional test is thus essential. The adherents of M'Naghten might say that such additional test is afforded by use of the term "disease of the mind." But since the meaning of this term is by no means fixed, it can hardly supply the needed interpretative aid in important borderline cases.

(2) IRRESISTIBLE IMPULSE

The M'Naghten test has been supplemented in many jurisdictions by the so-called irresistible impulse test, which exempts from punishment those who, while aware of the wrongfulness of their conduct, acted under an impulse which they were unable to resist. Criticism of the test has focussed on the term "impulse." It has been said that there are situations of grave mental illness, such as melancholia, characterized by brooding and meditation, where the ultimate criminal act is by no means spontaneous but was prepared and premeditated.[78] To meet this criticism, some tests modify the irresistible impulse test to read inability to conform

[76]Hall, *supra* note 11, at pp. 780, 784

[77]Hervey Cleckley, *The Mask of Sanity* (3d ed.; 1955), at pp. 21–2, points out that "one finds throughout the nation, and probably over the world, a horde of citizens who stoutly maintain beliefs regarded as absurd and contrary to fact by society as a whole. Often these people indulge in conduct that to others seems unquestionably irrational." Some of their practices are "no less fanciful than the delusions of patients confined in psychiatric hospitals."

[78]See *Royal Comm. Report* 110, *supra* note 9.

one's conduct to the appreciation of criminality. But the inadequacy of the irresistible impulse test lies not only in the use of the term "impulse" but also in the concept of the irresistible. When is a person unable to resist an urge or a temptation? Critics have called attention to the fact that many of those allegedly unable to resist do resist temptation when a "policeman is at the elbow."[79] Although the fact that such persons can restrain themselves under such, but not under other, circumstances does not indicate that they ought to be held responsible, it does indicate that incapacity to resist cannot serve as the proper standard of exemption or, at least, that it cannot serve as such standard without inclusion of additional circumstances. Thus, we are again referred to the question of what are the decisive circumstances for purposes of the exemption.

(3) THE MODEL PENAL CODE TESTS

The American Law Institute's Model Penal Code submits in a tentative draft one principal test and two alternative tests.[80] The principal test provides that a person is not responsible for criminal conduct if at the time of such conduct "as a result of mental disease or defect he lacks substantial capacity either to appreciate the criminality of his conduct or to conform his conduct to the requirements of law." In alternative (*a*) the capacity part is formulated differently: "his capacity either to appreciate the criminality of his conduct or to conform his conduct to the requirements of law is so substantially impaired that he cannot justly be held responsible." In alternative (*b*) that part reads: "he lacks substantial capacity to appreciate the criminality of his conduct or is in such state that the prospect of conviction and punishment cannot constitute a significant restraining influence upon him." Paragraph (2) reads uniformly: "The terms 'mental disease or defect' do not include an abnormality manifested only by repeated criminal or otherwise anti-social conduct."

Some features are common to all these tests: (i) each comprises two items: (*a*) description of a disability and (*b*) indication of the

[79]Model Penal Code, Tent. Draft No. 4, comments to §4.01, at p. 158. See also Davidson, *supra* note 36.

[80]Tent. Draft No. 4 (1955), §4.01, p. 27.

source of disability; (ii) in each test one disability variant is cognitive; this disability is uniformly described as lack of "capacity to appreciate the criminality of his [the actor's] conduct"; (iii) the disability in each test is related to the specific act charged; (iv) the source of disability is described in all tests as "mental disease or defect"; (v) in each test the disability must be "a result of mental disease or defect"; (vi) the term "substantial" recurs in all versions. I shall deal first with the common features and then discuss those aspects in which the tests vary from each other.

In *State* v. *Jones*,[81] Judge Ladd criticized the first M'Naghten answer by pointing out the inconsistency of denying an exemption to an actor if he "knew . . . that he was acting contrary to law, by which is meant the law of the land," while proceeding on the assumption that "[t]he law is administered upon the principle that *every one* must be taken conclusively to know the law of the land, without proof that he does know it." Judge Ladd was concerned with the problem of how the required knowledge of law was to be proven when such proof was barred by the conclusive presumption. The Model Code test, to be sure, requires not knowledge but capacity to appreciate, which is a distinct improvement. Still, one manner—perhaps the best—of proving defendant's capacity to appreciate the criminality of his conduct is proving that he did appreciate it. If the test is adopted, we will continue to witness the strange spectacle of evidence being adduced that a person alleging that he was mentally diseased or defective knew that what he was doing was a crime, when such knowledge is not required of a mentally healthy person.

Indeed, the strongest argument against use of any test requiring legal knowledge or capacity to know criminality is contained in this policy question: if knowledge of criminality is not a general requisite of responsibility, why should its absence or a lack of capacity to acquire it constitute an exemption ground? Surely, no serious contention is being advanced that the conclusive presumption of legal knowledge is based on a realistic belief that mentally healthy persons actually know the law or, indeed, appreciate it. A similar

[81](1871) 50 N.H. 369, at p. 386.

question is posed by the use of the term "appreciation" rather than "knowledge." Apparently, appreciation, as distinguished from knowledge, is intended to convey the notion of healthy knowledge, knowledge with attendant feeling, or meaningful knowledge, which some M'Naghtenites have read into the term knowledge. But why should capacity of such profound knowledge be required of the person whose mental incapacity is alleged when no profound knowledge is necessary in the case of a mentally healthy person?

Both capacity to appreciate and capacity to conform (or in alternative (*b*) deterrability by the prospect of punishment) are related to the specific crime that has been charged. Such relation is meaningful in M'Naghten, since relevant error of law is error regarding the specific prohibition which has been violated. But what meaning does this specificity have in the Model Code? As shown, knowledge is not in issue. Hence, capacity to know could be significant only as bearing on the nature or degree of the mental disease or defect. Assuming, then, that the crucial factor is mental disease or defect and that incapacity is but its symptom or a modifying factor, it is pertinent to inquire whether such incapacity actually has any bearing on the mental state of the actor. The answer is that this depends on the type of prohibition that happens to be in issue. If a person does not appreciate the criminality of killing a perfectly innocent neighbour,[82] such lack of appreciation has a clear bearing on his mental capacity within the mores of our society. But if the accused does not know that killing six hundred persons in order to save the lives of thousands is a crime, the German Bundesgerichtshof held that such error may be excusable,

[82]See *Pueblo* v. *Alsina* (1956), 79 D.P.R. 46. Alsina's killing of a neighbour, Aida Acosta, was completely unexpected. About a month before the act he purchased a revolver, and about two weeks before killing Aida he is supposed to have said that she was interfering with his matrimonial matters. *Ibid.*, at p. 49. The Court noticed that there was no evidence whatever of such interference on Aida's part. After diagnosing the accused's condition as "schizophrenia of the paranoid type," the psychiatric expert, Dr. Fernandez Marina, stated (at p. 51): "Such person, for instance, when asked whether it is bad to kill, says that it is bad to kill, but when asked whether it is bad to kill in self-defence, says that it is not bad, for he believes himself to be persecuted and thinks that when he kills the persons concerned he does so in self-defence and thus believes that it is not bad to kill at that moment."

since the prohibition of killing under such circumstances is by no means evident to most people and, indeed, constitutes a highly controversial ethical and legal issue.[83] A person who either does not or cannot appreciate the criminality of such killing or cannot conform to such prohibition need not be mentally ill. There are many provisions in the Penal Code of Puerto Rico as well as in other codes which I cannot appreciate.

While the requirement of "capacity to appreciate and to conform" (or to be motivated by the prospect of punishment) undoubtedly limits the class of those suffering from a mental disease or defect, use of the phrase "as a result of" rather suggests that the incapacity clause does not describe or define mental disease or defect for legal purposes, so that the latter is a subject of independent proof. Thus, we are referred back to the term "mental disease" that has been so vigorously criticized as vague and uncertain by opponents of the Durham test. In the Model Code psychopaths are specifically excluded from the exemption.[84] But what about neurotics? Are persons suffering from kleptomania or pyromania or the types of persons described in Alexander and Healy's *Roots of Crime*[85] mentally diseased persons? The Model Code does not answer these questions, since it does not, even to the extent that this is done in Durham,[86] define mental disease.

The phrase "as a result of" is but an equivalent of "product,"[87] so

[83]Decision rendered Nov. 28, 1952 (IV Strafsenat), reported [1953] *Neue Juristische Wochenschrift* [hereinafter cited N.J.W.] 513. For discussion see Silving, "Euthanasia: A Study in Comparative Criminal Law" (1954), 103 *U. Pa. L. R.* 350, at pp. 356–9.

[84]See par. (2) of §4.01, *supra*, text at note 80.

[85]Franz Alexander and William Healy, *Roots of Crime* (1935).

[86]In the *Durham Case, supra* note 20, at p. 875, "disease" is defined as "a condition which is considered capable of either improving or deteriorating," whereas "defect" is said to be "a condition which is not considered capable of either improving or deteriorating. . . ."

[87]The dictionary meaning of "to result" is "to proceed, spring, or arise, as a consequence, effect. . . ." *Webster's New International Dictionary* (2d ed.; 1953). After criticizing the Durham "product" notion, the draftsmen of the Model Code state: "While we agree . . . that mental disease or defect involves gradations of degree that should be recognized, we think the legal standard ought to focus on the *consequences* of disease or defect that have a bearing on the justice of conviction and of punishment." Comments to §4.01, at pp. 159–60. The dictionary meaning of "consequence" is "1. That which follows something on which it

that the criticism of the product notion of Durham, to be discussed when analyzing that case, is partially applicable to the phrase "as a result of" in the Model Code tests. True, there is a difference between the functions performed by the causation concept in Durham and in the Model Code tests. In Durham the disease is supposed to cause the commission of crime,[88] whereas in the Model Code it must cause the incapacity to appreciate or to conform. The latter statement might be taken to mean that the incapacity is an expression or a symptom of the disease, and in this sense is less objectionable than the statement that the disease produces criminal conduct. But the question remains whether it is possible to say that the defendant "would have been capable of conforming had he not suffered from the disease,"[89] which is implied in choice of the term "as a result of." Nor is this a "logician's nicety,"[90] but a matter involving the very usefulness of a test which affords no standard that is applicable in practice, the issue it raises not being answerable.

Since the Model Code definitions do not seem to render independent proof of mental disease dispensable and since "result of" plainly means "product of," it is submitted that the draftsmen's purposes might be better served if the phrase "as a result of" were replaced by the copula "and." But if this is done, it would become even more obvious that something is required as a test of responsibility where mental capacity is in issue that is not required in cases in which the issue does not arise.

There is no general objection to using the term "substantial" in law. It is often impossible to avoid the term, and while "substantial" does not make the meaning of a sentence quite determinate, it may make it less indeterminate than it would otherwise be. But the extent to which it adds to the determinateness of a sentence depends on the total framework within which it is used. "Substantial," of course, implies that the subject which it qualifies is

---

depends; that which is produced by a cause or ensues from any form of necessary connection; . . . 3. *a.* Chain of causes and effects; . . . *b.* Act of following something else as a result; relation of an effect to its cause."

88On this see particularly *Carter* v. *United States* (1957), 252 F.2d 608 (App. D.C., reh. den. 1957), at pp. 615–17.

89*Ibid.*

90*Ibid.* For the pertinent passages see *infra* text at note 154.

graded and indicates a relative degree, as compared with some standard. But the Model Code does not mention any standard of comparison. We learn from the comments[91] that "substantial incapacity" means that the incapacity need not be complete, as required in M'Naghten. The Code's draftsmen admit that there is in the reality of life no such thing as a complete impairment. While realizing the precariousness of the term "substantial" impairment when no principle is suggested "that measures how substantial it must be," they eventually dismiss the problem saying, "if capacity is greatly impaired, that presumably should be sufficient."[92] But the standard does not appear to be sufficient to the Reporter and a Council minority who suggest that it is necessary to state how substantial the impairment must be. With this, our attention is directed to alternative solutions suggested by Council minorities. Alternative (*a*) merely submits a less deceptive version, for it recommends no greater specificity but rather refers determination of the degree of incapacity that is necessary in order to exempt a defendant to the jury, which presumably is to decide on a case-to-case basis. This is implied in the version, "was so substantially impaired that he can not justly be held responsible," advocated by the Reporter. Other Council members rejoin that "it is unwise to present questions of justice to the jury."[93] The degree of jury discretion can be reduced by indication of the policy of the exemption, for in such event the impairment must be judged as "incapacity" with regard to the factor that is relevant in the light of such policy. Alternative (*b*) expresses such policy in the incapacity definition, "is in such state that the prospect of conviction and punishment cannot constitute a significant restraining influence." This phrase is more determinate than the phrase "lacks substantial capacity to conform." Without indication of a standard of comparison or of the policy of the test, lack of "capacity to conform . . . to the requirements of law" remains vague and uncertain, notwithstanding addition of the qualification "substantial." Nor could this test be much improved were the actual standard of comparison, "complete incapacity," expressly

[91]Comments to §4.01, at p. 158.
[92]*Ibid.*, at p. 159.
[93]*Ibid.*

incorporated in its wording. For since, admittedly, there is no such group as the totally incapacitated, it is virtually impossible to determine what constitutes a substantially greater impairment than that assumed to be present in such group. The capacity of average community members might afford a more realistic standard of comparison.

The concept of lack of "capacity to conform . . . to the requirements of law," which appears both in the principal test and in alternative (*a*), is most precarious. In discussing the German test, I shall deal at greater length with the objections raised against use of this concept. But to the extent that its shortcomings are evident from a critical reading of the Model Code and its comments, it is proper to indicate them in the present context. The Code commentators tell us that when using the phrase, "lacks substantial capacity to conform," they actually mean to convey the standard suggested by alternative (*b*). They inform us that "the question that is most precisely relevant for legal purposes" is "non-deterrability" and that the latter "is the determination that is sought," but that its assesment, meaning, an estimate of the subject's responsiveness to "a single influence, the threat of punishment," is "too difficult for psychiatric judgment," and that, for this reason, "non-deterrability . . . must be reached by probing general capacity to conform to the requirements of law."[94] In other words, incapacity to conform to the requirements of law is but a substitute for non-susceptibility to being influenced by the threat of punishment imposed by law upon violation of the prohibition. Is it then the draftsmen's contention that incapacity to conform to a given law can be psychiatrically proven whereas non-responsiveness to the threat which this law imposes cannot be proven? It would seem that the line between such incapacity to conform to a specific, given law and non-responsiveness to the threat which it imposes is rather tenuous. Indeed, it would seem that whether a person is capable of conforming is less answerable than whether he can be motivated by a threat. This, of course, should not be taken to imply approval of the test of alternative (*b*), for that test is based upon a doctrine of deter-

[94] *Ibid.*

rence, so that the critique of that doctrine submitted above is applicable to (*b*).

The main inadequacy of the majority test and alternative (*a*) lies in the limitation of incapacity to the spheres of knowledge and will. Is it really true that a person who in a state of melancholia kills his children because he believes that he is thus sparing them future suffering lacks either capacity to appreciate the legal prohibition against killing or capacity to conform his conduct to this requirement of law? Such person knows that killing is a crime and has sufficient self-control to resist a temptation to kill. His incapacity lies in a loss of a sense of reality, in a general collapse of total personality organization rather than in a specific failure of either knowledge or will power.

A significant objection addressed to all the versions is that their policy, as expressly stated in alternative (*b*) and as admittedly followed in the other versions, is not consistent. If this policy is to exempt persons who cannot be affected by punitive-correctional methods, that is, those who are not susceptible to deterrence, one might well ask why the Code specifically exempts in paragraph (2) those who are clearly "non-deterrable," namely, psychopaths.

Finally, none of these tests includes in the mental incapacity exemption apparently temporary mental disturbances, such as the disturbance of consciousness in Germany or the temporary mental disturbance in Spain. Persons acting in such mental states merit inclusion, provided that, contrary to the rules obtaining in civil law countries, when acquitted on the ground of mental incapacity, such persons ought to be subject to measures.

(4) GERMAN TESTS

The present German provision on mental incapacity reads thus: "Where the actor, at the time of the act, because of a disturbance of consciousness, because of a pathological disturbance of mental functioning or because of mental debility, is incapable of appreciating the impermissibility of the act or of acting in conformity to this appreciation, the act is not criminal [literally, there is no criminal act]" (section 51(1), German Penal Code).

Of the numerous tests, whether formerly in force or recommended by reform drafts and projects, I shall directly discuss only four: the one now in force; the tests of the Reform Drafts of 1956 and 1960; and the test recommended by Seelig. Common to the first-mentioned test, the tests of the Reform Drafts and the Model Code tests are (1) a dualistic approach expressed in the requirement that there be a defined incapacity and a defined source of such incapacity, at least as regards the principal exemption category; (2) specificity of incapacity, in the sense of its limitation to the specific act that has been committed; (3) division of incapacity into cognitive and conative incapacity. I shall first discuss the policy basis of the incapacity concept, since a uniform policy, reflected in a consistent treatment of the law of error and of that of mental incapacity, is one of the great merits of the German approach. It contrasts favourably with the lack of a consistent philosophy in the Model Code.

(a) *The philosophy of the "incapacity" concept*

The fact that "incapacity to appreciate" and "incapacity to conform" are related to the specific act that has been committed has a different import within the framework of German law from that which the same phenomenon has within the context of the Model Code. The German requirement that mental incapacity be one disabling the actor with regard to the specific act charged and the German stress on incapacity to know the law reflect a consistent policy oriented to an elaborate philosophy of guilt and punishment. The notion of guilt is principally expressed in German law in the rule on "error of law." The defence of such error has been admitted in Germany judicially, on the ground that it is implicit in the requirement of guilt. If an accused did not know the prohibition that he violated, he is excused, unless he acted negligently in not ascertaining the prohibition.[95] Hence there is a rational basis for inquiring whether he did or did not have capacity to know that prohibition or to conform to such knowledge, whereas raising the

[95] 2 B.G.H.St. 194 (1952), a landmark decision rendered by the Great Senate in Criminal Matters of the Supreme Court in Civil and Criminal Matters.

same questions within the Model Code is not consistent with its general adherence to the principle *error iuris nocet*. It may be interesting to note that the 1956 and the 1960 drafts of a new German Penal Code attempt to consolidate the law of mental incapacity with the law of error of law by gearing the "incapacity to appreciate" and "to conform to such appreciation" to illegality (*Unrecht*) of the act rather than—as is the case in present German law—to its being not permissible (*das Unerlaubte*),[96] which commonly means prohibited by either law or morality. While "*Unrecht*" is also ambiguous, it is the same term that is used in the drafts' provisions on legal error.[97]

(*b*) *So-called "mixed system"*

The approach reflected in the German tests is mixed or, as is usually said, "biologico-psychological," "biological" indicating the source of incapacity and "psychological" denoting the specific state of mind at the time of the act. Reference in legal literature to the source of incapacity as "biological" goes back to a time when mental disease was believed to have an exclusively biological foundation[98]—a belief that seems not to have been quite overcome in Germany. But though the term "biological" continues in use, it clearly includes psychic determinants of mental incapacity.[99] The phrase "mixed biologico-psychological" is interpreted to indicate that there must be a definite basis or source of "incapacity to appreciate or conform," so that the latter alone does not afford an exemption ground. The doctrinal stress that such a source must produce a specific incapacity to commit the act charged, while consistent with the dominant philosophy of guilt, is open to criticism on other grounds; it reflects a survival of obsolete psychiatric notions, akin to the persistence of the monomania notion in our law. Both the 1956 and the 1960 drafts explain direction of disease and incapacity to the specific act

96*Entwurf des Allgemeinen Teils eines Strafgesetzbuchs* 1956 (Bonn, 1958) (hereinafter cited as German draft 1956), comment to s. 23, at p. 30; *Entwurf eines Strafgesetzbuchs* (StGB) E 1960, Bundesrat Drucksache 270/60 (hereinafter cited as German draft 1960), comment to s. 24, at p. 132.

97Compare in the 1956 draft ss. 23 and 20, and in the 1960 draft ss. 24 and 21.

98Compare Judge Doe's view that mental disease is a physical state, *infra*.

99On this see German draft 1960, comment to s. 24, at p. 129.

by the relativity of incapacity to incur guilt.[100] The draftsmen point out that a man may at the time of the act be incapacitated with respect to some acts but not to others.[101] This is, of course, inconsistent with the view of modern psychology that a mental disability affects man's total personality and hence anything he may do. The newer insight is also obscured by the unrealistic specification of the faculties of appreciation and conformity. Relativity of capacity in German law is also inconsistent with formulation of incapacity itself in absolute terms, "is incapable" being the key word. The Model Code's substantial impairment of capacity is certainly more in accord with psychological reality.

(c) *Critique of the incapacity formula*

The criterion, "capacity to appreciate and to conform," has been introduced into the law in 1933 by the Law on Dangerous Habitual Criminals,[102] to replace the original version formulated in terms of exclusion of "free determination of the will." The substitution followed the advice of prominent psychiatrists, Aschaffenburg in Germany and Wagner v. Jauregg in Austria.[103] The psychiatrists' objection to the original version was that it unnecessarily involved the issue of free will. But the same objection now appears to be applicable to the substitute.

In 1948 the present version became the target of a vigorous critique by a leading psychiatrist, Dr. Kurt Schneider, who asserted that no man can answer the question of whether the accused possessed capacity of appreciation and conformance, adding that when psychiatrists answer such questions they actually rely solely on their finding the so-called biological basis either present or absent.[104] Schneider stated that section 51 "is based on a psychology of action that is not realistic and cannot be reconciled with contemporary psychological opinion." The jurist Seelig pointed out that this

[100]On this ground they reject a purely "biological" test, such as is, e.g., the test of the French Penal Code, art. 64, which defines the exemption simply as "*démence*."

[101]German draft 1960, comment to s. 24, at p. 130.

[102]Law of Nov. 24, 1933, [1933] Reichsgesetzblatt Part I, at p. 995.

[103]On this see Ernst Seelig, *supra* note 11, at pp. 214–16.

[104]*Ibid.*, at pp. 213–14.

critique does not apply to capacity to appreciate but does apply to capacity to conform. The latter, as formulated by Mezger and others, is reducible to capacity, at the time of the criminal conduct, "to act or not to act." To find whether the actor possessed capacity to conform, the observer must be able to ascertain whether the actor could have acted otherwise than he did act. This may be said to reopen the problem of free will, but, above all, when raised retrospectively, presents a most precarious, if not insoluble, issue. Mezger accordingly suggested that the ultimate problem of capacity to conform must be reduced to the question of "whether the actor can be justly held criminally responsible for his act."[105] This formula, of course, is precisely that advanced by Professor Wechsler. Seelig pointed out that it leaves the judge without any legal criterion, though supplying him with one was undoubtedly the purpose of qualifying the biological portion of the test. One might well inquire whether as thus conceived, the notion of capacity to conform serves any useful purpose.

Actually, the conformity test is but a disguised version of the older concept of "free determination of the will."[106] To demonstrate that it often misses the relevant issue, Seelig uses an example which resembles that presented by the Royal Commission on Capital Punishment in support of its critique of the irresistible impulse test. A schizophrenic teacher, Wagner of Degerloh killed his wife and children, whom he believed to suffer from an inheritable disease, set fire to buildings and fired from two pistols at all men in the community, allegedly in order to take revenge on his detractors.[107] Seelig correctly noted that the question of whether Wagner could have acted otherwise is not meaningful.

There is no objection, of course, to a basic free will policy, as reflected in, for example, the error of law defence.[108] But an attempt to integrate that policy in a legal text, such as the statutory test of

[105]*Ibid.*, at pp. 224–5.

[106]This, of course, is also a biblical idea. In the Bible, it is forcefully expressed in the Lord's words to Cain (Gen. 4:7): ". . . [S]in lies in wait at the door, and his desire is directed toward you, but you shall rule over him" (author's translation from the Hebrew).

[107]Reported in Seelig, *supra* note 103 at p. 220–1.

[108]See decision cited *supra* note 95.

mental incapacity, must fail, since a test of that type cannot operate functionally, being ultimately reducible to the issue "could the subject have acted otherwise than he did act?"

As will be shown, the source of incapacity in German law is not conceived as narrowly limited to cognitive and voluntaristic categories. But this neither eliminates nor modifies the shortcomings of the incapacity concept itself, although in decisions of law the incapacity test is often disregarded, as it is disregarded by psychiatric experts.

Seelig's submission that the present test of capacity to conform be replaced by a test of capacity to act in accordance with rational motivations deserves attention. It has the great advantage of emphasizing precisely that which a psychiatrist will take into consideration when inquiring into the mental state of a defendant, namely, his motivations,[109] whereas psychiatrists hardly ever examine whether the defendant could have acted otherwise than he acted.

My doubts regarding the usefulness of Seelig's test are mainly based on the observation that there are many queer people who believe and act upon notions that to others may seem absurd, for example, members of all types of quasi-religious sects, and who might therefore qualify for Seelig's exemption, though this is hardly what Seelig intended. "Incapacity to act in accordance with rational motivations" is a significant notion, when it operates within a broader test of mental incapacity, that takes account of the combined sociological-psychiatric aspect of the mental incapacity exemption, by stressing the impairment of a personality, as compared with the mental state of the average community member.

(d) The so-called biological basis

The biological source of incapacity in German law is broadly conceived. To be sure, merely a-typical personality features, such as excessive suggestibility, sexual dependence, character weakness, afford no basis of exemption.[110] But the exempting quality need

[109]Seelig, *supra* note 103, n. 2 at p. 224.

[110]Reinhart Maurach, *Deutsches Strafrecht, Allgemeiner Teil* (2d ed., 1958), at pp. 341–2.

not be a pathological one. A "disturbance of consciousness" within the meaning of section 51 may have its source in normal phenomena, such as drowsiness, exhaustion, affect, for a considerable reduction or a dimming of consciousness is sufficient. Thus, acts committed in states of extreme anger or anxiety have been excused.[111] To exempt, drunkenness need not be such as to exclude consciousness; impairment is sufficient, for example, a heavy drowsiness produced by alcohol consumption. Nor does mere capacity to remember the incident or proof of goal-directed conduct exclude the possibility of a disturbance of consciousness at the time of the act.[112] It is believed that the liberal treatment of so-called non-pathological states in German law is commendable, whereas the handling of pathological states is systematically less felicitous. I shall hence discuss the "disturbance of consciousness" and the "pathological states" in separate subdivisions, stressing the decisional aspects of the former.

(i) *Disturbance of consciousness*

The accused, a quiet, warmhearted, goodnatured person of conciliatory, peaceful disposition—but for years exposed to the nagging of both his domineering wife and a domineering mother-in-law—in the course of a violent controversy, accompanied by a struggle, cut his wife's throat with a potato-paring knife accidentally on hand. The Bundesgerichtshof held[113] that he had acted in a state of "disturbed consciousness" qualifying him for total exemption, even though he was declared by psychiatric experts to be perfectly normal. The trial court had found that he administered the cuts " 'in an excessive affect,' without at the time having regained control of himself." On the basis of expert opinion, it reached the conclusion that "due to the high-grade affect, the accused's capacity of cognition as well as his inhibitive capacity were possibly excluded." But the prosecution contended on appeal that a disturbance of

[111]Adolf Schönke, *Strafgesetzbuch, Kommentar*, ed. Schröder (7th rev. ed.; 1954), at pp. 222–3 (hereinafter cited *Schönke-Schröder*).

[112]Decision of the Bundesgerichtshof, in *Gotdammers Archiv für Strafrecht und Strafprozess* (1955), at p. 269, cited in Maurach, *supra* note 110, at p. 342.

[113]Decision of Oct. 10, 1957 (IV, Strafsenat), reported in (1958) 11 *N. J. W.* 266.

consciousness within section 51 requires that there be present certain specific circumstances such as sleep, drowsiness, hypnosis, brain damage, fever, or poisoning, and that a normal person, in the absence of "other defects in the mental and moral sphere," "even at the peak of excitement . . . remains capable 'to realize his own emotional excitement and motives of action focussed on the object.'" The Bundesgerichtshof rejected this view, supported by psychiatric literature and expert opinions in the case, relying on other psychiatric authorities and on a prior decision holding that "high-grade affects of anger and anxiety may exclude responsibility." "The loss of self-control," said the court, "may be based on a complete lack of self-consciousness in the sense of the actor's intellectual awareness of his own self and of his relation to the environment. But such loss can be also rooted in a profound disturbance of the emotional life and the drives, hence of the emotional sphere of the human personality." In answer to the prosecution's warning of the danger implicit in admitting exemption in cases such as that at bar where the alleged dimming of consciousness can only be inferred from the accused's self-serving assertion, since neither the victim nor third persons are available as witnesses, the court wisely pointed out that "as the instant case itself confirms and as life experience shows . . . sudden outbursts of affect do not accidentally arise in man, as a lightning coming from a clear sky, but . . . as a rule, such outburst is preceded by a long development and history. The latter are usually accessible to proof by witnesses even after the act."[114] The history of the accused's marriage, the constant tension to which he was exposed, the court said, are provable and have been proved in the case at bar; they abundantly show that at the moment of acting, he may well have reached a breaking point.

[114]The court was profoundly moved by the fact that after killing his wife, the accused had lifted her body and kissed her, saying: "Do it well, Irmgard." The history of the marriage was indeed pathetic. He was completely dependent on his wife sexually. She constantly threatened to divorce him. Before the crime she had come to his apartment to ask for the family book in order to initiate divorce proceedings. They nevertheless had sexual intercourse. Thereafter she repeated her insistence on divorce, asking for the family book. The struggle that followed began when he tried to prevent her from leaving and it then developed into a violent battle when she wanted to open the window so that neighbours might hear their quarrel.

On similar grounds, the First Senate of the Bundesgerichtshof had held in 1952,[115] where defendant had killed his brother with a hammer in the presence of two men, in alleged self-defence against an unarmed attack by the brother, that the provision on total exemption may have been applicable. The court below had found that there was present in the case "a sudden acting out of the bitterness which accumulated throughout the years against the degenerate brother," a violent habitual drunkard.

(ii) *Pathological states*

As pointed out before, this part of the German provision is not felicitously formulated, although on the whole decisional law has interpreted it in a commendable manner. There are two notions of pathological states, "pathological disturbance of mental functioning" and "mental debility." They will be discussed separately.

"Pathological disturbance of mental functioning." The Reichsgericht gradually enlarged the class of states within this category. Included are undoubtedly all the psychoses, whether inherited or acquired, whether somatogenic—those which are based on organic or physiological phenomena—or psychogenic—those in which, as the commentators of the 1960 draft put it,[116] "the organic bases . . . , referability to bodily causes, have not yet been clarified." An attempt is made to follow the development of psychiatric knowledge. Thus, the so-called *lucida intervalla*, that is, periods which in manic-depressive psychosis, for example, fall outside the stages of acute illness, and in which pursuant to older doctrine the accused was held responsible, are now believed not to disrupt the continuity of the process of disease; accordingly, in law, prevailing opinion demands exemption.[117] But beyond the psychoses, there is a measure of uncertainty which is reminiscent of our own experience with use of the term "mental disease." The disturbance must be diseased (*krankhaft*), pathological. But neuroses and psychopathies are not *a priori* excluded. In cases of the latter, characterized by "incapacity of conceiving moral notions," it has been held that an exemption

[115]3 B.G.H.St. 195 (I. Strafsenat), decided July 1, 1952, g.M.
[116]Comments to s. 24 at p. 130.
[117]Maurach, *supra* note 110, at p. 344.

will lie if the incapacity is based either on "a pathological cause or a defect of mental organization."[118] Doctrinally, a distinction is being drawn between instances in which the psychopathy is constitutionally acquired and cases in which it is due to environmental influences. The latter are without any clear reason believed not to fall within the exemption.[119] The same criterion is applied to kleptomanias, pyromanias, etc.[120] In sex offences, the test of exemption is said to be whether or not the deviation is of pathological origin.[121] "Pathological disturbance of mental functioning" also includes mental defect.

As may be readily seen, the same objections which have been advanced against use of the term "mental disease" in our law are also applicable to the notion of pathological disturbance of mental functioning.

"*Mental debility.*" There is considerable uncertainty regarding the meaning and scope of the final category, that of "mental debility," literally "mental weakness" (*Geistesschwäche*). The legislative purpose in adding this category was "to include, in an expression accessible to the layman, borderline cases."[122] The difference between this and the pathological disturbance category is said to be one of degree rather than of kind.[123] Mental debility, as well as pathological disturbance, may consist in a disturbance in the sphere of thought or in "the spheres of the will, feeling or drives."[124] Psychopathy is sometimes labelled "mental debility."

Recent reform drafts

The Reform Drafts of 1956 and 1960 commendably attempted to avoid the prevailing uncertainty regarding inclusion or exclusion of psychopaths and neurotics. The 1956 draft included them, the 1960 draft excluded them. The test of the former reads thus:

Section 23. *Incapacity to Incur Guilt Because of Mental Disturbances*
A person acts without guilt where, at the time of the act, he is

[118] RG DR 1939, cited *Schönke-Schröder*, *supra* note 111, at p. 223.
[119] Maurach, *supra* note 110, at p. 344.
[120] *Ibid.*, at p. 345.
[121] E.g., senility; *ibid.*, at p. 345.
[122] *Ibid.*
[123] Kohlrausch-Lange, *Strafgesetzbuch* (42d rev. ed.; 1959), comment to s. 51 VI, at p. 197.
[124] *Ibid.*

incapable, because of mental disturbance, which is pathological or based on a congenital or acquired deviation, or because of a temporary [transitory] disturbance of consciousness, to appreciate the illegality of the act or to act in conformity to this appreciation.

The comments to section 23[125] state that a "disturbance" caused by a "congenital or acquired deviation," as contrasted with a "pathological disturbance," includes "the neuroses, the causes of which may be found in situations of mental conflict; furthermore, disturbances in the drives, above all the psychopathies, which are conceived of as 'personality variants'. . . ." But the deviation from the norm of mental state must be considerable.

The test of the 1960 draft reads thus:

Section 24. *Incapacity to Incur Guilt Because of Mental Disturbances*

A person acts without guilt where, at the time of the act, he is incapable, because of a pathological mental disturbance, because of an equivalent disturbance of consciousness or because of mental deficiency, to appreciate the illegality of the act or to act in conformity to this appreciation.

In contrast to the prevailing law and the 1956 draft, that of 1960 formulates the biological basis of incapacity differently in the provision on total exemption and in that on diminished responsibility.[126] The total exemption provision does not apply to neuroses or to psychopathies.[127] The differentiation between psychoses, and neuroses, and psychopathies proceeds from a distinction between disturbances which affect "the core of personality" and those which have no such impact on personality,[128] a distinction which is hardly clear. The departure from present law is particularly regrettable since the latter has been elaborated in the course of years of judicial interpretation, which undoubtedly reflects a social need for enlargement of the group of those exempted. The draft expressly purports to narrow down the judicial constructions of "disturbance of mental functioning" and "mental debility" contained in leading decisions

[125]German draft 1956, at p. 29.
[126]German draft 1960, s. 25.
[127]*Ibid.*, comment to s. 24 at p. 130.
[128]*Ibid.*, at pp. 130–1.

of the Bundesgerichtshof and the Reichsgericht. According to the former court, "disturbance of mental functioning" "comprises, beyond the circle of mental diseases within the meaning of medical science, all disturbances which impair the conceptions [ideas, perceptions, *Vorstellungen*] and feelings that are present in a normal and mentally mature man making him capable of forming a will, whereby it is irrelevant whether the impairments in issue are those of the reasoning activity or those of the life of the will, of feelings or of the urges."[129] As stated before, the Reichsgericht had held "mental debility" to further extend the scope of the exemption.[130] It may be mentioned parenthetically that the phrase "an equivalent disturbance of consciousness" is most precarious and if adopted can be predicted to become the source of grave problems in practice.[131]

Group 2: *The New Hampshire Test; The Durham Rule; The Spanish Test*

(1) THE NEW HAMPSHIRE TEST

The New Hampshire cases follow a distinctive policy and a consistent method, as did the *M'Naghten Case*. Their reasoning proceeded from the assumption that crime, as well as a contract or a last will, must be the product of intent (or will); when anything that would be otherwise a contract, a will or a crime is produced by something other than intent, the requirements of law are not fulfilled; the otherwise criminal act is not punishable, the contract is void, the testament null. Said Judge Doe in *State* v. *Pike*: "[A] product of mental disease is not a contract, a will, or a crime."[132] This separation of conduct produced by mental disease from con-

[129]B.G.H., reported in (1955 *N.J.W.* 1726, No. 19, cited in 1960 draft comment to s. 24 at p. 131.

[130]73 Entscheidungen des Reichsgerichts in Strafsachen 121.

[131]The term "equivalent" mental abnormality is used in the Swedish Penal Code incapacity test, chap. 5, s. 5. For summary of the various mental incapacity laws see Hans Heinz Heldmann, "Zurechnungsfähigkeit, Zurechnungsunfähigkeit und verminderte Zurechnungsfähigkeit," in Institut für ausländisches und internationales Strafrecht in Freiburg i. Br., *Materialien zur Strafrechtsreform, Rechtsvergleichende Arbeiten I Allgemeiner Teil* ed. D. Lang-Hinrichsen (Bonn, 1954), Vol. II, p. 345.

[132](1870) 49 N.H. 399, at p. 438.

duct produced by intent followed the general doctrine that "if the alleged act of a defendant, was the act of his mental disease, it was not, in law, his act, and he is no more responsible for it than he would be if it had been the act of his involuntary intoxication, or of another person using the defendant's hand against his utmost resistence."[133]

The problem of incapacity exemption arising from this conception was quite simple: one had to establish that which produced the act; if this was not intent, the act was that of an extraneous force alien to the actor and he could not be held responsible for it. The question, "who or what produced the act?" could be answered either "John Doe did it" (John Doe's intent did it) or "The mental disease did it." This idea was by no means new in 1870. "Erskine said in *Hadfield's* case, that delusion is the test when it appears to have produced the act, but not when it does not appear to have produced the act."[134] The distinctive feature of the New Hampshire cases was that an attempt was made to reach a more general concept of that which may produce the act to the exclusion of intent, and this concept was found in mental disease. But "mental disease" or "insanity" in the New Hampshire cases, just as "delusion" in *Hadfield*, was conceived of rather as an ontological entity that entered the human being as an extraneous agent and that acted and produced effects independently of him, as though he had no part in this. It was apparently thought that the existence of this entity called insanity or mental disease and the activities and products of that entity were realities that had nothing to do with law: mental disease and its production of acts were phenomena which only science could observe, find, and attest to. Judge Ladd said that they were matters to be determined by the jury, "upon the question whether the act was the offspring of insanity; if it was, a criminal intent did not produce it; if it was not, a criminal intent did produce it, and it was crime."[135]

Judge Doe[136] exalted the achievements of modern science which

[133]*Ibid.*, at p. 441.
[134]*State* v. *Jones* (1871), 50 N.H. 369, at p. 394.
[135]*Ibid.*, at pp. 398–9.
[136]*State* v. *Pike*, *supra* note 23 at pp. 436–7.

had overcome the superstitious biblical belief that insanity was "demoniacal possession," disencumbered investigation of the subject of mental disease "of all theological complications," and thus found that "insanity is a disease." But his own notion of mental disease and its causal operations was still deeply ingrained in the demonic conception carried over from the Bible. In the Old Testament, insanity entered and left Saul as an "evil spirit."[137] Christ healed those "possessed with devils" by casting out "the spirits,"[138] sometimes by finding, at their request, a new home for them in swine.[139] Judge Doe emphatically disbelieved this. But he believed that insanity is a "physical disease or the result of physical disease" that had the power to cause acts independently of the actor, so that such acts were not "his acts," so to speak, not his "possessions" or "emanations" but the "possessions" or "emanations of mental disease."[140] As his notion that mental disease is an entity alien to its bearer, so was Judge Doe's notion of causation ontological. A century after Hume's critique of causation, Judge Doe apparently believed in the pre-Humean idea "that there exists an objective connection between cause and effect, a connection inherent in the things themselves—an inner bond such that the cause somehow brings about the effect. Hence, the cause is conceived of as an agent, a substance emitting force."[141] Professor Kelsen found a corresponding view supporting such notion of causality in "the experience of the operation of the will of man, who considered his ego or his 'soul' (a concept similar to that of force) as the 'cause' of his actions." In Judge Doe's and Judge Ladd's opinions the parallelism

[137]Compare the citations from I. Sam., *supra* note 59.

[138]Matt. 8:16.

[139]Matt. 8:28–32.

[140]A case cited in both *State* v. *Pike*, *supra* note 23 at p. 429, and *State* v. *Jones*, *supra* note 134 at p. 397, decided shortly before these cases, *Boardman* v. *Woodman*, 47 N.H. 120, held that a person possessed by a delusion could make a valid will unless the latter was the "offspring of the delusion." Judge Ladd pointed out in the *Jones Case* (at pp. 397–8) that accordingly one might say that a man "who labors under a delusion that his legs are made of glass, or that he is charged with controlling the motions of the planetary system, but is in other respects sane," need not be deemed incapable of making a valid will. But he refused to express either assent to or dissent from the manner in which the subject had been treated, since in criminal law delusion as cause of an act has been used as a criterion only in *Hadfield's Case*.

[141]Hans Kelsen, *Society and Nature* (1943), p. 249.

of such notion of causality operating by natural forces, on the one hand, and causality emanating from the will or intent of man, on the other hand, is strikingly reflected. In the opinion of the New Hampshire judges, either disease or intent is the moving force that causes the act, each of these forces functioning as an ontological entity endowed with an independent existence, as a substance emitting force.

When mental disease is thus conceived of as an existentially given entity, law is hardly the proper discipline to determine its necessary incidents, attributes, or the correct test or tests of proving it. Nor is law the proper authority to find whether an act was "caused by disease." If there are any pertinent laws that govern these matters, they are laws of nature, not legal laws. Law's attempts to determine by its own resources the proper test of mental disease or of its causal operations is hence absurd. Thus, there evolved the sentence which constitutes the core of the New Hampshire rule, that "the only general, universal element of law involved in the inquiry" into the exemption of mental incapacity is that the accused is not responsible if his act "was the offspring or product of mental disease."[142] All other issues—whether there is such a mental disease as dipsomania; what is the proper test of mental disease; indeed, whether there is a single test or several tests of such disease; when is an act a product of such disease—are by nature and logic issues of fact and not of law. Said Judge Ladd: "Whether the defendant had a mental disease . . . seems to be as much a question of fact as whether he had a bodily disease; and whether the killing of his wife was the product of that disease, was also as clearly a matter of fact as whether thirst and a quickened pulse are the product of fever."[143]

It is indeed interesting to note that doubts concerning the validity of these naïvely realistic philosophical and "scientific" assumptions were raised not by a lawyer but by a medical man, Dr. Isaac Ray. In a letter to Judge Doe, dated May 3, 1868, he pointed out that since the law recognized only a certain kind or degree of insanity

[142] *State* v. *Jones*, *supra* note 134, at p. 398.
[143] *Ibid.*

as having any legal consequences, the courts could not very well avoid the duty of defining by tests and rules what that kind or degree is. "If, then," Dr. Ray said, "insanity may or may not disqualify, must not this fact be recognized, in some way, by the statute?"[144]

(2) THE DURHAM TEST

The ontological concept of an intent or a disease producing the act has no longer any place in our age of de-substantialization of the universe. Not a trace is left of the notion of causation of the pre-Humean era—of causation as a connection that is inherent in the things themselves. Mental disease has ceased to be, as Judge Doe believed it to be, "only physical disease, or the result of physical disease."[145] The human mind is no longer thought of as divided into compartments, in which the will or intent occupies a separate place, that may be literally taken over or occupied by disease. Nor do we believe that disease is an alien intruder into man's mental life. We view it as distinguishable from health in degree rather than in kind. Indeed, there is no discrete concept of mental disease at all, which might be found to exist in any given case as a pure matter of fact. Our notions of logic, semantics, as well as of legal doctrine, particularly regarding the law-fact dichotomy, have undergone a thorough change. And yet, in the year 1954, Judge Bazelon enunciated in the District of Columbia the very same rule—except for one addition—that was proclaimed in New Hampshire in 1869–70 on the basis of conceptions of an act-producing metaphysical will and an act-producing ontologic entity, mental disease, which even in 1869–70 reflected obsolete ideas. The Durham test reads thus:

> The rule . . . is simply that an accused is not criminally responsible if his unlawful act was the product of mental disease or mental defect.
>
> We use "disease" in the sense of a condition which is considered capable of either improving or deteriorating. We use "defect" in the

[144]Quoted in Louis E. Reik, "The Doe-Ray Correspondence: A Pioneer Collaboration in the Jurisprudence of Mental Disease" (1953), 63 *Yale L. J.* 183, at pp. 188–9.

[145]Letter of Judge Doe to Tyler of Sept. 5, 1866, *ibid.*, at p. 187.

sense of a condition which is not considered capable of either improving or deteriorating and which may be either congenital, or the result of injury, or the residual effect of a physical or mental disease.[146]

Very little needs to be added to what has already been said about Durham. What was simple error in the New Hampshire cases turns into absurdity in Durham, the meaning of the very words used having undergone a revolutionary change. When the New Hampshire judges proclaimed mental disease that produces the act to constitute a logically necessary, a natural, exemption ground, and the questions of what are mental disease and its products to be pure matters of fact, they did so because they believed that when an act is the product of mental disease it is not the product of intent or indeed an act of the accused, and because they believed that the concepts of disease and product, and that of law and of fact are existentially given. Their reasoning, though proceeding from scientifically and jurisprudentially false premises, was methodologically correct. By contrast, today, the statement that an act is the product of mental disease is a presentation of psychological reality known to be fallacious, and the statement that what is mental disease and what are its products are matters of fact is misleading, since it appears to suggest a "givenness" of these notions which, in the light of contemporary knowledge, they do not possess. This raises the significant issue of the logics of Durham.

As pointed out by Dr. Roche,[147] the notions of "mental disease," of its relation to the act, of "intent," and so on, convey an entirely different meaning today from that they once possessed:

The term "mental disease" merely designates behavior which, in a given society, is regarded as maladapted; it designates an altered internal status of the indidivual vis à vis his external world as interpreted by others.[148]

. . . criminality and mental illness cease to be a demoniacal possession which has the self-contained faculty of turning itself on and off and "causes" one to do wrong; they become more meaningful processes

[146] *Durham* v. *United States*, *supra* note 20, at pp. 874–5.

[147] Roche, *supra* note 4, at pp. 88–9; also Roche, "Insanity and the Criminal Law" (1955), 22 *U. Chi. L. Rev.* 320.

[148] Roche, *supra* note 4, at p. 15.

reflecting the breakdown of psychic controls and the release of latent antisocial drives common to all.[149]

Mental illness does not cause one to commit a crime nor does mental illness produce a crime. Behavior and mental illness are inseparable—one and the same thing.[150]

. . . mental illness does not abolish intent but *releases* it.[151]

Since we no longer believe in any of the notions from which the New Hampshire cases proceeded—any more than we believe in an ether permeating the universe—to repeat the rule which these cases enunciated as though, by the same type of logical deduction, we could arrive at it in our times, is methodologically erroneous. Durham is not only wrong law. It is senseless. The defence of the Durham rule in *Carter* v. *United States*[152] affords a flagrant demonstration of its untenability. There the Court said: "When we say the defense of insanity requires that the act be a 'product of' a disease, we mean that the facts on the record are such that the trier of the facts is enabled to draw a reasonable inference that the accused would not have committed the act he did commit if he had not been diseased as he was."[153] The footnote to this passage is indeed illuminating.[154] After stating that the Government must prove "beyond a reasonable doubt" that there is a relationship between the disease and the act that is "critical in its effect in respect to the act," the Court explains the term "critical" thus:

By "critical" we mean decisive, determinative, causal; we mean to convey the idea inherent in the phrases "because of", "except for", "without which", "but for", "effect of", "result of", "causative factor"; the disease made the effective or decisive difference between doing and not doing the act. The short phrases "product of" and "causal connection" are not intended to be precise, as though they were chemical formulae. They mean that the facts concerning the disease and the facts concerning the act are such as to justify reasonably the conclusion that "But for this disease the act would not have been committed."

149"Insanity and the Criminal Law," *supra* note 147, at p. 323.

150*Ibid.*, at p. 322. Neither "disease" nor "production" are simple observable "facts."

151Roche, *supra* note 4, at p. 88.

152(1956) 252 F.2d 608 (App. D.C., reh. den. 1957).

153*Ibid.*, at p. 617.

154*Supra* note 16.

Should anyone puzzle how anything that is "not intended to be precise" can be proven "beyond a reasonable doubt," the answer apparently may be found in the following statement: "To the precise logician deduction of the foregoing inference involves a tacit assumption that if the disease had not existed the person would have been a law-abiding citizen. This latter is not necessarily factually true and can rarely, if ever, be proved, but in the ordinary conduct of these cases we make that tacit assumption. For ordinary purposes we make no mention of this logician's nicety."

Disregarding this confession of "logical failure" of the test—a failure which is hardly excusable by being labelled a "logician's nicety"—there remains the truly critical admission that the product feature of the test "can rarely, if ever, be proved." I submit with great respect that a test the essential elements of which are not provable is utterly meaningless and not merely wrong.

(3) THE SPANISH TEST

As shown, in the view of the New Hampshire judges, insanity excludes intent and thus must of logical necessity constitute a ground for exemption. It would be possible to argue that if the prosecution could establish the presence of intent (producing the act) notwithstanding insanity, the defence could be rebutted. This, however, is not the law, but no explanation is offered why it is not. Possibly, a reason may be found in the fact that intent or malice was not at common law an ultimately psychological phenomenon but a product of a peculiar mixture or indeed identification of primitive psychology, morality, religion, and law and that it retained this character even after insanity ceased to be regarded as a moral quality and was recognized as a medical-psychological phenomenon. It would require a special study in the history of legal concepts to ascertain how exactly the notion developed that "(t)he legal idea of malice includes the idea of sanity."[155] Perhaps a similar study would be necessary in order to explain the process of reasoning

[155]*State* v. *Pike, supra* note 23 at p. 431. The passage continues: "and the legal presumption of malice threw the burden of proving insanity on the defendant." Compare also *ibid.*, at p. 442: "Sanity being an essential element of malice, must be proved by the state beyond all reasonable doubt."

which leads from the Durham rule to the ultimate paragraph of the Durham opinion stating that the rule but reflects the settled doctrine of free will and intent.[156]

The role played by intent in the doctrine of the mental incapacity exemption in common law development is paralleled in civil law countries by the significance attributed to the notion of will. But in some penal codes the connection between the exemption and the concept of *dolus*, as consisting of knowledge and will, is made explicit, whereas in other penal codes this is not the case; upon closer scrutiny, it becomes clear that only rarely has the law actually reached an independent notion of the exempting quality or of the policy of the exemption. The idea persists that the mentally ill are exempt because they actually lack either knowledge or will.

In the Italian Penal Code the relationship of the incapacity exemption to *dolus* is clearly verbalized. "*Dolus*" is defined as "cognition (foresight) and will."[157] A person is responsible (*imputabile*) only if he possesses "capacity to understand and to will" (*capacità d'intendere e di volere*),[158] and is not responsible if at the time of action "he was, by reason of disease, in such state of mind as to exclude capacity of understanding or willing."[159] The terms "understanding" and "willing" are read literally. Clearly, no profound knowledge or will with feeling is taken to be required to render a

[156]Said Judge Bazelon in conclusion: "The legal and moral traditions of the western world require that those who, of their own free will and with evil intent (sometimes called *mens rea*), commit acts which violate the law, shall be criminally responsible for those acts. Our traditions also require that where such acts stem from and are the product of a mental disease or defect as those terms are used herein, moral blame shall not attach and hence there will not be criminal responsibility. The rule we state in this opinion is designed to meet these requirements." (*Supra* note 20 at p. 876.) This passage reflects the view expressed in the *Holloway Case* (supra note 16). But since Durham insists on the psychiatrists' freedom to give the jury all relevant and no irrelevant information—a position rejected in Holloway—it is pertinent to inquire whether the cited passage does or does not imply an ultimate concession to the Holloway philosophy of deceit as regards the role of intent in mental incapacity cases. That insanity actually excludes intent is seriously assumed in *Carter* v. *United States, supra* note 152, at p. 616; compare also Mr. Justice Frankfurter's view in *Leland* v. *Oregon, supra* note 13.

[157]Art. 43 of the Italian Penal Code (1930) defines crime as "dolose or pursuant to intent" (*doloso, o secondo l'intenzione*) when the result of action is "foreseen and willed [desired]" (*preveduto e voluto*).

[158]*Ibid.*, art. 85. Notice that not only "incapacity" but "capacity" also is defined.

[159]*Ibid.*, art. 88.

person responsible. The Corte di Cassazione explicitly declined to extend the exemption to a psychopath on the ground that a person of that type possesses "both cognitive and conative capacity and is incapacitated solely in the sphere of feeling," which is not enumerated in the statute defining the exemption.[160]

The history and wording of the Spanish test would appear to suggest a total departure from the obsolescent knowledge and will test. In fact, both in history and wording, this test is reminiscent of Durham. It was devised with expert psychiatric assistance to meet the demands of modern psychiatric insight. While defining felonies and misdemeanors as "voluntary acts and omissions,"[161] the Spanish Penal Code (1944) submits a distinctive definition of the mental incapacity exemption. This definition simply exempts "the alienated" (*el enajenado*), adding to this group that of the temporarily mentally disturbed.[162] As the American Durham rule had been, so the Spanish clause was hailed as a mark of great progress.[163] Yet, a look at doctrinal interpretation and decisional law shows that introduction of the new test has produced no revolutionary change in practice and that absence of knowledge and/or will continues to be used as the true criterion.[164] Thus, for example, Quintano

160Decision of the Corte di Cassazione (Sezione I) of April 15, 1955, reported in (1956) 61 *Giustizia Penale* II, 183. There the court said:

"La Hara, though possessing the capacity of distinguishing right from wrong and lawful from unlawful and though capable of determining his conduct in accordance with his own ideas, is nevertheless drawn to do wrong or to commit crime, because he does not feel any aversion against wrong and crime and is not disposed to obey the laws and to abide within the range of ordered social life, preferring to satisfy his low and egoistic instincts by *short-cut and illegal methods*. And, since of the mental faculties, that is, the feeling, the intelligence and the will, which subjectively characterize the opinion, the code in force, for purposes of responsibility, takes into consideration only the last two and not the first, the decision [below] which affirms the principle of the responsibility of constitutionally immoral persons is legally correct and not objectionable in the light of the prevailing rules.

"The expert had . . . found that La Hara did not suffer from any relevant defect in the field of 'ideation or critical faculties' or in that of 'volition,' but that he showed 'characterological features of abnormal affectivity' and 'preponderant instinctivity.' This does not fall within article 89, Penal Code [diminished responsibility]. The accused is responsible."

161Spanish Penal Code of 1944, art. 1.

162*Ibid.*, art. 8, al. 1°.

163Quintano Ripollés, *supra* note 52, at p. 66.

164For this criterion in Spain is a venerable one: it goes back to the Siete Partidas. Cf. *supra* note 52.

Ripollés[165] believes it to be self-evident that the function of psychiatrists in the administration of this test is strictly confined to submitting to the court a simple clinical diagnosis, a finding of the presence or absence of the reality of mental change, whereupon the court must decide whether "such change was or was not a determining factor in the commission of the act charged and *whether or not it affected the volitional and intellectual capacity of the actor*" (emphasis added). Compared with the test of the Spanish Code of 1870, which exempted "the imbecil and the lunatic, unless he acted in a lucid interval" (*el imbécil y el loco, a no ser que éste haya obrado en un intervalo de razón*),[166] the present test has been held to enlarge the exemption in conformity to changes in psychiatric opinion. Thus, under the new test, the Supreme Court, in a decision rendered on October 5, 1944,[167] abandoned the previous view that the relevant disease of the mind must have a physiological basis and held a person whose disease was diagnosed as rooted in psychic factors not to have been responsible. But although allegedly based on the new scientific formula, the decision rationalized its results by use of the ancient knowledge test.[168] Throughout, the court's pronouncements express continued adherence to the knowledge and will test.[169]

165*Ibid.*, at p. 67.

166*Ibid.*

167(Sala II), cited *ibid.*, at p. 76.

168A woman who drowned her child and attempted to commit suicide was found by the court to have committed these acts in a "moment of despair," "*without being aware of the acts* which she committed, and solely remembering that she had another disappointment with her husband" [emphasis added].

169In a single volume of a digest of decisions of the Supreme Court of Spain in criminal matters, the 1948–9 Appendix of Manuel Rodriguez Navarro, *Doctrina Penal del Tribunal Supremo*, Appendice II, see pp. 35–6 for pertinent cases, (1950), there are several statements expressing continued adherence to the knowledge and will test. The court required proof that the accused "acted in a state of complete annulment of his will, which put him in a state of unconsciousness or, at least a reduction of the latter." *Ibid.*, Sentencia 29–5–948; Rep. Jurisp. *Aranzadi*, p. 870. In another case the court held a finding of the court below of "a normal and perfect functioning of the accused's faculties of knowledge and action at the time of committing the offenses" to be "equivalent to a declaration of a perfect mental equilibrium on that occasion." S. 24–1–949; Rep. Jurisp. *Aranzadi*, p. 46. In a third case the court found the accused's "lucidity of judgment manifested during trial" to be inconsistent with an even transitory mental disturbance at the time of the act. S. 9–5–949; Rep. Jurisp. *Aranzadi*, p. 662.

Though the Spanish test does not in terms require the act to be the "product"

Thus, notwithstanding adoption of an allegedly scientific test, the criterion in Spain, as in other civil law countries, has remained the ancient one—that of knowledge and will. The knowledge portion is clearly derived in civil law countries, as in common-law jurisdictions, from the one-time law of legal error. Carrara, an author cited as much in as outside his native Italy, defined insanity (*pazzia*) as "a morbid state which, depriving man of the capacity of knowing the true relations of his acts to the law, has impelled him to violate it, without his being aware of such violation."[170]

Since in Spain knowledge and will rather than mental disease (*enajenación*) are the real issue, and since *enajenado* (the alienated), implying a non-temporary condition, does not cover all situations in which a person may be deprived of his cognitive and/or conative faculties, another supplementary test has been added. That test is called temporary mental disturbance (*trastorno mental transitorio*), which corresponds to our notion of temporary insanity. The test is considerably narrower than the German test of disturbance of consciousness. Since decisional law often requires total unconsciousness, meaning, "not a mere obfuscation of understanding but a total absence of the latter,"[171] there is reason to doubt that the test adds anything to the voluntary act requirement. The Supreme Court's insistence that the disturbance must be a "pathological one producing an (absolute or limited) annulment . . . of the capacity to know or to evaluate one's own acts or, which is the same, loss or limitation of will or free self-determination,"[172] reduces this test to but a variant of the principal one. Moreover, in contrast to German courts, the Spanish Supreme Court has shown no understanding whatever of mental realities such as were already known

of the mental disease, such requirement is being read into it. Thus, Quintano Ripollés, *supra* note 52, at p. 69, states that whether or not a kleptomaniac or pyromaniac will be held responsible for a crime depends on whether that crime "falls within the radius of his disease." Thus, the former will be held responsible if he commits arson but not if he commits larceny, and the latter will be punished if he commits larceny but not if he commits arson.

170 Francesco Carrara, *Programma del Corso di Diritto criminale*, Vol. I. (Spanish transl.; Madrid, 1922), cap. II, par. 248.

171 See decisions cited in Quintano Ripollés, *supra* note 52, at p. 76.

172 Sentencia 2–4–949; Rep. Jurisp. *Aranzadi*, p. 645, in Rodriguez Navarro, *supra* note 169, at p. 37.

in Dr. Ray's days, for example, that a person may act with "goal-direction" and apparent rationality and yet be in such mental condition as to make these factors but parts of a total, confused scheme of disease.[173]

B. *Partial Exemption Tests*

I understand by partial exemption: (1) the so-called partial responsibility, which is an exemption from responsibility not within all criminal law rules but within certain rules only; for example, a person thus exempt may be found incapable of premeditation, which means that he cannot be convicted of any crime which requires that state of mind; (2) the so-called diminished responsibility, which creates an intermediate notion between full mental capacity and full mental incapacity, leading to reduction of punishment without affecting the crime type or degree.

(1) PARTIAL RESPONSIBILITY

The principal case in the United States dealing with this concept is *Fisher* v. *United States*.[174] Petitioner, convicted of first-degree murder under the District of Columbia Code,[175] defining such murder as killing with "deliberate and premeditated malice," contended that though he was of sufficiently "sound memory and discretion" to commit murder in the second degree—defined as killing "with malice aforethought"[176]—he was not "capable" of "deliberation and premeditation," having been found to be a person of "psychopathic aggressive tendencies, low emotional response and borderline mental deficiency." Whether or not the Supreme Court's

[173]Thus, where "a chronic alcoholic, with psychopathic reactions, being in the afternoon of the act in a state of such extreme drunkenness as to suffer from vomiting spells," went to the house of a long-time friend whom she often visited and taking advantage of the latter's momentary absence (in the kitchen of the same apartment), entered an alcove, opened a safe with her own (the accused's) key and took 800 pesos, which she then kept until the police seized them," the Supreme Court reversed the acquittal based on an expert's opinion that the accused was in a state of temporary mental disturbance. The Supreme Court based this reversal on the alleged inconsistency of such temporary insanity with the "rationality" of her acts. S. 15–4–948; Rep. Jurisp. *Aranzadi*, at p. 572, in Rodriguez Navarro, *ibid.*, at pp. 37–8.

[174](1945) 328 U.S. 463, 90 L. Ed. 1382, 66 Sup. Ct. 1318.

[175]1940 ed., title 22, s. 2401.

[176]*Ibid.*, title 22, s. 2403.

affirming of the conviction and death sentence was correct depends on what is meant by "deliberation and premeditation" and whether or not the described qualities of the petitioner exclude or tend to exclude such deliberation and premeditation. "Malice aforethought" is not more than "intent," though the "intent" in murder need not always be directed at producing death.[177] "Malice aforethought" may be less than "intent" to kill but is never more than that.[178] "Premeditation and deliberation" at most add to the "intent" an element of "second thought" or an "appreciable time"[179] for thinking the matter over. In *Fisher* the time available for deliberation and premeditation was extremely short. Is it then contended that a person may be incapable of deliberating and premeditating for as much as half an hour and yet be mentally fit to be guilty of a serious crime? Can mental disease be dissected into such neat parts or discrete degrees? It is submitted that if *Fisher* proves anything, it proves the total inadequacy of our notions of intent and premeditation and of defining mental incapacity in terms of these notions.

The definition of partial responsibility submitted above also comprises what is known as diminished responsibility in Scottish law and in the English Homicide Act, 1957.[180] For the pertinent rules of the common law of Scotland and the new English rule[181] provide that in cases where the accused is found to fall within a mental category lesser than that of the M'Naghten rules, he is to be convicted not for murder but for a lesser crime, "manslaughter" in England and "culpable homicide" in Scotland.

[177]See Perkins *supra* note 56, pp. 38–40, for the various types of "intent" which qualify as "malice aforethought" or "man-endangering-state-of-mind."

[178]See *Turner* v. *Commonwealth* (1915), 167 Ky. 365, 180 S.W. 768, L. R.A. 1918 A. 329, for review of authorities. "Intent" as used in the text includes mere negligence as regards death.

[179]*Bullock* v. *United States* (1941), 122 F.2d 213–14 (App. D.C.); *Bostic* v. *United States* (1937), 94 F.2d 636, 639 (App. D.C.). In some of the States "premeditation and deliberation may be simultaneous with the formation of the intent to kill." *United States* v. *Wilson* (1959), 178 F.S. 881, 885 (Dist. Ct., D.C.).

[180]5 & 6 Eliz. II, c. 11. The pertinent provision is contained in s. 2(1).

[181]On these provisions see J. Ll. J. Edwards, "Diminished Responsibility," in Mueller, *supra* note 5, at p. 301; Hughes, "The English Homicide Act of 1957" (1959), 49 *J. Crim. Law Criminology & Pol. Sc.* 521; Prevezer, "The English Homicide Act: Attempt to Revise the Law of Murder" (1957), 57 *Colum. L. Rev.* 624.

The English test of such diminished responsibility provides that when a person kills another, he shall not be convicted of murder if "he was suffering from such abnormality of mind (whether arising from a condition of arrested or retarded development of mind or any inherent causes or induced by disease or injury) as substantially impaired his mental responsibility for his acts and omissions in doing or being a party to the killing." This test is vaguely reminiscent of that recommended by the majority of the Royal Commission on Capital Punishment, "to leave to the jury to determine whether at the time of the act the accused was suffering from disease of the mind (or mental deficiency) to such a degree that he ought not to be held responsible."[182]

That the diminished responsibility test of the Homicide Act 1957 hardly affords any guidance to judges may be seen from the fact that the English Bench is turning for illumination on instructions to juries, on the meaning and scope of such responsibility, to the practice of Scottish courts.[183] Such vagueness of a statutory test is hardly compatible with standards of "legality."

The criticism of partial responsibility as advocated in the *Fisher Case* is also applicable to the English and Scottish notion of so-called diminished responsibility. Is it realistic to assume that a person may not be sufficiently sane to be guilty of murder in the first degree—in England, of murder—but "sane enough" to be guilty of murder in the second degree—in England, of manslaughter, in Scotland, of culpable homicide? Implicit in such assumption is an unrealistic view of the mental element in crime. This is combined with a failure to realize that guilt in modern law should be conceived of functionally, as a policy-oriented social notion, rather than metaphysically. This failure accounts for the fact that no provisions were made at the outset for meeting the need for protection against the dangerousness of persons of diminished responsibility, though it is now expected that the necessary public protection will be afforded by provisions of the recently enacted Mental Health Act, 1959.[184] Similarly, the Model

[182]Royal Commission Report, p. 116.
[183]Edwards, *supra* note 181, at p. 319.
[184]7 & 8 Eliz. II, c. 72.

Penal Code, while specifically providing for admissibility of proof of mental disease or defect for the purpose of showing that the accused was not capable of the particular state of mind that is charged,[185] makes no provision for assigning such a person to a mental hospital or for any other measure of cure or care that might protect the community. We ought to face the fact that Fisher was dangerous.

(2) DIMINISHED RESPONSIBILITY

In instances where the accused is found to be partially responsible, a Scottish judge may, in addition, consider the reduced mental capacity in mitigation of punishment.[186] This implies that Scotland also admits diminished responsibility in the narrower sense in which this term is used in this paper. But the point is incidental and requires no elaboration.

The laws of many civil law countries have provisions on diminished responsibility. These provisions vary from country to country: in some, reduction is mandatory, in others, discretionary; some follow fixed reduction principles, for example, the German rule incorporates the reduction scheme established for cases of attempt;[187] others leave the matter entirely to judicial discretion, for example, the Swiss Federal Penal Code adopts such rule.[188] Of greatest importance are the provisions subjecting persons of diminished responsibility to measures. Since such persons are also amenable to punishment, though a reduced one, the problem of conflict between punishment and measures calls for resolution. There is a general tendency to permit punishment to yield to a measure, so that in an increasing number of cases such persons incur no punishment at all and are subjected only to a measure. But this result, generally believed to be desirable, may be reached directly by including persons of diminished responsibility in the group of those exempt from punishment and subject to measures,

[185] §4.02, Tent. Draft No. 4 (1955).
[186] For authorities see Edwards, *supra* note 181, at p. 306.
[187] Ss. 51 and 44, German Penal Code.
[188] Art. 11, Swiss Federal Penal Code of 1937.

rather than by deviation from an initial principle of combining punishment and measures.[189]

In the scheme advocated by this writer the length and extensiveness of permissible measures depends very decisively on the type of criminal act that has been committed, so that there is a certain concordance between punishment maxima and maxima in measures. But subject to certain limitations, a measure may—indeed, when its basis ceases to exist, must—be terminated at any time, so that on the whole a measure is realistically preferable to punishment. This should militate against adoption of a sweeping all or nothing, total mental incapacity rule, placing minor disabilities on the same level with major diseases when the prospect of early release in the former is extremely high whereas in the latter it is practically nonexistent, so that a person in the former category receives a perhaps unjustifiable advantage over the fully responsible one. However, since the concept of diminished responsibility is highly questionable and since in criminal law there obtains a general *favor libertatis*, borderline situations should be included in any definition which affords an advantage. Hence, the submission is that the category which would otherwise qualify for partial or diminished responsibility ought to be included in the class of those enjoying full punitive exemption.

Summary

In contrast to the older rules, neither their modern adaptations nor the newer rules are oriented to a consciously conceived and

[189]On this see Silving, "Rule of Law in Criminal Justice," *supra* note 5, at pp. 117–19 and 142–63.

There are two approaches to formulation of "diminished responsibility" tests: (1) repetition or incorporation by reference of the total incapacity test, with indication that the mental states and/or resulting faculties are present in smaller degree; (2) adoption of *sui generis* standards of diminished capacity. The German rule on diminished responsibility (s. 51(2), German Penal Code) adopts the former technique. A similar technique is advocated by the 1956 draft, art. 24. But the Swiss Federal "diminished capacity" test is distinctive (art. 11, Swiss Federal Penal Code), and the German draft 1960 adds to the sources of incapacity of appreciation or conformity, enumerated in the total incapacity rule, another special "diminished responsibility" clause: "because of another severe mental deviation" (s. 25). This clause is intended to apply the benefit of "diminished responsibility" to "psychopathies, neuroses and disturbances in the drives." See Comment at p. 133. But, of course, both the Swiss Federal Penal Code (arts. 14–16) and the German draft 1960 (s. 82) provide for application of measures to persons of "diminished capacity."

consistently followed criminal law policy. M'Naghten's rules are the product of a policy of protecting those engaged in error of fact or of law, for such error was once deemed to exclude an essential of crime, disobedience to law. The New Hampshire test purported to interpret intent and causation by intent, as understood by those who formulated the rule. Within the knowledge of the New Hampshire judges, the test was meaningful, for these judges thought that mental disease actually excludes a constituent element of crime, intent.

The modern rules which resemble M'Naghten, that is, the Model Penal Code rules and the mixed system civil law rules, such as the German one, are structured in terms of certain incapacities and sources of such incapacities. In none of these rules is it made clear whether the ground that justifies the exemption is the source, that is, the mental disease or defect, the incapacity indicating merely the degree of disease required for exemption, or the incapacity *per se*. This in itself makes it difficult to determine what policy these rules follow. The incapacity may affect the faculty of knowledge or that of conformity. Incapacity to appreciate or to know is but a modification of the M'Naghten knowledge test. Knowledge capacity must be related to the particular crime that is in issue. In our law this results in the paradoxical situation that when a person claims to have been insane, the law insists that he is not punishable if he had no capacity to know the law which he need not know if he is sane. Capacity to conform is particularly vulnerable, since it is ultimately reducible to capacity to have acted otherwise. Psychiatrists have asserted that it is impossible to answer the question, "Could John Doe have acted otherwise than he acted?" It is idle—perhaps, indeed, senseless to debate whether such a question is or is not absolutely unanswerable; for surely an answer could be given, if at all, only after a very long study of the person concerned that would acquaint the observer with all the motivations to which such person was subject and such a study cannot be made within the confines of criminal procedure. In fact, those who advocate this test often concede that it ultimately reduces itself to a problem of justice to be disposed of on a case-to-case basis. An alternative suggested by Seelig, that the issue be put in terms of capacity to be motivated by rational considerations, though preferable to the test of capacity for conformity to the legal rule, is particularly questionable in communities where there are large groups of persons who are not generally thus motivated.

The Durham test was adopted in order to accommodate psychiatric experts who themselves profess not to be able to supply the law with functional definitions or, indeed, to verbalize the grounds of individual diagnoses. Precisely because psychiatry is unsettled regarding such questions as whether comprehensive classes of mental states, psychopathies and neuroses, are included in the term "mental disease"—a term, *nota bene*, that does not appear in many pychiatric textbooks—Durham has chosen that term as the key concept of its definition of the mental incapacity exemption. This is actually intended to permit one psychiatric expert to testify that these categories are included while another expert testifies that they are not included. No objection could be raised against such allowance were it shown that such inclusion or exclusion is based on divergence of psychiatric insight into the nature of the pertinent mental states and that the points of divergence are relevent to a legal policy issue. But the fact is that the source of disagreement (or reversal) among psychiatrists is a variance in classification which, whatever meaning it may have in medical "communication," is for legal purposes purely verbal. Nor is the real ground of such classificatory testimony free from a normative moral taint that is rooted in the psychiatrist's desire to inculpate or exculpate. While juries are expected not to feel bound by psychiatric interpretations but to form an independent opinion, based on factual scientific data supplied by psychiatrists, the question whether an exemption is justified is put to them in terms of whether the accused suffered from a "mental disease," athough it is not even known to what discipline this concept belongs, since it is now declared not to be a psychiatric category. Moreover, the whole issue is obscured by interchangeable designation of the jury's task as consisting in finding presence or absence of mental disease, in a moral judgment, and in determination of a question of fact.

It is submitted that whether broad classes such as psychopathies or neuroses should afford a ground for exemption is a question of sufficiently general scope to be properly determinable by legislatures and not juries. This in a democracy is clearly a legislative task, much as it is a legislative task to define crime or any exemption from criminal responsibility. To be sure, it would be utopian to believe that legislatures can define either crime or a mental incapacity exemption with absolute certainty, that is, with such certainty as would make adjudication but a syllogistic operation. But questions of such degree of abstraction as whether psychopaths or neurotics should be exempt are certainly not of a type to admit no general answer that would afford a fair measure of equality in treatment. To this extent, legal certainty barring arbitrariness and inequality is of the essence of justice. Of course, legislative formulation of a sound exemption is predicated upon acquaintance with scientific data on how the human mind operates. These data should be supplied by psychologists and psychiatrists.

The most absurd feature of the attempt in the Durham test to be scientific is the use of sham scientific terminology. The phrase "product of mental disease or defect" has been shown by psychiatrists to be meaningless. Psychiatrists are truly unable to answer the question whether an act is or is not "the product of mental disease," whereas their assertion that they are unable to testify whether an accused "knew that what he was doing was wrong" is based on a fallacy in methodology. Nor is the former inability based on a "logician's nicety"; it is rather rooted in legally relevant psychiatric insight into the realities of mental life. In the light of this fact bearing on the practical aspects of psychiatric expert testimony, it is unnecessary to dwell on the jurisprudential question whether or not law can operate without logic.

In each and every respect, the reasoning behind the Durham test is methodologically fallacious, whereas the New Hampshire cases, being based on mistaken psychiatric, scientific, and philosophical "knowledge"—a wrong, but *bona fide*, "knowledge"—were disposed of by a correct methodology. There is as much difference between Durham and the New Hampshire cases as there would be between the trial of a witch today and such trial during the Middle Ages, when the belief prevailed that witchcraft was an actual craft that produced social harm, that might kill, injure, or render insane. Witches' trials were not immoral then, but they would be immoral today. In the same sense, the New Hampshire cases administered justice, whereas the same is not true of Durham. It may be interesting to note that Durham relies heavily on the *Holloway Case*, in which Judge Arnold turned into law his jurisprudential view that justice is not important, law being governed by the rule not of law but of popular illusion created by legal ritual.

Should there be a need for a practical demonstration of the fact that definition of the mental incapacity exemption simply as "mental disease" is not a functional policy disposition, such confirmation is afforded by the history of the administration of the Spanish test which defines the exemption by one word, *"enajenado."* The Spanish Supreme Court applies this test as if it did not exist. It simply continues to adjudicate cases on the basis of the old criterion of knowledge and will.

The notions of partial and diminished responsibility proceed from erroneous fundamental conceptions of the mental element in crime, premeditation and deliberation, malice aforethought, and so on. Moreover, the concept of such responsibility has the awkward practical result of calling for administration of criminal law on an assumption which defies recognition of a unitary notion of the human personality, namely, on the assumption that an individual may be partly sane and partly insane; this, in fact, is the implication of subjecting him to both punishment and measures administered successively, as is done in some civil law countries.

It would thus seem that we are left in a vacuum, all available tests and definitions having failed. To formulate a new test, we must return to fundamentals.

III. RECOMMENDED TEST

AS POINTED OUT in the first part of the paper, an exemption test ought to be based on the policy that is being pursued by the criminal law. In a punitive context, the policy of exempting from punishment should be derived negatively from the purpose of punishment; those persons whose punishment would not serve such purpose ought to be exempt. The purpose of punishment, as shown, is to document the relative social reprehensibleness of the offence that has been committed. The individual who is to be punished is selected as an object of such demonstration on the basis of his "guilt." Guilt in the criminal law of a democracy is not a theological or a metaphysical-philosophical notion. Nor is it a moral notion in the narrower sense of the term. It is a social-political concept to the effect that an individual, as a member of a community, is called to account for violating a social norm; in a sense, for having put in question the validity of the norm.

Such being the policy of punishment, its target is obviously the normal, average member of the community. A person who is not normal or average need not be punished; provided that, if he is dangerous, another purpose of law, namely, community protection giving rise to measures, may come into play. Normality thus postulated is not divisible into distinctive faculties. In many situations, of course, it may be possible to find specific, conspicuous symptoms of abnormality. Thus, a person is not normal if he has a conception of reality which is consistently divergent from that accepted by group consensus,[190] or has less power of self-control than average community members,[191] or shows emotional reactions that differ widely from those of the rest of the community. But it is not suggested that such specific symptoms be used to define mental incapacity.

[190]John C. Whitehorn, "Psychodynamic Approach to the Study of Psychoses," in Franz Alexander and Helen Ross, *Dynamic Psychiatry* (1952), p. 255, at p. 281, says: "In attempts to define psychosis, the point has often been made, descriptively, that psychotic thinking is unrealistic. Since reality is itself a concept difficult to define and to use with precision, the descriptive value of this statement is dubious. The discriminative value of the statement is also diminished by the observation that nonpsychotic persons also foster many illusions and carry on a large part of their mental operations with the use of prejudiced attitudes and folk beliefs which could scarcely be called realistic or even logical. A more useful criterion than reality is the consensus of the group."

[191]Average self-control depends much on expectation and habit within a given community. A Sicilian is not expected to possess as much self-control as an inhabitant of a Nordic community.

The policy implicit in the mental incapacity exemption formulated in terms of the socially "non-average" is also expressed in other types of exemptions, for example, in the general defence of so-called inexigibility of law-abidance or inexigibility of a different conduct, recognized in some civil law countries. The philosophy of this defence is that no one should be punished for a violation of law if he acted in circumstances in which most community members would have acted as he did. Just as heroism should not be expected by criminal law, so law that is devised for the average citizen should not be enforced indiscriminately against a person who has exceptional difficulties in meeting legal requirements. The correlation of non-exigibility and mental incapacity consists in the fact that the former applies when conduct otherwise illegal is average or normal, whereas the mental incapacity exemption is accorded to the "non-average" individual, with the proviso that if he is also dangerous, society must take steps to protect itself by measures.

The "non-average" must be understood as a psychiatric category. For in a democracy we cannot assume *a priori* that non-conformity is itself evidence of abnormality. There must be a serious failure in the individual's psychic organization, a grave impairment of his ego functioning. Since no one can be said to possess a perfectly balanced personality, abnormality must be assumed to begin at some discernible degree of imbalance. But since no mathematically precise variations in degree can be fixed, we must be satisfied with indications that the degree of imbalance is very great, as compared with the relative balance of average community members. There being no such thing as a universal normality, the particular community to which the individual belongs must be always assumed to afford the proper standard of comparison.

Normality is a precarious standard even if applied to a single community.[192] To make the mental incapacity test as definite and certain as the subject permits, it is proposed to be formulated in terms of comparison with the relative mental fitness of the majority

[192]On this see, e.g., Arthur P. Noyes and Lawrence C. Kolb, *Modern Clinical Psychiatry* (5th ed.; 1958), p. 130.

of community members rather than with a group average and of a very considerable deviation from the mental fitness of such majority. Specification of the area of unfitness as that of social adjustment is also expected to facilitate application of the test.

Except in cases of habitual criminals who engage in crime as a matter of routine, crime is not an average occurrence in the life of any individual, and so it may be assumed that at the time of its commission a normal individual acts in a state of impairment of ego functioning. It thus seems improper to limit the test either to the time of the act's commission or to a relation to that act. There is hardly any psychological realism in the usual limitation of mental incapacity to the state of mind obtaining "at the time of the act."[193] Nor could mental incapacity be established retrospectively with such precision. It is hence submitted that the formula use the words, "at the time of the act and for some time prior thereto." However, this should not be taken to exclude states of allegedly temporary mental disturbance from the exemption. As correctly pointed out by the German Bundesgerichtshof, "sudden outbursts of affect do not accidentally arise in man, as a lightning coming from a clear sky, but . . . as a rule, such outburst is preceded by a long development and history."[194]

As regards the relation of the mental state to social norms of conduct, reference to the criminality of the specific act charged implies recognition of "monomania," which has been discarded as a psychiatric category. Thus the test should be formulated in broader terms, namely, to relate to the actor's general capacity regarding social norms and rules.

In a previous publication I referred with approval to a test suggested by Bromberg and Cleckley, which poses the question of

[193]As pointed out by Roche, *supra* note 4, at pp. 84–5, "to the psychiatrist intent has the meaning of a behavioral event, the precursors of which operate within the accused in a structured manner having an instinctual source and having a flow into final pathways of action." The so-called union of act and intent doctrine is psychologically unrealistic as well as legally questionable. *Jackson* v. *Commonwealth* (1896), 100 Ky. 239, 38 S.W. 422, 66 Am. St. Rep. 336. For cases in which insistence on such "union" leads to absurd results see Albert J. Harno, *Cases and Materials on Criminal Law and Procedure* (4th ed.; 1957), p. 46, n. 2.

[194]Compare *supra*, text at note 114.

mental incapacity in the following terms: was the function of the accused's "ego so impaired that he could not, because of genuine disability, act within the limits of social demands and rules?"[195] However, I had reservations about using the terms "could not" and "genuine disability." Both appear to be vague, and the former lends itself to being nullified by deterministically oriented psychiatrists. I hence suggested the following modified version: "Was the accused's ego so impaired that he was very considerably less than the majority of the people within the community capable of conforming to social demands and rules?"

Having given further thought to this test, I became concerned with the use of the words "capable of conforming." In the context of mental incapacity, these words undoubtedly mean "being able to act otherwise." As pointed out above, such words, even when put in comparative terms, require an answer to a question which may be read as raising the issue of free will, and which either is not answerable by psychiatrists at all or would present practically insuperable difficulties. Hence I am now suggesting the following formulation of the exemption: "No punishment shall be imposed upon a person if at the time of engaging in criminal conduct and for some time prior thereto his ego functioning was so impaired that he had a very considerably greater mental difficulty in complying with social demands and rules than does the majority of the members of the community."

For purposes of defining the incapacity exemption the community should be that community which issues the norm that has been violated, in other words, the state. But there are many people whose life is so confined to narrower communities that it would be neither realistic nor just to apply to them such broad standard, as, for example, the state of mental health of the people of Puerto Rico. Hence the community should be understood to mean a narrower group, such as the population of the district from which, in the event of jury trial, a jury is drawn. But a community of persons living in a given geographical district is not necessarily homogeneous. There are varieties of social and cultural sub-groups,

[195]Silving, *supra* note 59, at p. 29.

some of which may be closer to similar sub-groups of other communities than they are to other sub-groups within their own community. Of particular importance is belonging to a group in which criminal habits are not distinctive, since the group generally practises such habits. When a person raised in a generally law-abiding group persistently follows criminal patterns, this in itself might in extreme cases point to mental deviation. But in a criminal group he may be a normal criminal, that is, a person "whose psychic organization is similar to that of the normal individual, except that he identified himself with criminal prototypes (sociological etiology).[196] Hence, in determining whether the accused's ego functioning was so impaired as to justify exemption, the court must assume as the standard of comparison not only the mental functioning of the broader community but also that of the particular group to which the accused belongs, whether social, educational, professional, and so on.

Summary

The recommended test exempts from punishment persons to whom the preferred philosophy of punishment does not apply: the psychologically-sociologically clearly and distinctively "non-average." This test defines as exempt persons whose ego is so impaired that they have considerably greater mental difficulty conforming to social demands and rules than the majority of community members. The community is the population of the district from which, in the event of jury trial, a jury would be drawn and the narrower community to which the accused belongs, whether it be educational, professional, or social. The disability is of general scope, affecting the subject's relationship to social demands and rules rather than merely his relationship to the specific conduct with which he is charged. The relevant time of impairment is broadened; the impairment must have existed at the time of conduct and for some time prior thereto.

This test is expected to eliminate the false assumption implicit

[196]Franz Alexander and Hugo Staub, *The Criminal, the Judge and the Public* (rev. ed.; 1956), p. 45, at pp. 210–11.

in other mental incapacity tests as though we were concerned with a specifically psychiatric issue. Law is a social discipline and is concerned with social and anti-social conduct. The psychiatric aspects such conduct presents are of merely indirect significance. The social nature of law ought to be emphasized in every legal rule, including that on mental incapacity. Forensic psychiatry should be clearly understood to be a distinctive discipline, a *sui generis* social science.

Sound law, that is, law based upon a rational social policy and operating on the basis of a rational view of psychological and social reality, must take into account the social purpose of a mental incapacity exemption and the teleological aspects of its prospective functioning. Psychology and psychiatry may throw light on the latter aspects. These sciences can tell us how men's minds operate. Our social philosophy must guide our judgment on the policy issue of how much we ought to demand of men.

Conclusion

In those rare situations in which a mental disability is of such nature as to actually negate "intent" or "premeditation" there is no need for a mental incapacity exemption. Exemption from punishment accorded to certain persons on the ground of mental disability is generally the result of policy considerations. But these are often disguised under a claim of inherent disability, constituting an exemption that is not conferred by decision makers but imposed upon them. A rational mental incapacity exemption should be based on a conscious policy guided by a clear notion of the ends of punishment and the conditions under which those ends are not applicable. In a democracy law addresses itself to the people and commands their obedience. In doing so, it must carefully consider both what is exigible and of whom it is exigible.[197]

[197]Problems of the administration of the suggested mental incapacity test will be discussed in a future publication.

Positive Law and the Moral Law

By MARK R. MACGUIGAN*

FEW JURISPRUDENTIAL SUBJECTS have been written about more often than the relationship between law and morals, but so much of the writing on the topic is polemical in nature that it is useful from time to time to discuss this relationship within the framework of a single point of view, without attempting to refute opposing theories. This paper is concerned solely with outlining St. Thomas Aquinas' conception of the relationship of law and morals and with drawing out and developing some of the conclusions which seem to be implicit in his doctrine.

It will be helpful to define at the outset the terms "law" and "morals" as used in this paper. By law I mean human positive law, the law of the political community or state. By morals or morality I do not mean the actual conduct, the mores, of a people or even of all peoples, nor do I mean rules of conduct based on revelation and disclosed to man by authoritative sources. I mean, on the one hand, *rules* of conduct rather than actual conduct, and, on the other hand, rules based on *human reason* rather than on revelation. Metaphysically speaking, morals is, in the words of Fr. Sertillanges, "the science of what a man ought to be by reason of what he is."[1] More concretely put, morals consists of principles of action as discovered and ordered by moral philosophy.

In the first part of the paper I shall deal with the more abstract aspects of the relationship of law and morals according to Thomistic principles. Then, in the second part, I shall attempt to determine

*Mark R. MacGuigan, Ph.D., LL.M., Assistant Professor of Law, University of Toronto. This article was written in partial fulfilment of the requirements for the degree of Doctor of the Science of Law in the Faculty of Law, Columbia University.

[1]A. D. Sertillanges, *Foundations of Thomistic Philosophy* (1931), p. 234.

some of the more practical jurisprudential consequences of these principles with reference to the legislator, the judge, and the citizen.

I

A. Natural Law

For St. Thomas natural law is that law implanted in man by nature, and man's nature is the immediate foundation of the natural law. So close is the association between natural law and human nature that the precepts of the former correspond to the inclinations of the latter (*Secundum . . . ordinem inclinationum naturalium est ordo praeceptorum legis naturae*).[2] Thus the first step in ascertaining the content of natural law is to discover the fundamental inclinations of human nature.

The most basic of all human inclinations—what Fr. Davitt calls "the master drive"[3]—is the inclination to good in general. Now good in general is a complex unity, containing all less general goods down to the most particular, and it is possible to distinguish within it the less than universal goods which together constitute it. Thus, included within the general inclination to good, there are the less general inclinations corresponding with the various levels of man's being: the inclination to the good of continued existence, that to the goods of animal nature, such as sexual union and the rearing of offspring, and that to the goods of human nature properly speaking, such as to know the truth about God and to live in society. These are man's basic "drives."

Following these inclinations are the principles of the natural law. The first and most general principle may be expressed either in the form "do good and avoid evil" or in the form "act according to reason." The four less universal principles into which the primary principle expands may be stated as follows: "seek the good of continued existence;" "seek the good of the marital community;"

[2]St. Thomas, *Summa Theologiae*, I-II, q.94, a.2. The analysis of the inclinations of human nature and of the principles of the natural law is taken from this text.

[3]T. Davitt, "St. Thomas Aquinas and the Natural Law," in Harding (ed.), *Origins of the Natural Law Tradition* (1954), p. 26, at p. 30.

"seek the good of truth about God;" and "seek the common good" or "do not harm those with whom you must live in society." The natural law may be thus expressed either as a single principle or as several principles because it is possible to look at it from different viewpoints, the viewpoint of the whole or that of the constitutive parts which together make up the whole. As Mortimer Adler points out, "precisely because human happiness is itself a complex unity, the natural law can be expressed in a single principle which derives its singleness from the unity of the end, or in several principles which derive their multiplicity from the complexity of the end."[4] The several principles are not deductions from the single principle, but are, singly, partial expressions of it, and, together, an equivalent expression of it. For St. Thomas no acts of judgment or of reasoning are necessary for the grasping of these principles of the natural law; no action of man's intellect is necessary beyond the grasping of the essences themselves. The principles of the natural law are self-evident to all who can conceive the terms which make them up, that is, they are known, not merely to the wise, but to all those who have reached the age of reason.

With regard to the content of natural law, there have been among disciples of St. Thomas two views as to its inclusiveness, views to which Dabin has given the names of "maximalist" and "minimalist."[5] The maximalists are those who give the natural law the greatest possible extension. They hold that it includes the whole content of the natural moral order, that is, all propositions that can be rationally deduced from the primal propositions. In order to make such a vast body of propositions logically manageable, they are forced to distinguish "primary," "secondary," "tertiary," and perhaps further kinds of precepts to indicate the extent of the deduction necessary for their derivation. The minimalists, on the other hand, are those who give the natural law the least possible extension. They hold that the natural law includes not all moral precepts which are according to nature but merely those few which

[4]M. J. Adler, "A Question about Law," in Brennan (ed.), *Essays on Thomism* (1942), pp. 205, 218.

[5]J. Dabin, *The Legal Philosophies of Lask, Radbruch, and Dabin* (1950), p. 420.

are self-evident, and to which the characteristics of universality, immutability, and necessity can be attributed.[6]

St. Thomas' own usage of the terms "primary" and "secondary" in relation to the precepts of natural law gives some shadow of authenticity to the maximalist position, but despite this occasionally inconsistent use of terms, his own words and the logical implications of his doctrine of natural law make it clear that for him natural law has a minimal extension, and includes only those principles that are self-evident, universal, immutable, and necessary.[7] To quote Adler again, "it is analytically inaccurate to extend the meaning of 'natural law' to include more than the first or indemonstrable principles. Strictly speaking, there are no secondary precepts of the natural law. . . ."[8] By the term "natural law," then, as I shall employ it henceforth in this paper, and as I believe St. Thomas understood it, I mean no more than the self-evident principles enumerated above. Further, in order to be consistent, I shall avoid referring to St. Thomas' philosophy of law as a natural law theory, since the term "natural law" correctly denominates only a small part of Thomistic legal philosophy.

Though Dabin himself endorses the minimalist conception of natural law, he maintains that a limitation on the extension of the natural law is of no interest to the jurist, because the jurist must in any case accept the whole moral order as given.[9] But the task of the jurist must not be thus narrowly conceived. The legal philosopher must not blind himself to theoretical nuances, even if they do not bear promise of practical import, let alone those which, as here, are of considerable practical significance. If the effect of observing the distinction were merely the psychological one of removing from the area of jurisprudential contention the term "natural law," juris-

[6]There are, of course, variations on both these views. For instance, J. Maritain, *Man and the State* (1951), pp. 85–93, holds a maximalist view with regard to the ontological element he discerns in natural law and a minimalist view with regard to the gnoseological element.

[7]For elucidation of this point see M. R. MacGuigan, "St. Thomas and Legal Obligation" (1961), 35 *New Scholasticism* 281, at pp. 294–300.

[8]Adler, *supra* note 4, at p. 214.

[9]Dabin, *supra* note 5, at pp. 455–6.

prudence would be the beneficiary, for the very term "natural law" has been one of the chief causes of confusion in jurisprudence. By restricting it to a precise and minimal meaning, we may thereby remove it from controversy, and at the same time we are enabled to see our problem as involving a "positive law–moral law" dichotomy rather than a "positive law–natural law" one. But the advantages to be derived from the employment of St. Thomas' restricted notion of natural law are greater yet, for this view makes it dramatically clear that the natural law is not a complete and ready-made code of action, nor even a set of certain precepts, but a principle which is the source of all law and contained within every law as its root. This lends enormous flexibility to the already assured generality of this conception of natural law. Natural law, as the principle and root of every law, is thus an intrinsic and formal cause of human law, and consequently is the foundation of legal as well as of moral obligation.[10] Natural law, as seen in minimalist terms, becomes an ultimate explanation rather than a proximate guide. In the words of Professor d'Entrèves, "perhaps the best description of natural law is that it provides a name for the point of intersection between law and morals."[11]

B. *Morality*

In approaching St. Thomas' conception of morality, we become aware at once that his is not a legalistic morality. The essence of legalism in ethics is the belief that a human act, that is, an act proceeding from reason and will, is not by itself a moral act, but that it becomes a moral act only by conforming to some extrinsic rule or law. The consequences of this view are that the norm of morality is conformity to law; that there can be morality only where there is law; and that since law is conceived of as being imposed on the individual extrinsically, morality is an extrinsicism. Moral rules are rules set by an authority and man must submit himself to them because, if he does not, he will be leading a life wholly lacking in

[10] For development of this conception see MacGuigan, *supra* note 7, at pp. 304–10.

[11] A. P. D'Entrèves, *Natural Law* (1951), p. 116.

moral worth. This, then, is the legalistic conception of moral life: action in submission to extrinsic rules.[12]

This view of morality is incompatible with that of St. Thomas Aquinas.[13] St. Thomas does not distinguish between a moral act and a human act (*idem sunt actus morales et actus humani*).[14] A human act is any act proceeding from reason and will.[15] It is reason, therefore, the distinguishing characteristic of the voluntary act, which is the norm of morality (*In actibus autem bonum et malum dicitur per comparationem ad rationem*).[16] Reason is not for Aquinas, as for the legalists, morally neutral, but is on the contrary the very standard of the moral life. Reason does not need to be dignified by any extrinsic rule in order to become moral. It is rather itself that which dignifies. A reasonable act, by the very fact that it is reasonable, is moral. Why, then, do we use the term "moral" at all, if it is identical with "human" and "rational"? Merely for the sake of emphasis. The value of the term "moral" is, as Fr. Tonneau suggests, "to point out and accentuate that which is suitable to man's distinctive and specific form, which is reason."[17]

In a moral universe such as that posited by Aquinas God is present not as legislator but as creator. Man does not take his moral rules from any extrinsic legislator, not even God. Morality comes from within the person, not from another person, not even if that other person is a divine person. Of course God has created man and

[12]Thus, J. Ford and G. Kelly, *Contemporary Moral Theology* (1958), Vol. I ("Questions in Fundamental Moral Theology"), p. 92, write: "[M]oral obligations are legal obligations, that is, have their source in divine law. . . . It is a dangerous thing . . . to decry a morality of duty, of law, and of obligation, because in the last analysis there is no other." Similarly W. Cahill, "Natural Law Jurisprudence in Legal Practice" (1958), 4 *Catholic Lawyer* 23, at p. 34, states: "No individual, by his act done in absence of law, can bind himself to another or another to himself, either legally or morally."

[13]Cf. I. T. Eschmann, "St. Thomas's Approach to Moral Philosophy" (1957), 31 *Proc. Amer. Cath. Philos. Ass'n* 25, at p. 32: "A moralist of the twentieth century, author of a recent compendium of Moral Theology, begins his book with the statement: Catholic Moral Theology is legalistic. This statement literally contradicts every line of the *Summa* of St. Thomas."

[14]St. Thomas, *supra* note 2, I-II, q.1, a.3.

[15]*Ibid.*, a.1.

[16]*Ibid.*, q.18, a.5. Cf. St. Thomas, *In II Sents.*, d.39, q.2, a.1; *De Malo*, q.2, a.4.

[17]J. Tonneau, "At the Threshold of the 'Secunda Pars': Morality and Theology," in *Man and His Happiness* (Theology Library, 1956), Vol. III, pp. xvii, xxxviii.

his nature and so is in this indirect sense the author of morals. Hence God in a sense imposes morality upon man, but not by legislating it. He imposes it only by, as it were, imposing upon man his nature. God makes man and man makes morality—or rather man finds morality, in his own nature and in other natures.

Now when he says that the rule of morality is reason, St. Thomas does not mean by reason the faculty itself but rather norms which are the products of that faculty. Indeed he often refers to the rule of morals as "right" reason.[18] The determination of these norms of morality involves an activity of reason, an ordering by reason, but it also presupposes non-rational activity of the intellect. As we have seen, man's nature is not a neutral nature, indifferent as between good and evil, but is inherently orientated to good, and consequent upon the most general orientation of human nature to good there follow principles of human action, naturally and intuitively known by the human intellect through the virtue of synderesis,[19] which we call the natural law. Reason, understood as a discursive power involving a movement from principles to conclusion, has no part in the grasping of these principles, any more than it has in grasping the first principles of the speculative order.[20]

The principles of natural law are the beginning of the moral order, but, though the moral order is the domain of reason, reason (understood as a discursive power) plays no part in its inception. The principles of the natural law are a "given" to reason; reason accepts them and begins its work of deduction and analysis. Just as that which belongs to man naturally and unchangeably is the foundation and principle of all else that can be said to belong to him,[21] so those principles which he knows naturally and infallibly

[18]St. Thomas, *supra* note 2, q.93, a.3c and ad 2; also q.73, a.2 and q.73, a.7 ad 3. O. Lottin, *Morale Fondamentale* (1954), pp. 165–73, points out that St. Thomas has two different formulae for the norm of morality: (1) the rule of morality is the end; (2) the rule of morality is right reason. In his later works St. Thomas prefers the second formulation, but there is no opposition between the two formulae, for the latter is explicitly subordinated to the former: see St. Thomas, *ibid.*, q.90, a.1.

[19]*Ibid.*, q.94, a.1 ad 2.

[20]On the first principles of the speculative order see *ibid.*, I, q.79, a.8. St. Thomas compares the first principles of the speculative and practical orders, *ibid.*, I-II, q.94, a.1 and a.2.

[21]*Ibid.*, I, q.82, a.1.

are the basis and the source of the whole order of human action.[22]

Reason's role in morality is the analysis and comparison of natures. The ends of human life are set by nature and, embodied as principles of action, are given to reason as the natural law; but reason must determine, from analysis of human nature, the necessary content of these principles. Further, it must analyse the natures of other things to ascertain their necessary aspects. Then it must compare the necessities of other things with those of human nature, and it is this comparison of necessities which gives rise to moral obligation.[23]

All obligation involves necessity, and moral obligation involves what is called "moral" or "hypothetical" necessity. For St. Thomas the most general division of necessity is into intrinsic and extrinsic. Intrinsic necessity comes either from the matter or from the form of the thing and is called "natural" or "absolute" necessity, since it is imposed by nature and is thus inevitable. Extrinsic necessity is either "necessity of coaction" or "necessity of end." Necessity of coaction arises when someone is coerced by an extrinsic agent; since it involves violence, it is wholly opposed to the freedom of the will, for it contravenes the inclination of the will. The necessity inherent in moral obligation, therefore, is not found in necessity of coaction, nor in intrinsic necessity, but exists only in necessity of end.

Necessity of end arises, St. Thomas says, when an end can be attained either not at all or not well without a particular means, as one cannot maintain life without food, nor travel without a horse.[24] Now all necessity of end, all finality, is not moral, even though all morality is based on finality. In St. Thomas' examples there is a moral obligation on man to use the necessary means, food, to maintain the necessary end, life, but there is no moral obligation to use a horse, the most fitting means (in his day) to the end of travelling, because the end, travelling, is not itself necessary. Hence morality involves not merely a necessary means but also a necessary end.

[22]*Ibid.*, I-II, q.94, a.1: *praecepta legis naturalis . . . sunt prima principia operum humanorum.*

[23]That there are definite kinds of operations appropriate to definite kinds of natures is not a great step for St. Thomas to take, for in his thought operation is consequent upon nature: see *Summa Contra Gentiles*, Vol. III, c. 129.

[24]*Ibid.*, I, q.82, a.1.

Moral obligation is, in the words of Fr. Farrell, "the relation of a necessary act to a necessary end."[25] The kind of necessity which constitutes moral obligation is called "hypothetical," "suppositional," or "moral" necessity. It is that kind of necessity in which, to quote Fr. Farrell again, "the means are necessary, supposing the necessity of the end."[26] Therefore, as something lived, morality is the doing or omitting of certain acts in view of an end. As Fr. Sertillanges puts it, "according to St. Thomas, morality is the art of attaining our end."[27]

Human acts, for St. Thomas, are of three kinds: those which are good in themselves, abstracting from concrete circumstances; those which are bad in themselves; and those which are in themselves indifferent as to good and evil.[28] Acts of the first two kinds are said to have "intrinsic morality" and to belong to the "natural moral order." Reason, inasmuch as it is the principle of the natural moral order, may be called "natural reason," reason analysing the natures of things and especially of man. Now one may identify natural reason with right reason, as Lottin suggests,[29] but one may not identify it with the natural law, as he does,[30] because natural law consists of merely the first and self-evident principles of natural reason. It is, of course, true that all the moral precepts discovered by natural reason are "according to nature," for they are derived from the analysis of natures, but that is not to say that they are principles of the natural law.[31] They are not, to be sure, ontologically distinct from the natural law, since all are equally in accord with nature, but they are gnoseologically distinct from it:[32] for natural law principles are grasped intellectually but not rationally, whereas the derived precepts are attained only through reasoning—and often only with great labour.

[25]W. Farrell, "The Roots of Obligation" (1939), 1 *The Thomist* 14, at p. 24.
[26]*Ibid.*, at p. 20.
[27]Sertillanges, *supra* note 1, at pp. 248–9.
[28]St. Thomas, *supra* note 2, q.92, a.2.
[29]Lottin, *supra* note 18, at p. 117, n. 2.
[30]*Ibid.*, at p. 123.
[31]Davitt, *The Elements of Law* (1959), p. 125, points out that not all things which may be said to be "according to the natural law" belong to the natural law in the strict sense.
[32]On this distinction see Maritain, *supra* note 6, at pp. 85–93.

The number of acts which are generically good or bad and which thus fall within the natural moral order is quite small in comparison with the number of those which are morally indifferent. Among the acts which present themselves to reason as necessarily evil in themselves are murder, suicide, theft, lying, calumny, drunkenness, adultery, and polyandry. On the other hand, such institutions as government and private property appear to reason as necessarily good in themselves. It would be a major undertaking to discover all the precepts of action within the realm of natural reason; this is the task of moral philosophy and will not be considered in this paper. My purpose is not to determine the contents of the natural moral order, but its formal relationship to the order of human positive law.

C. Law

Professor Adler has divided the judgments of the practical reason into four groups: primary and indemonstrable truths, necessary conclusions from these primary truths, contingent general determinations of these conclusions, and singular applications of these determinations. He has proposed that these four groups be referred to as "principles," "precepts," "rules," and "decisions" respectively.[33] I think that this is a valuable proposal for purposes of clarifying jurisprudential issues and I shall adhere to this usage throughout the paper. Our investigation thus far leads us to the conclusion that the primary truths or "principles" belong to the natural law and that the necessary conclusions from them, "precepts," belong to morals. We must now discover what type of judgment is peculiar to law.

All human law, St. Thomas says, insofar as it has the character of law, is to this extent derived from natural law. Something can be derived from natural law in two ways, he continues: either deductively or by specification. St. Thomas' example of derivation of the first kind is that the precept "one ought not to kill anyone" is

[33]Adler, *supra* note 4, at p. 212. Adler has also observed, *ibid.*, at p. 389, n. 7, that this division corresponds well with the usual division of practical thinking: thus principles and precepts may be said to belong to the realm of the speculatively-practical, rules to that of the practically-practical, and decisions to that of the purely practical or prudential.

derived as a conclusion from the principle "one ought not to do harm to anyone." His example of the second type of derivation is that the natural law goes no further than to say that he who does evil should be punished, leaving undetermined what punishment should be inflicted upon him; human law therefore may prescribe the form of punishment.[34] This passage in Aquinas means that human law contains not only rules and decisions, the products of derivation of the second kind, but also, since it involves derivation of the first kind as well, precepts, which, as we have seen, are characteristic of the moral order. Here we begin to see the interlocking of law and morals.

St. Thomas was not unaware of the differences between the legal and the moral orders. He points out that, since men cannot judge interior acts, human law is quite incapable of regulating them and that another law is needed for this purpose.[35] For St. Thomas, therefore, morals deals with internal and external acts, whereas law deals only with external acts. On the other hand, he frequently refers to a power which law has over and above morals, the power of coercion.[36] Indeed, he finds in its possession of this power a justification for the existence of human law; men who are prone to vice must be prevented by force and fear from performing evil.[37] So important is the power of coercion that Fr. Cahill declares that "it is this attribute of 'coercibility'—the legal precept's quality of being able to achieve its objective where the subject's will does not embrace the law's objective, and even where the subject's will positively rejects the law's objective—which distinguishes the law from all other precepts in the moral order."[38] St. Thomas is well aware that law and morals are not identical.

[34]St. Thomas, *supra* note 2, q.95, a.2. St. Thomas refers to a determination made by human law as a determination of the natural law (*quaedam determinatio legis naturae*), but it is clear that it is such only mediately and that immediately it is a determination of a necessary conclusion of the natural law, i.e., of a moral precept.

[35]*Ibid.*, q.91, a.4. Cf. also q.100, a.9.

[36]*Ibid.*, q.90, a.3 ad 2; q.96, a.5.

[37]*Ibid.*, q.96, a.5.

[38]Cahill, *supra* note 12, at p. 28. This does not mean, however, that law aims at producing merely externally good acts; its intention is always to produce acts wholly good, but it is unable to be an effective cause of this result.

But, while keeping their differences in mind, St. Thomas stresses the link between them, namely, the rational nature of each. Morals is wholly rational; law is rational, but not wholly so, for the will too has a role to play.[39] All law arises from the reason and the will of the legislator.[40] But though equally necessary, reason and will are not equal partners in law. There is a priority among the constitutive elements; and the rational element is the primary one, the volitional element being secondary. The will is the moving or efficient element in law, but reason is the directive or ordering element, and thus St. Thomas says that law comes from will regulated by reason (*a voluntate hominis ratione regulata*).[41]

Since reason is the norm of law as well as of morals, there is considerable congruence between the two orders. Indeed, if law were only reason, as morals is, they would be identical. But law is much more than reason, for only that which is reasonable and at the same time willed by the legislator is law. Indeed the most obvious element in human law is will. Yet law is not untrammelled will; the arbitrary fiat of the legislator is not law. An unjust edict of the legislator, one directly contrary to moral (rational and necessary) precepts is not law but a perversion of law.[42]

Morals is potentially part of law to the extent that it bears a relation to the common good because, though morals is concerned with both individual good and the common good, law for St. Thomas is concerned only with the common good.[43] Adler calls that part of morality which is concerned with the common good *ius gentium*, stating that it "consists only of those conclusions which are propositions about the universal means to be employed in the sphere of social conduct, means ordained to the social common good as

[39]St. Thomas, *supra* note 2, q.90, a.1c and ad 3.

[40]*Ibid.*, q.97, a.3.

[41]*Ibid.* In a will theory of law the will is necessarily both the efficient and the directive element, for it moves the reason not only as to exercise (as it does even in a reason theory) but also as to specification. Thus reason's role in a will theory is a decidedly subordinate one; it may help in the mechanics of formulating the legal proposition and making it consistent with other legal propositions, but the justification for the substance of the proposition will be found, not in the reason, but only in the will.

[42]*Ibid.*, q.90, a.1 ad 3; q.95, a.2; q.96, a.4.

[43]*Ibid.*, q.90, a.2.

proximate end, rather than to the ultimate end, happiness."[44] It is this *ius gentium* part of morality that has a relationship to law, and consequently it is only this part of morals that we shall be concerned with. But *ius gentium* is not a part of morals which can be clearly set off from the rest of the science because the boundary between it and the rest is continually shifting, as is the boundary between law and morals.

The effect of morals upon law varies according to the derivation of the legal rules involved. As we have seen, legal rules are derived from natural law through the moral "law" in two ways, by conclusion and by determination. We might cast this difference in derivation into the traditional common law distinction between *mala per se* and *mala prohibita*, but I prefer to adopt the terminology suggested by Dr. Brendan Brown and refer to these rules as "static" and "dynamic" norms respectively.[45] Static norms are those which are ascertained deductively, whereas dynamic norms are those which are instituted with the aid of induction. The more basic judge-made rules and many constitutional and equitable norms are static or deduced, but by far the greater number of explicit legal rules are dynamic and not logically necessary. However, underlying the dynamic rules in almost every part of law there are unspoken static rules which are implicitly part of law. For example, underlying the law that one who fraudulently and without colour of right takes anything with the intention of depriving the owner of it is guilty of theft and is subject to certain penalties there is the implicit moral judgment that theft is wrong. The fact, therefore, that static rules are in an explicit way such a small part of law is no gauge of their importance, for implicitly they are the basis of all law.

[44]Adler, *supra* note 4, at p. 393, n. 17a. It is not clear that St. Thomas used the term "*ius gentium*" in this sense, and certainly the ancient Romans did not. Lottin, *supra* note 18, at p. 185, feels that the term can be dropped entirely without appreciable loss.

[45]B. Brown, "Natural Law: Dynamic Basis of Law and Morals in the Twentieth Century," in Brown (ed.), *The Natural Law Reader* (1960), pp. 158, 167. Adler, *supra* note 4, at p. 402, n. 63, says that positive rules can be divided into those which are just formally as well as finally and those which are just only finally. Cf. St. Thomas, *supra* note 2, q.99, a.4 ad 2, where he points out that judicial precepts have something in common with moral precepts and something in common with ceremonial precepts.

Morals has a substantive effect upon the static norms of positive law and a merely adjectival effect upon the dynamic norms. The static norms, since they can be deduced from the principles of the natural law, fall within natural morality. They are concerned with things good or bad in themselves and are thus necessary conclusions from the principles. Hence the content of the rule as formulated by the science of morals is taken over into law; for the legislator, though he does have the choice—except in the case of moral precepts absolutely necessary for the preservation of society, such as the prohibition of murder—whether to adopt a moral precept or not and make it a static norm, does not have the option of changing the content of the rule, since it is the product of right reason and just as binding on the legislator as on the moralist. Morals, therefore, dictates the very substance of the static norms.

The effect of morals upon dynamic norms is different because these norms govern morally indifferent acts. They operate in a sphere in which institution rather than rationality predominates, though reason is not, of course, excluded. Here the legislator has no obligation regarding the contents of the laws he makes. His sole obligation is to proceed reasonably. This obligation, though single, is not inconsiderable. St. Thomas says that laws must be just in a threefold way: in their end, that is, they must be ordained to the common good; in their author, that is, their making must be within the legislator's power; and in their form, that is, their incidence must be according to a proportional equality established by the common good. To be wholly just, a law must be just in all of these ways.[46] The first requirement is clearly substantive but the second is adjectival and the third has at least a strong adjectival aspect. Thus, though morals affects the substance of the static rules, it affects the dynamic rules only by imposing procedural requirements.

But the relationship of law and morals comprises more than the penetration of morals into law. There is a mutual interpenetration of law and morals. Again the effect depends upon whether static or dynamic legal norms are involved. Static norms cannot affect the

[46]St. Thomas, *supra* note 2, q.96, a.4.

natural moral order because they are repetitions of what is already in it, adding merely the authoritative command of the state to the internal command of reason. Dynamic norms, however, contribute to the contents of morality. They cannot, of course, add to the natural moral order, except accidentally,[47] because the acts which they command or forbid are in themselves morally indifferent. But the totality of morality, morality in the concrete, is more than intrinsic morality. Indeed in the concrete every act is either good or bad: for an act has goodness or badness not only from its object, which determines its species, but also from the circumstances accidental to it, and every act has some circumstance which makes it good or bad, even if it is only the end it intends.[48] Thus, though dynamic legal rules are incapable of adding to the natural moral order, since they are not in themselves either good or bad, they are able to add to the sum total of morality. This is possible because the necessity of a political authority to guide the many to the attainment of the common good of the community is an inescapable conclusion from the natural law principle of seeking the common good, and because this authority, once established, proceeds by instituting rules of conduct which are the most feasible and convenient means to the attainment of the end, the common good; and, once the means have been determined by the superior wisdom of the legislator, the citizens must accept them as *the* ways of achieving the common good, or else the very purpose of the legislator's authority

[47]Though law can have no direct effect upon intrinsic morality, it can have an indirect and accidental effect. J. Connery, "Prudence and Morality" (1952), 13 *Theological Studies* 564, at p. 582, writes: "[P]rudence must play an important part in formulating the more remote conclusions of the moral law. Such conclusions, it is true, are virtually contained in the principles themselves and might, at least in theory, be deduced from them. But in practice metaphysical relations are often obscure. They are brought to the surface often enough only as the result of experience. . . . Thus, prudence has a function not only in regard to individual acts, but also, though more remotely, in regard to moral science itself. It will never, of course, play the constitutive part it has in regard to positive law. In moral science, its function will be merely to bring to the surface the relations between moral principles and the more remote conclusions which are frequently hidden from the speculative intellect." Brown, *supra* note 45, at p. 161, gives as an example of the inductive advance of moral science the adoption of the empirical observation that excessive inbreeding interferes with the primary end of marriage, *i.e.*, the healthy propagation of the human race.

[48]St. Thomas, *supra* note 2, q.18, a.9.

will be frustrated.[49] Thus obedience to the commands of the legislator becomes a moral obligation in the concrete, even though it is not a moral obligation in the abstract because of the absence of a necessary relationship to the natural law. The determination of the ruler, even though merely prudential and contingent, binds the subject in conscience.[50]

Human laws, says St. Thomas, are either just or unjust (that is, either conformable or contrary to intrinsic morality), and if they are just, they have the power of obliging in conscience from the eternal law, from which they are derived.[51] Now it is clear from the whole "Treatise on Law" that the eternal law is related to human law only through the mediation of the natural law, and so Aquinas is in effect maintaining that all human laws derive their obligatory force from the natural law.[52] This is hardly a surprise in the light of the fact that he considers all human law to be derived from the natural law; but the natural law is not the only cause of legal obligation. The natural law is the general and formal cause of legal obligation, but the legislator is the particularizing and efficient cause. These causes work together harmoniously: each requires the

[49]Authority is a moral necessity. It is such not only for those unable to govern themselves—children and the feeble-minded; authority is necessary even for those who are not intellectually deficient. It would be necessary even in a wholly adult community in order to assure the unity of the action of the multitude. In the words of Y. Simon, *Nature and Function of Authority* (1940), pp. 17–18, "a multitude aiming at a common good, which can be attained only through a common action, must be united in its action by some steady principle. This principle is precisely what we call authority." Because the certainty of speculative truth is not possible in the practical order, disagreement as to what to do is certain. The community in certain matters must act as one and the function of authority is to ensure that it does. Thus authority, government, is a necessary means towards the necessary end, human association in political society. Since authority is morally necessary in order to ensure unity of action, it is morally necessary that the multitude obey the commands of authority within its duly constituted sphere or the effectiveness of this necessary end will be impaired, or even destroyed.

[50]It will be obvious from this statement that I do not admit the validity of the so-called "purely penal" law. T. Davitt, *The Nature of Law* (1951), pp. 140–6, shows that the notion of purely penal law is wholly incompatible with the doctrine of St. Thomas. R. Bégin, *Natural Law and Positive Law* (1959), pp. 137–8, n. 101, points out that many violations of laws which some would consider to be purely penal laws are to be disregarded, not because the laws do not bind in conscience, but because of the extreme slightness of the matter.

[51]St. Thomas, *supra* note 2, q.96, a.4.

[52]On this and the following points, see MacGuigan, *supra* note 7, pp. 307–10.

co-operation of the other for its own causality to be efficacious, and so there is mutual fulfilment without conflict. The legislator is an extrinsic cause of legal obligation, but the natural law is an intrinsic cause: for the natural law, being for St. Thomas a principle, exists within every derived law as its root.

The natural law is the source of both moral and legal obligation. Moral obligation in the realm of natural morality is purely intrinsic, arising solely from the perception by reason of the exigencies of ends and means. Legal obligation is not purely intrinsic, since it has an extrinsic efficient cause as well as its intrinsic formal cause, the natural law. But the natural law exercises its causality upon law through the mediation of the moral "law," and so there is a large measure of identity between moral and legal obligation. The obligation of static legal norms is wholly and in itself moral obligation, but the obligation of dynamic legal norms is a secondary and derived kind of moral obligation, arising not in the realm of nature or of science but in that of prudence, for an act, morally neutral in itself, becomes morally obligatory once commanded by the legislator. Thus all legal obligation is moral, either primarily or secondarily, for all law binds in conscience to the performance of the thing commanded or to the avoidance of the thing forbidden by the legislator—either because the act is a necessary conclusion of the natural law or because it is a prudential determination of the natural law.

Thus there is for St. Thomas a mutual interpenetration of law and morals. Some moral obligations are also legal obligations (static norms), and all legal obligations are moral obligations, either primarily and necessarily (static norms) or secondarily and prudentially (dynamic norms). In fact, St. Thomas even goes so far as to say that legislative determinations which are unjust (and therefore, by his own definition, not law at all) may sometimes be binding in conscience for prudential reasons, that is, in order to avoid the greater evils of scandal and disturbance.[53] St. Thomas does not confuse the moral and legal orders. He clearly sees the essential features of each and distinguishes them effectively. But for him

[53]St. Thomas, *supra* note 2, q.96, a.4c and ad 3.

distinction is not separation, and so far is he from adopting a theory of the separation of law and morals that he posits a massive penetration of each into the realm of the other.

II

IN THIS PART I shall deal with what I consider to be the most important consequences of the Thomistic theory of the interpenetration of law and morals on the legislator, the judge, and the citizen.

A. The Legislator[54]

For St. Thomas the proper effect of law is to make those subject to it good.[55] Not only is this the intrinsic effect of law but it is also the subjective intention of the good legislator.[56] St. Thomas, however, does not mean to impose upon the legislator the burden of enacting into positive law all the precepts of the moral law, for there are certain limitations inherent in the legislator's role. The first is that law is not concerned with good in general, but with the common good.[57] St. Thomas brings this out when dealing with the question of whether human law is obliged to prescribe acts of all the virtues. His answer is that there is no virtue whose acts cannot be prescribed by law because every virtue is capable of standing in relation to the common and the individual good. For example, the virtue of fortitude can be employed either to protect the community or to uphold the rights of a friend. Though law can prescribe acts of every virtue, it does not, he maintains, prescribe all the acts of every virtue, but only those which are related to the common good either immediately, that is, in itself and directly, or mediately, that is, for the sake of justice and peace in the community.[58] An example of something mediately directed to the common good is the keeping of contracts among individuals, which is not in itself necessary for

[54]I use the term "legislator" rather than "legislature" to avoid any connotation of the doctrine of the separation of powers. Even the work of the judge may be legislative in character.

[55]St. Thomas, *supra* note 2, q.92, a.1.

[56]*Ibid.*, q.96, a.2 arg. 2.

[57]*Ibid.*, q.90, a.2.

[58]*Ibid.*, q.96, a.3.

the common good, though it may be necessary for the peace of the community to enact laws regulating it.

Dabin has an excellent analysis of the proximity of moral precepts to the common good and their potentiality for incorporation into the law.[59] He distinguishes, first, between precepts governing duties towards others and those governing duties towards God and one's self, and points out that the latter, in contrast with the former, can affect the common good only incidentally. Second, within the group of precepts relating to our duties towards others, he distinguishes those which relate to an obligation capable of exaction and those which do not, and thus he is able to conclude that matters involving the virtue of justice are the natural and primary subject matter for the legislator. Regarding moral precepts concerning other virtues, he says that "the measure of interest the jurist accords them will depend on the degree of their proximity to justice."[60]

The second limitation on legislation is that laws must always be relative to the particular conditions of the community for which they are made. Law is for St. Thomas a rule and measure, and, since a measure must be homogeneous with what it measures, law must be imposed upon men only in accordance with their condition. St. Thomas takes a supremely realistic view of the condition of mankind, recognizing that most men are not perfect in virtue. Thus, he holds, human laws should not prohibit all the vices from which those who are fully virtuous are able to abstain, but only the more grievous ones, from which it is possible for most men to abstain, and especially those evils which are harmful to other persons and without the prohibition of which human society could not be preserved, such as murder and theft.[61]

St. Thomas justifies his view of the minimal function of the legislator on the ground that the purpose of human law is to lead men to virtue not all at once but gradually. Thus law does not immediately impose on the masses, who are imperfect, the standards of conduct of those who are virtuous. Otherwise, he continues, the imperfect, not being able to bear such precepts, would break out

[59]Dabin, *supra* note 5, at pp. 461–70.
[60]*Ibid.*, at p. 462.
[61]St. Thomas, *supra* note 2, q.96, a.2.

into greater evils; as Scripture says, he who blows his nose excessively brings forth blood.[62] Thus Aquinas clearly imposes only minimal duties on the legislator with regard to the incorporation of moral precepts into the law.

The work of the legislator involves the exercise of the virtue of prudence, for both in deciding what his legislation should attempt to do and in working out the best way of achieving his purpose the legislator is in a realm where abstract considerations do not take him very far. Prudence is a virtue which seems to be much misunderstood today. At best, it is likely to be identified with a cautious conservatism; at worst, it is likely to be thought of as the expediency of the worldly wise. For St. Thomas Aquinas, however, prudence is pre-eminent among the virtues, for it is demanded by the other virtues for their completion,[63] and is indeed the cause of their being virtues.[64] Prudence is the right way of doing things;[65] more particularly, it is right judgment about human good in single things to be done.[66] In the words of Professor O'Neil, it is "rightness in knowledge, the right knowledge of what is to be done here and now in circumstantial concreteness."[67] Thus prudence is concerned with individual acts rather than with science; it deals not with human ends, which are determined by nature, but with means, which are left indeterminate by nature.[68]

Prudence is an intellectual virtue, but of the practical intellect.[69] Hence, though it belongs to the intellect, it is able to be fully as much a virtue as the moral virtues.[70] It therefore has two aspects, the cognitive and the preceptive.[71] As Pieper puts it, "prudence looks two ways . . . but the cognitive aspect is prior and sets a standard."[72] The priority of the cognitive aspect reveals that moral

[62]*Ibid.*, a.2 ad 2.
[63]*Ibid.*, q.64, a.3.
[64]St. Thomas, *De Virt. In Comm.*, a.6.
[65]St. Thomas, *supra* note 2, q.57, a.4.
[66]St. Thomas, *supra* note 64.
[67]C. O'Neil, "Prudence, The Incommunicable Wisdom," in Brennan (ed.), *Essays In Thomism* (1942), pp. 185, 196.
[68]St. Thomas, *supra* note 2, II-II, q.47, a.1 ad 2.
[69]*Ibid.*, a.2.
[70]*Ibid.*, a.4.
[71]*Ibid.*, q.48, a.1.
[72]J. Pieper, *Prudence* (1959), p. 27.

action is according to reason in means as well as in ends. Fr. Connery declares that "Thomistic morality is essentially rational not only in the goals it pursues but also in their realization."[73]

Prudence can dispense neither with its relationship to knowledge nor with its relationship to action. It is indeed wholly concerned with the singular, but in order for it to grasp the singular in its totality it must know it in its relation to general moral precepts as well as in isolation. To be sure, general principles alone are not enough for the moral life; but they remain necessary as the foundation of concrete moral decisions. "Although the proper mystery of the prudential determinations cannot be discarded," Yves Simon wisely observes, "the truly prudent man, the true man of action, wants to have his prudence enlightened by principles."[74] The principles themselves settle no concrete political issues; concrete issues are settled by prudence. But prudence does not operate in a "principleless" vacuum. It must not only consider circumstances but also apply principles.

From the viewpoint of the moral lives of the citizens, laws are not, strictly speaking, prudential directives, for although in comparison with the principles of the natural law and even with moral precepts they are concrete, they still retain a certain generality; they are, for example, made not for one particular citizen but for all the citizens. Law is the realm of the practically practical, in contrast with the speculatively practical realm of moral science and the purely practical realm of prudence strictly taken.[75] However, from the viewpoint of the legislator himself, there is no question that law is the expression of a prudential judgment, both with regard to means in general and with regard to singular means here and now.

What is expected of the legislator in the realm of prudential determination is not easy. Prudence is always a difficult virtue. Some

[73]Connery, *supra* note 47, at p. 573.

[74]Simon, *supra* note 49, at pp. 3–4. It is in accordance with this insight that Simon formulates (*ibid.*, at 46–7) the principles of authority and autonomy as the necessary preliminaries to the prudential life in the field of politics.

[75]Thus law does not come under the principal act of prudence, the act of command, see St. Thomas, *supra* note 2, II-II, q.47, a.8. Nevertheless it may loosely be termed prudential; St. Thomas himself, *ibid.*, q.57, a.1 ad 2, so refers to it (*quaedam prudentiae regula*).

of the prerequisites which St. Thomas says are necessary for prudence are memory, docility, ingenuity in new situations, foresight, circumspection, and caution.[76] Even if the legislator possesses all of these attributes, things may not turn out as he expects, either because the law he makes may not have the result he intended, or, if it does, the result he intended may, contrary to his expectations, turn out to be bad; the certitude of the theoretical order is not possible in practical matters. But all is not hopeless. The legislator can, on the basis both of his own experience and of that of others, formulate political generalizations which will work more often than not; a well worked-out theory of interests would prove invaluable to him in this process. Further, the legislator can rest easy in his conscience about his mistakes in prudential judgment, for the truth of practical knowledge does not consist, like that of speculative knowledge, in conformity with reality, but rather in conformity with a rectified will.[77] If he is acting in good faith, his actions are formally good. Needless to say, this does not dispense him from his obligation to enlighten himself on pertinent facts.

Reinhold Niebuhr maintains that "the mistake of Catholic moral casuistry [is] to derive relative moral judgments too simply from the presuppositions of its natural law,"[78] and he charges with this fault, not modern Catholic thought, much of which is unfortunately so tainted, but St. Thomas Aquinas, of whom it is emphatically not true. St. Thomas was not wont to over-emphasize the easiness of the moral life, either from the viewpoint of knowledge or from that of will. For him the most important of all the virtues is prudence; prudence is involved in every act of every virtue. Where there is prudence, the answer cannot be cut and dried, and often there is more than one valid answer. What St. Thomas expects of the legislator is in keeping with this: that he have true moral precepts and apply them as well as he can through his own virtue of prudence.

[76]*Ibid.*, q.49, a.1 ff.

[77]*Ibid.*, I-II, q.57, a.5 ad 3.

[78]Quoted by C. de Koninck, "General Standards and Particular Situations in Relation to the Natural Law" (1950), 24 *Proc. Amer. Cath. Philos. Ass'n* 28.

B. The Judge

There is some reason for thinking that St. Thomas favours a limited conception of the judicial function. For one thing, he expressly agrees with Aristotle's dictum that as many matters as possible should be determined by laws and as few as possible by judges, and he repeats Aristotle's reasons in support of this view. First, he says that it is easier to find a few wise men for legislators than many wise men for judges. Second, legislators have sufficient leisure to consider matters beforehand and in the universal and do not have to deal with cases in the singular and as soon as they arise. Third, legislators are able to judge in the abstract and for the future, whereas judges are likely to be influenced by their feelings towards the parties.[79] He seems to conceive of the judge's function as primarily one of determining matters of fact as contrasted with matters of law; for he says that certain singular matters which cannot be comprehended by the law must necessarily be left to judges, as, for example, whether something has or has not happened.[80]

St. Thomas further indicates support for a restricted view of the judicial function by maintaining that judgment should be given according to the letter of the law (*secundum legis scripturam*).[81] It is of course to be expected that St. Thomas would add the qualification that judgment can be according to the letter of the law only where the written law contains nothing contrary to natural right, for otherwise it would be unjust and so lacking in binding power.[82] But it is significant that he also adds the qualification that, because of the generality of the law and the consequent fact that it cannot take account of all particular cases, in some cases recourse must be had to equity rather than to the letter of law.[83]

He develops his concept of equity more fully in another text.[84]

[79]St. Thomas, *supra* note 2, q.95, a.1 ad 2. The Aristotelian text is Rhetoric I, 1, 1354a32–b15.

[80]St. Thomas, *supra* note 2, q.95, a.1 ad 3. This is also in accordance with Aristotle.

[81]*Ibid.*, II-II, q.60, a.5.

[82]*Ibid.*, ad 1.

[83]*Ibid.*, ad 2.

[84]*Ibid.*, q.120, a.1.

There he points out that human acts, the subject matter of laws, consist of an infinite variety of singular contingent things and that it is consequently impossible to make a rule of law which will cover every conceivable instance without fail. Further, the legislator must direct his attention to those things which happen for the most part, and make laws with regard to them; even if he were able to foresee every individual instance in framing the law, he ought not to do so because this would make the law too detailed and confusing.[85] Therefore, in some cases it would be contrary to the equality of justice and to the common good, which the law itself intends, to follow the letter of the law. He gives as an example the legal rule that things deposited ought to be returned to the depositor on request, a rule which is for the most part just; but it would be wrong to follow it if someone who had deposited his sword demanded it again while in a fury, or to fight against his country. In such cases it would be wrong to follow the law and right to go beyond the words of the law to follow what justice and the common good demand. Thus to act pertains to the virtue of *epikeia* or equity. St. Thomas points out that such dispensations from the letter of the law normally ought to be given only by those in authority, and that a man ought not to dispense himself except in case of emergency.[86] Apparently, therefore, a judge need not always follow the letter of the law but must always see that justice is done, as the law intends.

For St. Thomas the object of the judge is always justice. The name "judge" (*iudex*) is, he says, taken from his act of pronouncing the right (*ius dicens*), and the right is the object of justice.[87] Indeed he refers to the judge as the living embodiment of justice (*iustitia animata*).[88] This in itself would not necessarily indicate an awareness of the creativity involved in judicial activity, but St. Thomas also remarks that he who gives judgment in a way interprets the letter of the law by the very fact of applying it to a particular situation (*ille qui iudicium fert legis dictum quodammodo interpretatur*,

85*Ibid.*, I-II, q.96, a.6 ad 3.
86*Ibid.*, a.6.
87*Ibid.*, II-II, q.60, a.1.
88*Ibid.*, I-II, q.95, a.1 ad 2.

applicando ipsum ad particulare negotium).[89] Finally, he recognizes a likeness to the legislator's in the judge's activity, for he declares that the judge's decision is, with reference to the particular fact-situation, like a particular law (*sententia iudicis est quasi quaedam particularis lex in aliquo particulari facto*).[90]

It is obvious that the Greek and Roman legal systems with which St. Thomas was familiar through his reading were not at all like the Anglo-American legal system of today, and it is no easy task to disengage his principles from his application of them to these systems. It seems clear that his most fundamental principle is that the judge must attempt to achieve justice, and this principle logically implies that the judge's role cannot be a wholly passive one. But how active a role St. Thomas would allow the judge is hard to say. In one text he agrees with the Roman law principle that no one other than the legislator can interpret the law when it is not clear,[91] but on the other hand we have seen that he allows the judge some latitude in interpretation. Obviously, in a legal system in which there is a complete written code, though there is certainly scope for the judicial creation of law it must be wholly within the context of legislative creation. Therefore, we can hardly take St. Thomas' application of his basic principle to such a system as setting the pattern for its application to a legal system in which legislation is not only interstitial but even viewed in the light of the judicial tradition, and the primary responsibility for the attainment of justice rests upon the judiciary. At least in the context of the Anglo-American legal system, Professor Brown's view that the Thomistic

[89] *Ibid.*, II-II, q.60, a.6.

[90] *Ibid.*, q.67, a.1. He says, *ibid.*, III, q.59, a.1, that the judge's prime need is wisdom, since it is vital for formulating his judgment. J. Dolan, "Natural Law and the Judicial Function" (1960), 16 *Laval Théologique et Philosophique* 94, at p. 128, observes that "while there is in St. Thomas no minute examination of interpretative methods, we know that the judicial office is not conceived mechanically. For it is above all by his *prudence* that the judge applies the common precept of law to the singular cases." However, Fr. Dolan does not enter into a consideration of how St. Thomas' principles apply to the common law, but is content to reiterate St. Thomas' own viewpoint; thus he sees the function of judge as one of legislating "'interstitially' where 'gaps' occur in the law." *Ibid.*, at p. 113

[91] St. Thomas, *supra* note 2, II-II, q.120, a.1 ad 3.

jurist ought to "subject the rule of *stare decisis* to the test of reason, justice, and experience"[92] seems to be the proper application of St. Thomas' basic principle. Dean O'Meara has recently suggested that only such a creative conception of the judicial function can make a theory of the interpenetration of law and morals practicable in a common law system:

> [W]hat role is there for natural law to play? What contribution can it make? Comparatively little, so far as I can see, if law be no more than an aggregation of already existing rules. But law must be regarded as a great deal more than that. It seems to me convenient and useful to think of law as a living process for the just resolution of never-ending controversies. If law is regarded in this light, as a process of decision, it comes alive, is responsive to changing human needs; and the way is cleared for a positive contribution by natural law. . . .
>
> This, of course, presupposes that the judge is not an automaton proceeding mechanically according to predetermined rules.[93]

In the light of this conception of law as a process of decision in which the judge performs a creative function, Dean O'Meara feels that "the sharp distinction, commonly drawn, between the law-that-is and the law-that-ought-to-be is unrealistic, for the simple reason that the so-called law-that-*is* in important part is a myth";[94] law must be recognized to be not something which *is* but something which is *becoming*. In such a conception the judge has in the last analysis "nothing to rely on but his own intellect, experience and conscience,"[95] and his exercise of discretion ought to be guided, *inter alia*, by principles of morality; "when the nature of the case warrants, the judge should turn for guidance to relevant ethical principles. . . ."[96]

If the view of Dean O'Meara is right, and it seems to be, this would mean that the Thomistic theory of the interpenetration of law and morals, as applied to the common law, is wholly incom-

[92]Brown, "A Scholastic Critique of Case Law," in Brown, *supra* note 45, at pp. 154, 157.

[93]J. O'Meara, "Natural Law and Everyday Law" (1960), 5 *Natural Law Forum* 83, at pp. 84–5.

[94]*Ibid.*, at p. 90.

[95]*Ibid.*, at p. 97.

[96]*Ibid.*, at p. 98.

patible with the Blackstonian fiction that judges do not make but merely find the law. Such an interpretation is supported by St. Thomas' indicated approval of a creative function for the judiciary with regard to static legal norms, those which have to do with acts which are immoral or moral in themselves; for he states—in dealing with the question of whether judgment should be given according to the laws as written—that, if the letter of the law contains anything contrary to natural right (that is, to the natural moral order), it is unjust and has no binding power,[97] and the plain implication of his words is that in such a case the judge should refuse to follow the command of the legislator and should substitute the proper legal rule.

In this area of the judge's responsibility with regard to an unjust law, there has been considerable development in Catholic thought since the days of St. Thomas Aquinas, but it has been development consonant with the thought of St. Thomas. Of greatest importance is the declaration of Pope Pius XII in 1949 that "a judge cannot simply throw responsibility for his decision from his own shoulders, causing it to fall on the law and its authors. Undoubtedly the authors are principally responsible for the effects of such a law. But the judge who applies it to a particular case by his sentence is a joint cause and thus jointly responsible for these effects."[98]

The basic moral precept in this realm is that a person may not perform an act which concurs in the wrongdoing of another. Concurrence in wrongdoing is called scandal where the other person has not yet resolved upon doing evil, and it is called co-operation in wrongdoing where the other has already determined to do wrong. Concurrence in evil is formal where the person concurring intends the evil which the other's act involves, and formal concurrence is always evil in itself. Concurrence is material where the person concurring does not intend but merely permits the evil which the other does, and material concurrence is sometimes morally permissible in order to prevent a greater evil.[99] Where a judge's co-

[97]St. Thomas, *supra* note 2, II-II, q.60, a.5 ad 1.

[98]Pius XII, "Duties of Catholic Jurists" (1950), 48 *Catholic Mind* 53, at p. 57.

[99]Cf. W. Cahill, "Some General Criteria of Morality" (1958), 4 *Catholic Lawyer* 41, at pp. 52–4.

operation with the legislator in evil is formal, that is, where the judge too intends the evil law, his action is never morally licit. But where his co-operation is merely material, he may in some circumstances allow the evil law to take effect.

The late Holy Father in the same address quoted above applies the principles of co-operation in evil to the work of the judge, laying down three principles by way of guidance. The first principle he states is that "[a] judge may never by his decision oblige anyone to commit an act intrinsically immoral, that is to say, an act which is by its very nature contrary to the law of God and the Church."[100] This first principle does not go very far. It merely forbids the judge ever to order the doing of something intrinsically evil, such as taking the life of an innocent person, or performing eugenic sterilization.[101] By the "law of God" the Pontiff refers to the law God established by virtue of the act of creation, that is, the precepts of the natural moral order. By the "law of the Church" he refers, not to the positive legislation of the Church, but rather to "actions forbidden by the Church acting as the teacher of the law God has implanted in nature."[102] The number of cases which might conceivably come under this principle in common law jurisdictions is almost nil, for the legislatures in these jurisdictions habitually respect the moral "law."

The late Pontiff's second principle is that a judge "can in no case expressly recognize and approve an unjust law—which for that matter would never constitute the foundation for a judgment valid in conscience and before God."[103] This principle means that a judge cannot expressly approve of an unjust law, even one not intrinsically

[100]Pius XII, *supra* note 98, at p. 57. For the substance of my analysis of these principles I am indebted to J. Davis, *The Moral Obligations of Catholic Civil Judges* (1953), pp. 111–38.

[101]The U.S. case of *Buck* v. *Bell* (1927), 274 U.S. 200 involved a Virginia statute which allowed eugenic sterilization of persons afflicted with hereditary forms of insanity, idiocy, imbecility, feeble-mindedness, or epilepsy. Mr. Justice Holmes, speaking for the court, declared: "The principle that sustains compulsory vaccination is broad enough to cover cutting the Fallopian tubes. . . . Three generations of imbeciles are enough." *Ibid.*, at p. 207. The court's decision in this case infringed the third rather than the first of the Pope's principles, since the court did not order but merely permitted the application of the statute.

[102]Davis, *supra* note 100, at p. 123.

[103]Pius XII, *supra* note 98, at p. 57.

evil. A judge may declare neither publicly nor privately his approval of an unjust law. This principle, like the first, seems to impose no particular hardship on a judge in the common law world.

The third principle clarifies the second:

> Nevertheless, not every application of an unjust law is equivalent to its recognition or approval. In this case, a judge may–sometimes, perhaps, must–allow an unjust law to take its course, whenever this may be the only means of impeding much greater evil. He may inflict a penalty for transgression of an unjust law if it is of such a kind that a person who is affected by it is reasonably disposed to submit to it in order to avoid that harm or assure a good of very much higher importance, and if the judge knows, or can prudently suppose, that such sanction will be willingly accepted by the transgressor for higher motives.[104]

This final principle makes it clear that not every application of an unjust law implies approval and is consequently forbidden. Often a judge may apply an unjust law, and sometimes he even must apply it. Of course, there must be sufficient reason for a judge so to apply an unjust law, and the judge must make a prudential judgment that application of the law is a lesser evil than the evil which would probably result if he did not apply it.

We must distinguish between the application of the content of unjust laws and the application of the penalty attached to them. With regard to the application of the content, we may observe that there are four types of unjust laws, and whether a judge may ever apply an unjust law depends upon what type it is. The first type of unjust law is that which is contrary to the natural moral order; the judge may *never* command such a law to be obeyed. The second type is a law contrary only to the divine positive law. Here we must distinguish between negative and affirmative divine laws. A negative divine law is one that forbids an evil action; for example, the first and second commandments of God forbid the worship of false gods and the blaspheming of the true God. A judge may *never* apply a law which would force a person to contravene such divine precepts. An affirmative divine law is one which commands some-

[104] *Ibid.*

thing good to be done; examples of affirmative divine laws are the commandment to keep holy the Lord's Day and the commandment to profess the true faith openly. An affirmative divine law by its very nature does not bind to continual but rather to periodic performance; we are not bound to make a continual profession of our faith but may await a more propitious time. To avoid a greater evil a judge may sometimes *permit* an unjust law opposed to affirmative divine law to take its course. The third type of unjust law is that which is contrary only to ecclesiastical law. The judge may in some circumstances apply such a law, though, if circumstances permit, he ought first to obtain permission from the proper Church authorities. The fourth type of unjust law is one that is contrary only to human good; again the judge may in some circumstances apply such a law. With regard to penalties, the judge may in some circumstances punish an innocent person—innocent, that is, because what he violated was no law—regardless of which class of law is involved, provided that two conditions are satisfied: the penalty must not be out of proportion to the good obtained—the penalty of death is always disproportionate—and the judge must be able reasonably to presume willingness on the part of the victim to suffer the penalty.

The most common case of material co-operation in evil to arise before common law judges is in divorce actions where there is a valid marriage according to both ecclesiastical and civil law and where presumably at least one of the parties will attempt a new marriage if the divorce decree is granted. The view of the majority of Catholic theologians is that the action of a judge in pronouncing a decree of divorce is not in itself an evil act, but that he is guilty of proximate mediate material co-operation in the evil of the new marriage which will subsequently be attempted; and since the judge would thus be guilty only of material co-operation, he is permitted to grant a divorce when there is a sufficiently weighty reason to do so. On what constitutes a sufficiently weighty reason Fr. Davis writes:

> In our own United States in our day it may safely be said that Catholic judges have at times sufficiently weighty reasons for granting divorces from marriages valid before God and the Church, even when

> there is a probability or certainty of remarriage. Should a Catholic judge . . . refuse to do so, in all probability he would suffer serious abuse, criticism, loss of prestige and probably the loss of his office. . . . Theologians in the United States consider these reasons sufficiently present and weighty for Catholic judges here to grant such divorces when they must do so in the course of fulfilling the duties of their office.[105]

The opinions of theologians in other common law jurisdictions would unquestionably be the same as those of American theologians.

It is clear from the foregoing discussion that the judge must play a creative role with regard to static norms, for he must determine whether the moral status which they possess in themselves is or is not in accord with moral precepts, and, if it is not, whether he may nevertheless apply the legal rules in question. In this area of static legal norms it is clear that the judge cannot simply shrug off responsibility and allow an unjust legislative enactment to take effect without deciding that he may morally do so; he is himself morally responsible for all his judgments. But, as Professor Hart has rightly observed, not all legal norms are in themselves moral,[106] and it is not clear from the necessity of judicial creativity with respect to legal rules which are in themselves moral or immoral that there should be judicial creativity concerning all legal rules. However, it would seem inappropriate to hold that the judge's role is creative only with regard to static norms, for, although these norms are few in number, they are the most fundamental and the most important of all legal norms, and it would seem that the judge should have equal power in dealing with the less important norms. Further, the judge's responsibility to achieve justice would not seem to be satisfied merely by attaining an abstract justice; logically it should be satisfied only with the achievement of a just prudential decision in the instant case. In St. Thomas' application of his legal principles the primary responsibility for the achievement of justice is that of the legislator, but in our system, where often the first "say" and always the last "say" as to what law governs a situation is that

[105]Davis, *supra* note 100, at pp. 190–1.

[106]H. L. A. Hart, "Positivism and the Separation of Law and Morals" (1958), 71 *Harv. L. Rev.* 593, at p. 613.

of the judge, it would seem that the primary responsibility is largely reversed, and that our application of St. Thomas' principles would have to be different from his.

The problem of personal justice does not arise in any more acute form for a Thomistic theory of judicial creativity than for any other such theory, but one issue which does arise is the fear that acceptance of a Thomistic theory of the interpenetration of law and morals opens the way for the domination of the realm of law by the Catholic Church through its authoritative interpretation of the natural moral order. The reason for the Church's concern with the natural moral order is that, because of the fallibility of human reason, as soon as men begin to draw conclusions from the principles of the natural law through their own unaided judgment error arises. To give us certitude as to some of the conclusions, God has given us his divine positive law which repeats the most important requirements of the natural moral order, and so there is a considerable area of coincidence between moral precepts as known by faith and as known by reason. Further, since error is even more possible in the remote conclusions, God has provided us with an infallible teaching authority in the realm of faith and morals, not only to give us supernatural truths but also to help us to draw the right conclusions in the natural order. But, as Dr. Brown has well said, "the tenet that the Catholic Church, through its divine mission, has the right and duty to decide the content of the natural law [i.e., the natural moral order] when reasonable men disagree is not a part of the natural law but of supernatural law."[107] Thus the Church's interpretation of the natural moral order is not binding on those who accept the validity of the natural moral order merely because they accept that order; it is a question of faith and entirely beyond the natural order. The fact of authoritative ecclesiastical interpretation is not a datum contained within the natural moral order itself.

Of course, the judge who freely accepts the authority of the Church is bound to follow the Church's interpretation of the natural moral order as far as he can. But, as we have seen, the

[107]Brown, book review of "The Philosophy of Law in Historical Perspective," by Carl Joachim Friedrich, in Brown, *supra* note 45, at pp. 101, 104.

Catholic judge has considerable leeway in view of prudential considerations. In a pluralistic society prudential considerations will normally prevent the Catholic judge's attempting to force his moral views upon those who do not share them.

C. The Citizen

By definition the citizen stands in no position of public trust. He has no duties of office to which he must be faithful, and so his resolution of the problem of conscience raised by a conflict between law and morals is somewhat different from that of the judge.

For St. Thomas there are two general kinds of unjust laws, those which are unjust because they are opposed to human good and those which are unjust because they are opposed to divine good.[108] Let us first consider those unjust according to human good.

As laws are just when just in end, authority, and form, so they are correspondingly unjust when unjust from any of these three viewpoints. First, a law is unjust if it is not directed to the end of law, that is, to the common good, for example, a law imposing a burden which is not for the good of the community but merely for the cupidity or glory of the legislator. A contemporary example would be a tax law with an unduly high depreciation allowance for a business or industry in which the legislator has a personal interest. Second, a law is unjust if the author does not have competence to legislate in the field. This is primarily a question of jurisdiction. Third, a law is unjust if it is inequitable in form, that is, if it distributes its benefits or burdens inequitably among the citizens. A good example of this would be a tax law which hits with undue severity certain sectors of the community.

To determine whether or not a law is contrary to human good is obviously a difficult task. Abstract precepts will rarely be able to solve a problem alone—and, of course, there is not always a consensus among moral philosophers or theologians as to how the precepts should be applied, even where there is agreement about the precepts. What is inequitable is a matter for prudential judgment involving a knowledge and evaluation of all the facts present in a

[108]St. Thomas, *supra* note 2, q.96, a.4.

given situation. There is a presumption that a law is just, and so, where it is not clear that it is unjust, it is always presumed to be just.[109] The reason for this presumption is, as Fr. Cahill points out, that we are dealing with matters not susceptible of metaphysical, mathematical, or physical certainty:

> We regard some generalities, of fact or of principle, as being "in possession," because they are the carefully gathered and interpreted data of common and prolonged human experience. Conclusions contrary to those generalities, though they have been reached by careful inquiry and though they are so clear as to enjoy some probability, may have to be set aside while the moral judgment follows the generality which is "in possession." This must be done until the contrary conclusion has been demonstrated to have the "weight of probability," or even to be probable beyond reasonable doubt, depending upon the moral interests secured by maintaining the generality in possession.[110]

This presumption binds the judge as well as the citizen, but it has even more force in the case of the citizen because of his lack of authority to interpret or change the law. Analogizing to St. Thomas' statement that equity should be invoked against the letter of the law only by those in authority, except in case of great necessity,[111] we may conclude that, since such instances of necessity are extremely rare, the citizen should almost invariably obey a law which is doubtfully just.

In those few cases where it can be clearly determined that legislative enactments are unjust, these enactments are in St. Thomas' eyes acts of violence rather than laws. They do not, therefore, oblige in conscience and so need not be obeyed. However, St. Thomas cautions, although such laws have in themselves no obligatory power, they may accidentally oblige in conscience in order to avoid scandal or disturbance, which are such great evils that the citizen sometimes must cede his legal rights in order to avoid them.[112] Whether or not such laws, even if clearly unjust, may be disobeyed depends on a prudential judgment. If the evil resulting from

[109]Cf. Davis, *supra* note 100, at p. 138. He quotes St. Alphonsus' maxim: *lex in dubio praesumitur iusta.* Cf. also Bégin, *supra* note 50, at p. 138.

[110]Cahill, *supra* note 12, at p. 40.

[111]St. Thomas, *supra* note 2, q.96, a.6.

[112]*Ibid.*, a.4.

observance of the law were small, disobedience would not usually be justifiable. Revolution against constituted authority, though sanctioned by St. Thomas in some situations where the ruler has turned into a tyrant,[113] is obviously a last resort and almost any evil is to be preferred to it.

Laws may also be unjust through contrariety to divine good. Examples of such laws are edicts of tyrants commanding the worship of idols or something else contrary to divine law. In "divine good" St. Thomas obviously includes the principles of the natural law and the precepts of the moral "law." It is also apparent from his example that he includes in "divine good" the dictates of the divine law, as, for example, the first table of the Decalogue. There is no leeway for prudence to operate with regard to such laws, for they simply must not be obeyed. However, a prudential judgment would be necessary as to whether to engage in passive or active resistance.[114]

So far we have been dealing with the area of conflict between law and morals, in which law is subservient to morals (or, more precisely, what is not in accord with morals is not law), but this is the less important aspect of the interpenetration of law and morals. What is of much greater significance is the vast majority of instances in which law and morals are in agreement and in which legal obligation is either primarily or secondarily moral obligation. For St. Thomas certain acts which are neither good nor evil in their species are said to be indifferent, but in the concrete every act

[113]Cajetan, *Commentarium in Summa Theologiae*, II-II, q.64, a.3, makes a distinction between a tyrant who has gained power legitimately and one who has usurped power; the latter, he believes, may rightly be killed by a private person, whereas the former may not, no matter how iniquitous his rule. This distinction was implied by St. Thomas himself, *Scriptum Super Sententiis*, II, d.44, q.2, a.2 ad 5. However, these texts do not settle the problem of active resistance or revolution, since a revolt does not necessarily involve killing the tyrant. St. Thomas, *supra* note 2, II-II, q.104, a.6 ad 3, says that a subject is not bound to obey a ruler who has either usurped power or who, though legitimate, is ruling unjustly, unless perhaps to avoid scandal or greater evil, but there is no indication that he is sanctioning anything more than disobedience or passive resistance. In the *De Regno*, c.6, where he directly considers the question of revolution, St. Thomas maintains that a people which has the right of providing itself with a king has the right to depose a king who becomes an intolerable tyrant. Modern Catholic thought considers that every people has these rights, but it is not clear that St. Thomas thought so.

[114]The kind of prudence needed by the subject is not the same as that needed by the ruler: see St. Thomas *supra* note 2, II-II, q.47, a.12.

which a man performs is either moral or immoral, because of the surrounding circumstances. Thus an edict of the legislator commanding or forbidding an act morally indifferent in species makes that act secondarily moral or immoral, as the case may be. In this realm of morally neutral acts the citizen ought to be grateful to the legislator for enlightening him on the prudential demands of the common good. (And, it is necessary to add, the legislator should be one supremely in possession of the highest kind of prudence.)[115]

Of course, the mere fact that the citizens make their lives outwardly conform to the commands of the legislator does not of itself mean that they are living the moral life. But the Kantian dichotomy between law and morals is a wholly false one. The fact that a thing is done in conformity with a command from a superior does not mean that it is necessarily without moral worth. It is true that the saints have been said not to be under the law even when the law applies to the very act they are performing, but what this means is that, since they obey the law out of love rather than out of fear of its coercive force, they do not find it burdensome.[116] It is not that the just are not obliged to obey the law, but that they are of themselves inclined to do what is just even without a law.[117] Thus they are, like the ruler, subject to the directive force of law though free of its coercive force.[118] Further, the existence of law gives them a greater opportunity for the practice of virtue than they could have without the law.

Law is morally beneficial not only for those who come under the *vis directiva* but also for those subject to the *vis coactiva.* The fact that they obey the law out of fear of punishment is itself of no moral benefit, though it is useful to the community in that it secures civil concord, but it is an excellent training in virtuous action and it may in time lead to their performing the same actions voluntarily. Professor Simon brings this point out well: "This elevated conception of the pedagogical function of coercion rests upon the psychological

[115] *Ibid.*

[116] *Ibid.*, I-II, q.93, a.6 ad 1.

[117] St. Thomas, *Summa Contra Gentiles,* Vol. III, c.128.

[118] See St. Thomas, *supra* note 2, q.96, a.5 for the distinction between *vis directiva* and *vis coactiva.*

fact that a good habit generated by fear, although non-virtuous in its origin, makes virtue easier, the substitution of good will for fear taking place easily when the exterior acts of a virtue have become habitual. Coercion, in the long run, paves the way for persuasion, because habitual automatism turns to voluntariness. Let us recall the famous analysis of Pascal on religious habits as a preparation to faith."[119] Sanctions have a pedagogical function as well as a protective function. Thus coercion prepares the way for persuasion, the truly human means of government.

III

THE THOMISTIC THEORY of the interpenetration of law and morals is frequently criticized for the reason that in the event of conflict between a command of the ruler and a moral precept it takes the view that the command of the ruler is not only immoral but that it is not even law. Professor Hart has recently suggested that this view is subversive of morals in that it fails to make clear the moral choice with which the citizen is faced by a wicked "law,"[120] but the more usual criticism is that the Thomistic view is subversive of law. However, the instances in which in a democratic society there are conflicts between law and morality are few in the extreme, and, moreover, as Professor Fuller has pointed out, "If the matter is examined candidly it will be found that there is no one who cannot imagine himself, even as a judge, being faced by a law so infamous that he would feel bound to disobey it."[121] If this is true, attacks on the Thomistic theory from this viewpoint will not carry great conviction.

But there is another viewpoint from which the Thomistic theory is open to attack. This may be stated in the words of Mr. Constable, who is outlining this criticism only to reject it: "It would seem that natural law jurisprudence is bad in that its alleged rules have no good uses. . . . The absence of good uses is evident from the fact

[119]Simon, *supra* note 49, at p. 54, n. 3.
[120]Hart, *supra* note 106, at pp. 620–1.
[121]L. Fuller, "American Legal Philosophy at Mid-Century," in Brown, *supra* note 45, at pp. 202, 203.

that these rules give to the citizen in general, and to legislators, judges and lawyers in particular, no perceptible help in solving the innumerable concrete practical problems daily confronting them."[122] This contention that Thomistic jurisprudence is of "no perceptible help in solving the innumerable concrete practical problems" seems basic to Professor Friedmann's criticisms in the *Canadian Bar Review* controversy some years ago. His principal criticisms were that "natural law" formulas "do not supply a sufficiently definite and practical test for the borderline cases in which justice and positive law conflict," and that "their use creates an illusion of higher and unchallengeable authority which may lead to the intolerance and suppression of conflicting faiths."[123] It seems that Professor Friedmann's fear that the recognition of a theory of natural law would lead to "an illusion of higher and unchallengeable authority" loses force in the face of the minimalist conception of natural law which I have expounded here, since this conception confines the natural law to the universal and near-universal principles of the practical order, concerning which there is general agreement. Of a minimalist natural law even more than of a maximalist natural law it is true that, as Charles Curtis puts it, it will "give us only a direction, not directions."[124] Similarly Fr. Davitt remarks that "The relation of Natural Law to the man-made law of legislation and adjudication is similar to the relation of a compass to navigation. A compass indicates basic direction, but it will not navigate."[125]

However, the increased generality of natural law in a minimalist conception seems merely to add fuel to Professor Friedmann's first criticism, viz., that it is too general to be of practical value. It is, of course, true that, in the words of Professor Crabb, "the nature of something so fundamental as the law is a question of legitimate intellectual interest, particularly to those whose professional life is deeply involved in it, regardless of whether the argument bears promise of practical results,"[126] but in the practical order we must also consider

[122]G. Constable, "What Does Natural Law Jurisprudence Offer?" (1954), 4 *Catholic U. L. Rev.* 1, 2.

[123]W. Friedmann, Correspondence (1954) in 32 *Can. B. Rev.* 593, at p. 596.

[124]C. Curtis, *Law as Large as Life* (1959), p. 12.

[125]Davitt, *supra* note 3, at p. 40.

[126]J. H. Crabb, Comment (1960), 12 *J. Legal Ed.* 548, at p. 550.

the relationship of principles to practice. Now the principles of the natural law are admittedly so general as to be far removed from the concrete world, but from the natural law are deduced the precepts of the natural moral order which, though still possessing a certain generality, are sufficiently close to the concrete to be significant guides in concrete situations. Thus the natural law, powerless in itself to solve concrete problems, gives birth by way of rationally deduced conclusions to the moral "law," which is a proximate guide to human action, including the action of the legislator. As we have seen, the effect of moral precepts on law varies according to whether the legal rules affected are static or dynamic, and in the case of the latter norms the effect is merely a procedural one, but it is important to bear in mind that moral precepts have a substantive effect upon the fundamental legal rules and are with regard to them a proximate and ready guide to action.

Professor Friedmann would not deny the proximate utility of these moral rules, but he would take issue with their status as knowledge, for he cites the disagreement of theologians and philosophers on the issues of war, private property, birth control, human equality, and the fulfilling of contracts. However, disagreement indicates that some views are wrong, but not necessarily all views; for one must distinguish between certitude and certainty, demonstration and persuasion, proof and conviction, the objective and the subjective. Professor Friedmann's presupposition, in the light of which disagreement appears as a sign that proof of ethical propositions is impossible, is that "ultimate values must be believed, they cannot be proved."[127] This view is based on the premise that there is only one scientific method, that of the experimental sciences, and that the method of moral philosophy is not truly scientific.

In actuality, however, there is not a single scientific method, which alone gives rise to demonstrative proof, but many scientific methods, all capable of producing demonstration, but not all capable of producing the same degree of subjective certitude because of the differences in their objects. St. Thomas believes that mathematics is the mode of scientific knowledge most commensurate with the

[127] W. Friedmann, *Legal Theory* (3d ed.; 1953), p. xvi.

human mind, and therefore both easier and more certain than the knowledge attained in the philosophy of nature, metaphysics, or the moral sciences.[128] In the non-mathematical sciences truth is more difficult of attainment and of verification, but it is still possible. Since the principles of the natural law are known by sheer intellection, without reasoning, they are capable of general agreement, but the moral precepts deduced from them are subject to disagreement, for since reason is fallible, all men will not arrive at the right conclusion. But truth is possible, though not everyone may be able to see it. Professor Friedmann considers the recognition of moral precepts the assertion of a particular "political faith"; this is an acceptable designation, provided that it is understood that the word "faith" is used loosely and not as opposed to science. Admittedly it is not easy for natural reason to establish the true moral science nor to persuade all men of its truth. But that this is not an impossible task is shown by the fact that in common law countries there is a consensus as to the moral worth of just war, private property, human equality, and the observance of covenants, even though there is not on birth control; the area of existing agreement is considerably more than minimal.

What, then, are the advantages of the Thomistic theory of the interpenetration of law and morals? I hope this paper has indicated that there are two advantages. First, the guidance given to law by the natural law and its derivative, natural morality, though not descending to the purely practical level of prudence, is considerable. Second, by making all legal rules moral precepts, either primarily or secondarily, this theory makes possible a moral and rational explanation of all law; legal obligation becomes explicable in rational terms and law thus gains the support of reason as well as the adherence of will. The Thomistic theory of the interpenetration of law and morals gives both speculative satisfaction and practical assistance to man as political animal.

[128] St. Thomas, *In de Trinitate*, q.6, a.1.

International Business Law:

A NEW LAW MERCHANT

By CLIVE M. SCHMITTHOFF*

THE RISE of international business law is one of the most significant legal developments of our time although it has received comparatively little attention from academic law teachers. Those engaged in commercial legal practice as attorneys or house counsel have constantly to deal with problems of international business law but normally have neither time nor inclination to study the wider implications of their work; and those who, as law teachers or research workers, should explore and expound the new development usually do not have sufficient factual material from which to draw general conclusions. This new branch of law is elusive: it is not found in the usual statute or case materials, but its main source is in custom and practice; in this sense, it is extra-legal. It is intended in this article to indicate the historical background of international business law and to attempt an evaluation of its function in modern world society.

THE MEANING OF INTERNATIONAL BUSINESS LAW

FIRST, however, it is necessary to attempt to define the term "international business law." The concept of business law, as understood in the United Kingdom, is a modern development of orthodox commercial law. "Whilst conventional mercantile law contents itself

*C. M. Schmitthoff, LL.D. (London and Berlin); Barrister at Law; Senior Lecturer in Law, The City of London College; Editor of the *Journal of Business Law*.

with the description of the positive rules of law regulating the organization and transactions of business, business law includes into its ambit a treatment of the practical application of these principles which it attempts to relate to their economic and social environment."[1]

International business law is not identical with international economic law. The latter forms part of public international law, the former is a branch of private law but does not pertain to private international law. International economic law is concerned with multilateral conventions, such as the General Agreement on Tariffs and Trade (GATT), and bilateral Treaties between states, such as treaties of commerce and friendship; it also includes the treatment of international economic organizations constituted by sovereign states, such as the International Monetary Fund, the World Bank, and the International Finance Corporation. International business law, on the other hand, deals with the legal organization of international business transacted on the level of private law. The subjects of international business law are, in the countries of free market economy, individuals and companies and, in the countries of planned socialist economy, foreign trade corporations. International business law has two main branches, namely, the law of international trade[2] of which the sale of goods abroad is the most fundamental part though the legal aspects of international banking, insurance, and carriage of goods by air, sea, and inland transport also pertain to it; and, secondly, the law of international companies, that is, companies incorporated under the laws of one country but having business interests in other countries, whether these interests take the form of shareholdings or managerial participation in subsidiary or associated companies incorporated in the other countries or another form.[3]

International business law and international economic law overlap in two respects: first, arrangements creating regional trade groups and double taxation agreements pertain, strictly speaking, to

[1]Statement of Aims of the series "Business Law and Administration," printed in C. M. Schmitthoff, *Sale of Goods* (London, 1951), p. 273.

[2]On this topic see C. M. Schmitthoff, *The Export Trade, A Manual of the Law of International Trade* (4th ed.; London, 1961).

[3]On this topic see W. G. Friedmann and R. C. Pugh, *Legal Aspects of Foreign Investment* (Boston, 1959).

international economic law but, to the considerable extent to which they affect the individual importer and exporter, they also form part of international business law. The planning of an international business transaction would be incomplete if the tariff requirements and the incidence of taxation in the country to which the transaction extends were disregarded. Secondly, in some branches of international business, contracts between states, on the one hand, and subjects of private law on the other, are not unusual. An illustration of these "mixed" contracts are agreements dealing with a grant of oil or mineral concessions.[4] These contracts have many unusual features: they often contain clauses relating to the right of the foreign private investor to repatriate his income and capital, or provide for protection against future nationalisation or for fair compensation in that case.[5] These mixed contracts pertain both to international business law and international economic law.

THE STAGES OF DEVELOPMENT OF INTERNATIONAL BUSINESS LAW

HISTORICALLY, international business law has developed in three stages: in the Middle Ages it appeared in the form of the law merchant, a body of truly international customary rules governing the cosmopolitan community of international merchants who travelled through the civilized world, from port to port and fair to fair, wherever business offered itself. The second phase began with the universal acceptance of the idea of national sovereignty: in this phase the law merchant was incorporated into the various municipal systems of law, a process which, though universal, was carried out in the various countries for different reasons, in different manners, and in differing degrees. The third and contemporary stage of the development has commenced when the exaltation of national sovereignty characteristic of the nineteenth century has given way to a more detached and critical attitude, except, perhaps, in the young

[4]D. A. Godwin Sarre and A. Unler, "Modern Oil Law," [1960] *J. Bus. L.* 161.
[5]M. Brandon, "An International Investment Code: Current Plans," *ibid.*, at p. 7; D. A. V. Boyle, "Some Proposals for a World Investment Convention," *ibid.*, at pp. 18, 155.

countries of Asia and Africa in which the experience of national statehood is still new. World society is again beginning to think internationally, as evinced by the activities of the United Nations and the plethora of specialized international agencies. On the level of private law, this tendency manifests itself in the economic empires of our time, the great international companies which are weaving a worldwide and very powerful economic superstructure upon the old international pattern of national communities. Complementary to the return to internationalism in the political and economic field is, in the legal sphere, the return to the international concept of commercial law, the emergence of a new *lex mercatoria* which tends to develop into an autonomous international business law, that is, a law of universal character that, though applied by authority of the national sovereign, attempts to shed the national peculiarities of municipal laws. This development deserves closer attention.

THE OLD LAW MERCHANT

THE INTERNATIONAL character of the old law merchant is too well known to require elaboration. It is perhaps most delightfully expressed in those lines from Chaucer's *Man of Law's Tale*:

> In Syria once there dwelt a company
> Of wealthy merchants, serious, straight and wise,
> That had a far-flung trade in spicery
> And cloth-of-gold and satin of rich dyes . . .
> It happened that some merchants of this sort
> Made up their minds to venture out to Rome . . .
> They were not satisfied to stay at home
> And send [out agents] but crossed the foam
> In person thither; and where their expectation
> Of profit lay they found accommodation.[6]

Four main factors contributed to the international character of the old *lex mercatoria* and preserved its uniformity throughout the Middle Ages:[7] the unifying character of the law of the fairs, the

[6]Geoffery Chaucer, *The Canterbury Tales* (Penguin Classics ed.; 1951), p. 149.

[7]On the history of the law merchant see T. F. T. Plunkett, *A Concise History of the Common Law* (5th ed.; London, 1956), p. 657 *et seq.*; W. A. Bewes, *The Romance of the Law Merchant* (1923).

universality of the customs of the sea, the special courts dealing with commercial disputes, and the activities of the notary public, that ubiquitous and versatile mediaeval practitioner in whose hands lay a good deal of commercial legal work. As regards the law of the fairs, whether they were held in Flanders, France, England, or elsewhere, the following observations of Professor M. Huvelin give an accurate account of the position:

The law of the fairs, born of the peace of commerce, is acting strongly on institutions under the ordinary law still imbued with its ancient rigours. . . . The tendency to uniformity is strengthened. In the midst of the diversity of local law, the law of the great fairs everywhere remains the same in its essential features. This law is universal almost by the same right as the Canon law. And thus emerges the conception of the law merchant, outside and above civil statutes and local commercial usages. . . . Thus the fairs, this original form of terrestrial commerce, have been in the history of civilisation incomparable instruments of reconciliation, of unification and of peace.[8]

Not less remarkable is the uniformity of the other branch of the law merchant, the customs of the sea. Here again the development is well known: it led from the sea laws of the Phoenicians and Greeks to the laws of Rhodes which, in the form in which they have come down to us, date between A.D. 600 to 800; thence to the *Consulado del Mar* of Barcelona which became the maritime code of the Mediterranean, the judgments of Oleron (1160) which became the foundation of English maritime law,[9] and the Sea Laws of Wisby which were applied in the Baltic. Many principles of maritime law were common to these codifications, for example, those relating to general average and to the power of the master of the ship to sell the consignor's goods in order to raise funds for necessaries. Professor René A. Wormser sums up the character of these customs of the sea when he states that "the explanation of this universality is, of course, that the sea law was developed by merchants themselves and was not the law of territorial princes."[10]

[8]M. Huvelin, *Essai historique sur les marchés et les foires* (1895), quoted by Bewes, *ibid.*, at p. 138.

[9]Cf., Lord Justice Willmer, "The Sixth Century of the Admiralty Court," [1960] *J. Bus. L.* 276.

[10]R. A. Wormser, *The Law* (New York, 1949), p. 500.

Thirdly, the itinerant merchants travelling with their wares from port to port and fair to fair had their own courts to settle their differences, in particular the courts of Piepowder. Normally, so-called half-tongue juries sat in these courts, that is, half the jury consisted of indigenous and the other half of foreign merchants and it might well have happened that a merchant would one day act as a juryman in an English court and a few days later as a juryman in a foreign court.[11] The proceedings in these Courts were informal, pleas were begun without writ and proceedings were *de hora in horam*.[12] Although Coke's explanation, according to which the Court of Piepowder was a court in which justice was done as speedily "for the amendment and traffick as the dust can fall from [the merchants'] feet",[13] was more imaginative than etymologically correct, since the word "Piepowder" was in fact derived from the French "Prudhommes," there is no doubt that these commercial courts were unique; they were in the nature of modern conciliation and arbitration tribunals rather than courts in the strict sense of the word. Moreover, to use modern terminology, they had the characteristics of permanent international arbitral tribunals, the lay arbitrators being called upon to decide issues at various localities and clearly administering the same commercial custom whatever the venue of the tribunal and the local variety of that custom.

The fourth factor which contributed to the universality of the law merchant were the activities of the notary public. From the year 1326 on, fair contracts in Champagne had to be made in the notarial form and from the middle of the thirteenth century notarial contracts were common in Italy. It is reported that a single notary in Marseilles drafted more than a thousand commercial documents in a single year (1245), while one notary drafted nearly 60 in a single day.[14] Many of these notarial contracts were obviously what we would call today "standard contracts," that is, they were copied or adapted from a model standard form such as a charterparty (*carta partita*).

[11]A. T. Carter, *A History of the English Courts* (7th ed.; London, 1944), p. 265.

[12](1908) 23 *Selden Society* xxvi.

[13]Coke, *4th Inst.*, p. 271.

[14]Bewes, *supra* note 7, at p. 6.

It would be tempting to examine in detail the points in which the old law merchant differed from the common law, the gradual admission of the rule of market overt, the development of the concepts of assignability and negotiability, the disregard of the requirement of the seal, the disinclination to require consideration in simple contracts, the acceptance of stoppage *in transitu* and general average, and many other commercial concepts which the common law did not initially admit. However, this temptation must be resisted in the context of this article. It is enough to sum up the position in the words of Professor Rudolf B. Schlesinger:

> The main characteristics of the substantive law which was created by the commercial courts, were emphasis on freedom of contract and on freedom of alienability of movable property, both tangible and intangible; abrogation of legal technicalities; and, most importantly, a tendency to decide cases *ex aequo et bono* rather than by abstract scholastic deductions from Roman texts. No wonder, then, that commercial law was a highly successful institution. Cosmopolitan in nature and inherently superior to the general law, the law merchant by the end of the medieval period had become the very foundation of an expanding commerce throughout the Western world.[15]

It is sometimes said that the cosmopolitan character of the law merchant is a modern, rather than a contemporary, evaluation of that law. Holdsworth observes: "I very much doubt whether these features would have seemed peculiar to a medieval merchant or lawyer. The merchants were simply one of the sharply defined classes of medieval society, and the customs of all these classes possessed cosmopolitan characteristics similar in kind if less in extent; while the civil and canon law possess them in a far higher degree."[16] These observations may be perfectly correct; they refer to the stratification of world society before the rise of the national state. They do not detract from the accuracy of the present analysis since the fact that other branches of law were equally or more cosmopolitan in no way diminishes the cosmopolitan character of the law merchant itself.

[15]R. B. Schlesinger, *Comparative Law* (2nd ed.; Brooklyn, 1960), p. 185.

[16]Sir W. S. Holdsworth, *History of English Law* (London, 1937), Vol. V, p. 61.

THE INCORPORATION OF THE LAW MERCHANT INTO MUNICIPAL LAW

THE INCORPORATION of the law merchant into the municipal laws of the various countries took place in the eighteenth and nineteenth centuries, although the theory of national sovereignty on which the concept of municipal law is founded is much older, it being pronounced first by Grotius. The incorporation of the law merchant into municipal law did not proceed on uniform lines but was motivated by very different political and social causes and carried out in different ways.

In France codification on a national scale was first carried out by the Ordinance *sur le commerce* of Louis XIV of 1673 and Colbert's Ordinance *de la marine* of 1681. A revision of this legislation was commenced in 1787 but was interrupted by the French Revolution. Only at the beginning of the nineteenth century was work resumed and in 1807 the *Code de Commerce*, one of the five codes of Napoleon, was enacted.[17] The Napoleonic codes gave final expression to the political ideals and the philosophy of the French Revolution. The fundamental concepts of the Napoleonic codification are freedom of contract and the assertion of ownership as an absolute right. The Napoleonic codes have been described as ratifying the triumph of the *tiers état* in which, as we know, the *commerçants* and the liberal professions were prominent.[18] The French codification is thus the final seal of a victorious political movement.

Very different is the political character of the German codification of commercial law which, unlike the French codification, preceded that of the general private law.[19] In Germany the creation of the commercial code was the legal reflection of the struggle for political unity; it was a deliberate attempt to give impetus to the movement for German political unification by means of the creation of a uniform law.[20] It was only natural that commercial law was chosen

[17]A. Marx, *Die Französische Handelsgesetzgebung* (1911), p. 1.

[18]Schlesinger, *supra* note 15, at p. 323.

[19]France (Commercial Code: 1807; Civil Courts: 1804); Germany (Commercial Code: 1807; Civil Courts: 1804).

[20]See Brunner-Heymann, *Grundzüge der deutschen Rechtsgerichte* (7th ed.), p. 276.

as the first subject for unification of German law because it is a general experience that uniformity of law is most needed and most easily obtained in commercial matters. Thus, in 1834 the *Zollverein* sponsored a Uniform German Bills of Exchange Act which was duly promulgated in 1848. In 1856 the German Confederation convened the first conference for the creation of a Uniform Commercial Code. A resulting draft code was published in 1861 and was adopted by most members of the German Confederation, including Austria and Prussia. This code is still the law of Austria, but the German Reich adopted a new Commercial Code in 1897. These dates indicate that, as the political unification of Germany progressed, the codification of commercial law continually became more ambitious. The political aspects of this codification are obvious.

In England the main motive for the final incorporation of the law merchant into the common law was economic rather than political. Trade, particularly with foreign countries, had become part of the life of the nation. In the middle of the eighteenth century and after the decline of the special commercial courts, it was an unrealistic anachronism for the common law courts to insist, in every case tried by them, on specific proof of universally accepted commercial custom; the precise meaning of such custom and its general acceptance was very difficult to ascertain. The reform which Lord Mansfield carried out when sitting with his special jurymen at the Guildhall of London, was ostensibly aimed at the simplification of commercial procedure, but was, in fact, much more: its purpose was the creation of a body of substantive commercial law, logical, just, modern in character and, at the same time, in harmony with the principles of the common law. It was due to Lord Mansfield's genius that the harmonization of commercial custom and the common law was carried out with an almost complete understanding of the requirements of the commercial community and the fundamental principles of the old law and that that marriage of ideas proved acceptable to both the merchants and the lawyers.

In summing up this brief historical survey the following observations may be added: while the process of incorporating the law merchant into the municipal laws of the various countries was undoubtedly unavoidable in view of the general political and social trend, and while the codification of commercial law, whether in the statutory form favoured on the continent of Europe or in the judicial form adopted by the common law, at the beginning clearly benefited the countries which effected it, today we are looking at this development in a more detached and critical manner and are beginning to doubt whether, in the long run, the disadvantages did not outweigh the benefits. Professor André Tunc, in an examination of English and Continental commercial law, speaks of the "nationalism which has been introduced in the field of law as the unfortunate result of the French codification and of the German historical jurisprudence,"[21] and Professor Rudolf B. Schlesinger notes "the intellectual isolation of each national legal system which resulted from the codifications."[22]

It is a significant feature of the integration of commercial law into the municipal systems of law that none of these systems carried out the integration completely. Traces of the international complexion of commercial law remained even in this period, visible to those who understood the origin and nature of that branch of law. Lord Mansfield himself had no intention of severing the law merchant from its old roots; on the contrary, he repeatedly expressed the view that the law merchant was founded on an international basis. In *Pelly* v. *Royal Exchange Assurance* he said: "The mercantile law, in this respect, is the same all over the world. For from the same premises, the same conclusions of reason and justice must universally be the same."[23]

Sir Frederick Pollock, writing at the beginning of the twentieth century, emphasizes that the old international source of commercial custom from which English commercial law developed was still open. He wrote: "Yet the law merchant has not wholly lost its old character. It has not forgotten its descent from the medieval law of nature which claimed to be a rule of universal reason embodied in the various forms of cosmopolitan usage. Conforming to English procedure and legal method, it can still be reinforced by additions

[21]A. Tunc, "English and Commerical Law," [1961] *J. Bus. L.* 234, at p. 237.
[22]Schlesinger, *supra* note 15, at p. 188.
[23](1757) Burr. 341, 347.

drawn from established general custom."[24] This characteristic of English commercial law is remarkable since English jurisprudence does not consider commercial law as the law of a class of persons, for example, the traders, but rather as part of the general law of the country.[25] On the continent of Europe where the national integration of the law merchant was effected more strictly and thoroughly than in the common law, at least some jurists recognized the special character of commercial law. The German scholar, Professor Julius von Gierke, regards it as a feature of German commercial law that it is a "*Sonderrecht für Kaufleute, nämlich für grössere Kaufleutë*" and adds that one of its characteristics is its international complexion due to the fact that the international exchange of goods occupies a central position in commercial law.[26]

THE RETURN TO INTERNATIONALISM— A COMMON PLATFORM OF THE EAST AND WEST

THE THIRD STAGE in the development of international business law is represented by a return to the concept of internationalism which characterized the old law merchant. "We are beginning to rediscover the international character of commercial law and the circle now completes itself: the general trend of commercial law everywhere is to move away from the restrictions of national law to a universal, international conception of the law of international trade."[27] This view is shared by eminent commercial lawyers in many countries, both of free market economy and of planned economy. Professor André Tunc of France, after noting this trend, states that the international aspects of commercial law "may bring about radical

[24]Sir Frederick Pollock in his Introduction to the *Commercial Law of Great Britain, and Ireland: I*, ed. William Bowstead and Sir Thomas E. Scrutton (Vol. XIII of *The Commercial Laws of the World*), p. 11.

[25]C. M. Schmitthoff, *A Bibliographical Guide to the Law of the United Kingdom* (London, 1956), p. 67.

[26]J. von Gierke, *Handelsrecht und Schiffahrtsrecht* (8th ed.; 1958), p. 4.

[27]C. M. Schmitthoff, "Modern Trends in English Commercial Law," an address to Helsinki University appearing in *Tidskrift, Utgiven av Juridiska Foreningen in Finland* (1957), p. 354.

changes for which we should be ready."[28] In his view this new trend has three causes: the similarity of commercial experience in the various countries, the political and economic importance of some countries—the "radiation" of their law—and the drafting and ratification of international conventions.[29] Professor Aleksander Goldštajn of Yugoslavia writes: "Notwithstanding the differences in the political, economic and legal systems of the world a new law merchant is rapidly developing in the world of international trade. It is time that recognition be given to the existence of an autonomous commercial law that has grown independent of the national systems of law."[30] Professor Roman Piotrowski of Poland has expressed a similar view.[31]

A particular aspect—and value—of the rediscovered international conception of commercial law is that it represents a common platform for the jurists of the East and West. The view is widely held, particularly by lawyers from the East, that ideological, political, or economic differences are no obstacle to the global uniformity of the law of international trade. Professor Piotrowski writes: "As shown by Professor Bratuš and Professor Ostrovitianov in the Soviet Union, by Dr. Goldštajn in Yugoslavia, by Professor Schmitthoff in Great Britain, and similarly by other authors in various other parts of our world, commercial law greatly facilitates co-operation between all capitalist and socialist countries."[32] Professor Bystricky of Czechoslovakia has likewise expressed the view that the difference in purpose prevailing in various political and economic systems does not alter the fact that contracts of sale in all legal systems show certain similarities in respect of their essential nature and legal regulations.[33] These similarities have become more marked in recent years because in the countries of socialist economy foreign trade is now carried on on the level of private law. It has been delegated to foreign trade corporations which, as far as their external activities

[28]Tunc, *supra* note 21, at p. 237.

[29]*Ibid.*, at pp. 237–46.

[30]A. Goldštajn, "The New Law Merchant," [1961] *J. Bus. L.* 12.

[31]R. Piatrowski, "The Great Importance of Commercial Law for Peaceful Economic Collaboration of All Nations" (1958), 9 *New Yugoslav Law* 6–8.

[32]Piatrowski, *ibid.*, at p. 8.

[33]Goldštajn, *supra* note 30, at p. 16.

are concerned, are similar to the corporations or companies of the countries of free market economy, although their internal constitution is very different: they have no shareholders and, like nationalized enterprises in the countries of free economy, are either self-accounting or accountable to the state.[34] Of course, western and eastern jurists, when noting these similarities in the legal technique of international trade, do not wish to blur or minimize the fundamental differences in purpose and aim pursued with these transactions in the countries of free market economy and socialist economy. These differences remain, in spite of the fact that a new law merchant common to both economies is developing. However, if, as is to be hoped, the competition between the countries of the East and the West, and in particular their struggle for the soul of the "uncommitted" nations, will take the form of trade competition and not that of armed conflict or cold war, a uniform law of international trade will have the task of establishing the "rules of the game" which all participants in that competition will have to observe as a necessary condition for the state of peaceful co-existence.

Moreover, the similarity of the business law of the East and West might not be restricted to the law of international trade. It may well be that it may extend to the legal aspects of management of business corporations. No less a person than Adolf J. Berle, one of the most advanced thinkers of company theory, has observed that the organization of the business corporation in the East and West will not lead to a fundamental conflict between the countries of free market economy and the socialist countries.[35] Indeed, the problems of large-scale business management, in their legal aspects, might not be so different whether the manager is guided by the principles of social responsibility, as directors of large public companies in the countries of free market economy should be, or by strict state-planning, as in the case with regard to the managers of large business concerns in the socialist countries. At present these problems are not yet ripe for legal examination, but one day, and perhaps

[34]C. M. Schmitthoff, "A New Approach to East-West Trade," [1958] *J. Bus. L.* 141; S. Shafer, "Some Legal Aspects of East-West Trade," *ibid.*, at p. 50.

[35]A. A. Berle, Jr., *Power without Property* (New York, 1960), p. 175.

sooner than some of us might think, they will have to be examined in a dispassionate, politically unbiased manner, possibly in joint research by lawyers from the East and West.

At present, let us revert to the law of international trade. While it is obviously impossible in the compass of this article to discuss in detail the rules of the new law merchant, its nature and sources may well be outlined here.

THE NEW LAW MERCHANT AND REGIONAL UNIFICATIONS OF COMMERCIAL LAW

THE NEW law merchant, as was Chaucer's older variety, is international in character. Thus, unification of commercial law on a regional basis presents many problems peculiar to federal or other inherently related groupings. Recent illustrations of the regional unification of commercial law are many: the Uniform Commercial Code of the United States has been given statutory force in six American states.[36] The General Conditions of Delivery of Goods, 1958, has been adopted by the member countries of the Council for Mutual Economic Aid, the eastern block of which is under the leadership of the Soviet Union.[37] These conditions have been widely used by foreign trade corporations of the countries of the eastern European block in their dealings with each other. Further, the Treaty of Rome of March 25, 1957, which created the European Common Market, provides in article 3(h) that the activities of the Community shall include: "The approximation of their respective municipal law to the extent necessary for the functioning of the Common Market." In pursuance of this aim, the six countries of the Common Market are at present engaged in the "harmonization" of their municipal commercial laws; but it is already evident that that phase will, as far as business transactions are concerned, be transi-

[36]Connecticut, Kentucky, Massachusetts, New Hampshire, Pennsylvania, and Rhode Island.

[37]H. J. Berman, "Unification of Contract Clauses in Trade between Member-Countries of the Council for Mutual Economic Aid" (1958), 7 *Int'l & Comp. L. Q.* 659.

tional only and the development will be similar to that in the Zollverein and the Deutsche Bund, that is, towards an eventual unification of the commercial law of the Common Market. At present the member states of the Common Market are studying two projects of unification: the adoption, by them, of the third Draft Convention of a Uniform Law of International Sale of Goods, 1956, suggested by the International Institute for the Unification of Private Law in Rome,[38] and the creation of a European company.[39] In the field of anti-trust regulation the members of the Common Market are even closer to the goal of a uniform law, as shown by the draft of the First Enabling Regulation of October 28, 1960, which was issued in pursuance of articles 85 and 86 of the Treaty of Rome;[40] this regulation leaves already existing restrictive trade agreements virtually unaffected but prohibits the creation of new ones. Further illustration of regional unification exists elsewhere, for instance, in Scandinavia where several countries have adopted a uniform law of sales[41] and are at present exploring the possibility of a uniform company law.

The relationship between universal and regional unification has been explored by Mr. Mario Matteuci, the Secretary General of the International Institute for the Unification of Private Law at Rome.[42] He points out that it cannot be denied that regional unification interferes with the aims of unification on a universal scale of the same topics.[43] Mr. Matteuci illustrates the difficulties which regional unification might raise by the following example: if a uniform law of international sales is evolved by the Common Market countries, and another uniform law on the same subject is accepted by the Benelux countries, and eventually the Rome Draft of the

[38]G. Lagergren, "A Uniform Law of International Sales of Goods," [1958] *J. Bus. L.* 131; B. A. Worltey, "A Uniform Law of International Sales of Goods (1958), 7 *Int'l & Comp. L. Q.* 1.

[39]I. Seidl-Hohenveldern, "European Companies," [1959] *J. Bus. L.* 120.

[40]Seidl-Hohenveldern, "The First Draft Regulation of the Common Market on Restrictive Practices," [1961] *ibid.*, at p. 132.

[41]Sweden (1905); Denmark (1906); Norway (1907); Iceland (1922). See Schmitthoff, *supra* note 1, at p. 4, n. 7.

[42]M. Matteuci, "L'Evolution en matière d'unification du droit" (1961), 13 *Revue de droit comparé* 285 *et seq.*

[43]*Ibid.*, at p. 288.

Uniform Law of International Sale of Goods is accepted, judges and counsel in some of the six Common Market countries will, at least for some time, have to deal with four systems of law, their own municipal law, and three different "uniform" systems. Mr. Matteuci concludes that the only remedy, in order to avoid the inconvenience of regional unification, is to submit topics of general character (he includes in this category most topics of commercial law) to universal unification and to proceed to regional unification only if this aim cannot be realized.

In many instances, however, regional codification can be regarded as valuable because it reduces the number of commercial legal systems of the world and may be the forerunner of global unification. In any event, whatever the value of regional unification it cannot be denied that it is different in character from the universal custom of international merchants on which, in the last resort, the new law of international trade is founded.

THE NEW LAW MERCHANT AS AN AUTONOMOUS BODY OF LAW

THE NEW law merchant is in the nature of an "autonomous" law and, as such, it attempts to provide its own legal regulation without reference to, and independent of, any municipal system of law. Therefore, the question arises: what is the legal basis on which such "self-supporting" regulation can be founded?

In most legal systems the parties to a contract are allowed a considerable measure of autonomy in the making of the contract, the terms which they wish to adopt, and the choice of law which they wish to apply to their bargain. "The universal recognition and confirmation of the two principles of freedom of contract and *pacta sunt servanda* is an accepted fact," writes Professor Goldštajn.[44] As the principle of party autonomy in the law of contract is recognized by most countries of the East and West, none of the legal systems raises a theoretical objection to an attempt of the parties to a con-

[44]Goldštajn, *supra* note 30, at p. 17.

tract to go to the extreme and to adopt a legal regulation which makes redundant a reference to a national system of law.

This raises the critical question whether it is possible for a legal regulation, even if founded on the autonomy of the parties' will, to be independent of a territorial law. In short, is the concept of an autonomous law merchant a practical possibility or is it merely a professional chimera? When examining this question we have first to acknowledge that the concept of an autonomous legal regulation is subject to certain qualifications which, it is thought, are obvious and incontrovertible. The new law merchant, as an autonomous legal regulation, can apply in a municipal jurisdiction only by leave and licence of the municipal sovereign; that, however, causes little practical difficulty because experience shows that most sovereigns admit it without objection. Further, as Professor Yntema explains,[45] the principle of party autonomy in the law of contract is subject to various restrictions in the different municipal laws and is not interpreted everywhere in the same manner; these restrictions are mainly imposed for reasons of public policy or in the public interest. The qualifications of the concept of an autonomous law merchant, imposed by the principles of territorial sovereignty and public policy, are self-evident and do not require further comment; in view of their general application they do not cause practical difficulty.

Much more important from the practical point of view is the question whether, in view of the multitude of unforeseeable difficulties which might arise in the performance of a contract, it is possible to devise a regulation which is truly autonomous, or whether, in the last resort, a reference to a national system of law will become necessary. If the latter view is correct, it would be safer to state the proper law already in the contract; if the former view is correct, the definition of the proper law in the contract becomes redundant.

Experience has shown that a practically workable degree of autonomy can only be achieved if the autonomous regulation is complemented by an arbitration agreement. Arbitration tribunals do not always apply strict rules of municipal law but are inclined to

[45]H. E. Yntema, "'Autonomy' in Choice of Law" (1952), 1 *J. Comp. L.* 341.

found their award on what Lord Mansfield called "the same conclusions of reason and justice." If no arbitration clause is inserted into the agreement of the parties, a reference to a national system of law becomes unavoidable.

These observations indicate that an automatic contractual regulation, truly independent of municipal law, is a practical, and not merely a theoretical, possibility. What is more, the new law merchant, founded on the combination of party autonomy in matters of contract and arbitration, exists already in its beginnings. This is perhaps best illustrated by the General Conditions of Sale and Standard Forms of Contracts sponsored by the United Nations Economic Commission for Europe. Mr. Peter Benjamin, when discussing their purpose and effect, writes: "The general conditions and standard forms of contract, in fact, render it somewhat redundant to refer to a national legal system. These instruments take as their point of departure the fact that under nearly all legal systems the proper law of a contract is determined by ascertaining the free will of the parties and applying it to the contract. In other words, the parties to the contract can generally make their own law and this need not be a system of national law."[46] Mr. Benjamin then points out that all the General Conditions of Sale contain an arbitration clause and that the vast majority of these clauses contains no reference to a national system of law.[47] The older sets of General Conditions contained a choice of law clause but in the more recent General Conditions the arbitration clause does not contain such reference "as this has been considered to be unnecessary."

Professor Goldštajn, when discussing "the existence of an autonomous commercial law that has grown independent of the national systems of law," observes: "Two legal factors have made this development possible in the laws of Western countries: the optional character of the law relating to the purchase and sale of goods, and the ever-growing use of arbitration in commercial disputes."[48]

Professor Henry Batiffol has commented on the use of the autono-

[46]P. Benjamin, "E.C.E. General Conditions of Sale and Standard Forms of Contract," [1961] *J. Bus. L.* 113, at p. 116.

[47]*Ibid.*, at p. 117.

[48]Goldštajn, *supra* note 30, at p. 13.

mous regulation in a special case—that of a corporation of international character.[49] He refers by way of illustration to the statute of the Bank of International Settlement, created by the Convention of January 20, 1930, and the statute of the Scandinavian Airlines System. In both cases the statute intends to provide an autonomous regulation. In the former instance the convention provides that legal personality should be conferred upon the bank by a resolution of the Federal Swiss Council, but adds that the statute creating the bank should take effect in spite of any contradiction with the provisions of present or future Swiss law. The statute of the Scandinavian Airlines System contains an arbitration clause which provides that differences between the associated companies are to be submitted to an arbitral tribunal composed of three members and that the tribunal should determine, *inter alia*, "the national jurisdiction" which is to be applied. Professor Batiffol concludes that the "recent experiments, such as that of Scandinavian Airlines system, show that the refusal to subject the contract or creative statute of a company to a particular body of [national] law raises the necessity of providing for an arbitral jurisdiction that will create the rules necessary for the fulfilment of the contract of statute."[50]

These illustrations indicate that in both branches of international business law the new law merchant, as an autonomous legal regulation, is founded on the complementary interaction of party autonomy and arbitration.

THE AUTONOMOUS LAW MERCHANT AS A MEANS OF CONFLICT AVOIDANCE

IT HAS been explained elsewhere[51] that it is one of the tasks of those planning an international business transaction to avoid a conflict of laws. "In the conflict of laws, two approaches are possible for the disposal of a conflict problem: the preventive method of conflict

[49]H. Batiffol, "Conflict Avoidance in European Law" (1956), 11 *Law & Contemp. Prob.* 570, at pp. 577–80.
[50]*Ibid.*, at p. 579.
[51]P. 130, *ante*.

avoidance and the clinical method of conflict solution."[52] From the practical point of view in international business law, avoidance of conflict is infinitely more important than solution of conflict. Generally speaking, conflict on the private level can be avoided either by localizing a transaction in a particular country, thereby equating it to a municipal transaction, or by adopting an autonomous regulation for the transaction in question. Important total localization devices are, for example, the confirmed commercial credit where the obligation of the foreign buyer is confirmed by a bank in the country of the seller, or the local subsidiary of a foreign controlling company.[53] The autonomous regulation of an international transaction, such as that attempted by the E.C.E. General Conditions of Sale and Standard Forms of Contract, is another means of averting conflict.

The efficiency of these conflict avoidance devices may be judged by the relative paucity of litigation on conflicts arising from international contracts, as compared with the frequent court cases concerning issues which are not governed by the autonomy of the parties' will, such as the validity of divorces or other matrimonial causes.

THE SOURCES OF INTERNATIONAL BUSINESS LAW

IT IS UNNECESSARY to give here a full account of the sources from which modern international business law, as an autonomous body of law, is derived. This topic will be considered in detail in September, 1962, by a small study group of lawyers from the East and West at a Colloquium convened by the International Association of Legal Science in conjunction with UNESCO. The subject of the Colloquium, for which the writer is acting as General Reporter, is "The

[52]C. M. Schmitthoff, "Conflict Avoidance in Practice and Theory" (1956), 11 *Law & Contemp. Prob.* 429.

[53]*Ibid.*, at p. 446. It should be noted that a total localization device cannot abolish or eradicate the international character of a transaction, but can only transfer it from a highly vulnerable area of conflict of interests to a less vulnerable one in which such a conflict is less likely to occur. Cf. *ibid.*, at p. 454.

New Sources of the Law of International Trade, with special reference to East-West Trade."

However, it should be stated here that the two main sources from which international business law is derived are mercantile custom and international legislation. These two terms describe inadequately the processes at work: traditional concepts, in law as well as in other fields of human activity, are moulded by past experience and are, for that reason, but imperfect vehicles of thought when reference is made to trends which are just emerging and not yet expressed in generally accepted terminology.

It is the traditional view, supported, amongst others, by the authority of Lord Justice Devlin,[54] that mercantile custom has ceased to be a source of law of consequence because custom will only be recognized by the courts if it is "reasonable, certain and notorious."[55] "Notorious" in this connection means "generally accepted," a requirement which is difficult to establish in evidence and can be easily disproved by showing that responsible businessmen did not act in conformity with the alleged custom. This view reflects the fact that custom normally grows slowly and takes some time before becoming generally accepted. This fact, however, should not mislead us into thinking that custom today is less active as a law-creating agency than it was in old days. Illustrations of international commercial customs of relatively recent growth which have become part of the commercial laws of the world are the c.i.f. contract, the true character of which was finally established in England as late as 1911,[56] and the confirmed commercial credit which came into general use only after the First World War.[57] On the contrary, the all-important function of formulation of international mercantile custom is probably more developed in our days than it was in earlier times, thanks to the contribution of many international bodies; reference may be made here only to two, the International Chamber of Commerce which has sponsored the

[54]Lord Justice Devlin, "The Relation between Commercial Law and Commercial Practice" (1951), 14 *Modern L. Rev.* 249, at p. 251.

[55]*Devonald* v. *Rosser and Sons,* [1906] 2 K.B. 728, 743.

[56]*E. Clemens Horst Co.* v. *Biddell Bros.,* [1912] A.C. 18.

[57]Cf. Lord Sumner in *The Kronprinsessan Margareta,* [1921] 1 A.C. 486, 510.

Uniform Customs and Practice for Commercial Documentary Credits and Incoterms, and the United Nations Economic Commission for Europe which has sponsored numerous General Conditions of Sale and Standard Forms of Contract.

With respect to international legislation as a source of the autonomous law of international business, the reservation made earlier with respect to the inadequacy of traditional terminology fully applies. In our system of national sovereignties all legislation affecting municipal law is clearly national; by "international legislation" is understood the technique by which a deliberate normative regulation is devised internationally and then introduced into the municipal laws by national legislation. International legislation, in that sense, is carried out by two methods: the adoption, by states, of a multilateral international convention or the formulation of a uniform model law which may be adopted by a state unilaterally. In comparing these two methods Mr. Matteuci lists as the main advantage of the convention method its greater certainty, although he does not overlook that the uniform character of a convention might be diminished by reservations when the convention is ratified by the various countries and by a different interpretation of its provisions by national judges.[58] According to Mr. Matteuci the adoption of a uniform law is a more elastic method and for that reason has a greater chance of success in some fields of commercial law. The two methods are best illustrated by reference to the law of the United States of America: the Carriage of Goods by Sea Act, 1936, is founded on the Brussels Convention of 1922 which gave effect to the Hague Rules of 1921 on Bills of Lading, while the Uniform Commercial Code is an example of a uniform law. It is not correct to think that the convention method, which undoubtedly is the older method in the international field, is obsolete today: the New York Convention on the Recognition and Enforcement of Foreign Arbitral Awards of June 10, 1958,[59] and the Geneva

[58]M. Matteuci, "The Unification of Commercial Law," [1960] *J. Bus. L.* 137, at p. 142.

[59]For the text of the convention see: [1958] *J. Bus. L.* 393–400; also see articles by S. Pisar, "The United Nations Convention on Foreign Arbitral Awards," [1959] *ibid.*, p. 219, and "The Law Governing Arbitration," *ibid.*, at p. 342.

European Convention on International Commercial Arbitration of April 21, 1961, are recent examples of international conventions occurring in the law of arbitration.

The assessment of the relationship of international mercantile customs and international legislation as contributory factors to the creation of international business law as an autonomous body of law is extremely difficult. It is tempting to state simply that international custom represents the process of law-making grown from commercial practice while international legislation is a deliberate act of law creation. That, however, would be a dangerous and fallacious over-simplification. It has already been pointed out that in our days the facilities for the deliberate formulation of commercial custom are well developed. The true difference is, then, between unformulated and formulated custom. The formulation of custom, for example, by the International Chamber of Commerce or by the competent committee of the United Nations Economic Commission of Europe, is as deliberate an act as that of the draftsman of an international convention or of a uniform law. Mr. Matteuci is closer to the truth when, in a searching analysis of the relationship between the two sources of international business law, he writes that "unification by legislation and unification by model contract . . . integrate and do not exclude each other since their aims are different and they cover different areas."[60] International legislation is required where a compulsory normative regulation is intended, such as the prohibition of "contracting out" by article III, paragraph 8, of the Hague Rules relating to Bills of Lading, or the recognition of foreign arbitral awards in article III of the New York Convention. Further, in the words of Mr. Matteuci, "as a corollary of the contractual activities and as a limitation of them, the action of the international lawmaker is indispensable, in order to harmonize, by the instrument of the uniform law, the unavoidable conflict of economic interests, in the light of social justice."[61]

Apart from the necessity for international legislation in cases in which a compulsory normative regulation is intended, the relation-

[60]Matteuci, *supra* note 58, at p. 140.
[61]*Ibid.*, at p. 141.

ship between formulated commercial custom and international legislation appears to be much the same as, in municipal law, the relationship between the contractual regulation and the normative regulation of municipal law. The former is founded on the autonomy of the parties' will, the latter forms part of the law of the country which applies *proprio vigore* although it might admit that the parties may make other arrangements. Thus, the model contract, to give an example of the former, applies because the parties, in the area within their discretion, have adopted it; the convention which has been incorporated into municipal law has become part of the municipal system of law, superseding the former normative regulation and applying to the relationship of the parties without requiring adoption on their part.

CONCLUSION

THESE BRIEF OBSERVATIONS have indicated, it is hoped, that human progress is not limited to the field of science, spectacular as the advance is in that field of human activity. In commercial law we are rediscovering the international horizon. The law of international trade emerges in our day as a body of autonomous legal rules, to a large measure independent of national systems of law, founded on the universally recognized twin principles of freedom of contracting and recognition of commercial arbitral awards, and supplemented by international legislation dealing with specific topics. This new *lex mercatoria* is formulated in general conditions of sale and standard forms of contract accepted by the international business community and in international conventions and uniform statutes incorporated by states into their municipal law. Founded as it is on the universal practice of international business, on the commonsense of businessmen in all parts of the globe, the new law merchant is common to all countries engaged in international trade and is a platform of mutual understanding for the common lawyer and the civil lawyer, the lawyer in the countries of free market economy and the socialist lawyer. If mankind is sane enough to avoid a clash of arms, the international exchange of goods, the activities of international companies, and industrial aid to the developing countries will be greatly intensified in the period of peaceful coexistence which lies ahead. The new law merchant will then become the first common law of the world, it will provide the background to that period in which trade will take the place of arms but which, in other respects, will be no less competitive and fateful for mankind than the preceding periods. This development will produce radical changes in the commercial law of all countries but, then, law has always meant change. We need not fear these changes; we can leave it to the skill and learning of judges and jurists to integrate them into the traditional pattern of commercial law.

The Development of International Liability Rules Governing Aerial Collisions

By GERALD F. FITZGERALD*

AN AERIAL COLLISION between aircraft of different nationalities can give rise to legal problems for which there is no easy solution.[1] The substantive liability rules applicable to such cases vary from jurisdiction to jurisdiction, and a civil action with a particular pattern of fact can produce results that differ from country to country. The purpose of this article is to describe current efforts to unify substantive and procedural rules on aerial collisions and to view the latest drafts against the background of existing aviation conventions. Occasional reference will be made to aspects of liability in maritime collisions.[2]

*Gerald F. FitzGerald, B.C.L., Ph.D., Senior Legal Officer, International Civil Aviation Organization, Montreal; Lecturer at the Institute of Air and Space Law, McGill University; member of the New Brunswick Bar. This article was written in a private capacity; responsibility for the opinions expressed is the the author's.

[1]For examples of the complications involved see W. Guldimann, "Méthode de travail du comité juridique" (1960), 14 *Revue française de Droit aérien* 1, at pp. 20–7; see also *Report of the Subcommittee on Aerial Collisions* (Paris, 1961), ICAO LC/SC/Aerial Collisions no. 71, 27/3/61.

[2]Reference to maritime principles is made merely as a matter of general interest. The American delegation to the Fourth International Conference on Private Air Law, Brussels, 1938, "pointed out in connection with the proposed collision convention that because of lack of sufficient aviation data and experience, a readiness to draw upon the body of maritime rules had been observed; that the same freedom of opportunity to evolve laws suitable to the operation of aircraft should be afforded as had been accorded to other forms of transportation, and that to persist in assimilating to air navigation analogous principles applicable to other forms of transportation might have unfortunate results." Latchford, "Brussels Air Law Conference" (1939), 10 *J. Air L. & Com.* 147, at pp. 154–5. The text placed before the conference was adopted by the CITEJA at Berne in 1936. CITEJA Doc. no. 320. For an American translation of this text see (1937) 8 *J. Air L. & Com.* 320.

As long ago as 1930, the *Comité international technique d'experts juridiques aériens* (CITEJA)[3] began working on a convention on collisions. Their text was developed between the years 1930–6, and though it was placed before the Fourth International Conference on Private Air Law held at Brussels in 1938,[4] it was not considered by the conference. The topic was then dropped until it was taken up by the Legal Committee of the International Civil Aviation Organization.[5] In March, 1961, ICAO's Subcommittee on Aerial Collisions, meeting in Paris, drew up a draft convention which will be discussed presently. It will be remembered that much of the air carrier's or air operator's liability has been subject to international rules for some time past. Thus the carrier's liability for the international carriage of passengers, baggage, and cargo is governed, for some fifty-seven states,[6] by the well-known Warsaw Convention for the Unification of Certain Rules Relating to International Carriage by Air, 1929,[7] and the operator's liability for surface damage is

[3]CITEJA functioned from 1926 to 1947 for the purpose of developing conventions on private air law. It comprised experts on air law named by various states. Drafts prepared by CITEJA were sent for adoption to international conferences on private air law.

[4]See *supra* note 2.

[5]ICAO is a specialized agency of the United Nations. The ICAO Legal Committee is open to all 84 contracting states, although average attendance is about a quarter of that number. Draft conventions prepared by the Legal Committee are submitted for final adoption to diplomatic conferences. At first, the ICAO Legal Committee studied aerial collisions in conjunction with the question of damage caused by foreign aircraft to third parties on the surface. For discussions and documents see Minutes and Documents of the Legal Committee as follows: ICAO Doc. 6014 LC/111, Second Session (May, 1948); ICAO Doc. 6024 LC/121, Third Session (Sept.-Oct., 1948); ICAO Doc. 6027 LC/124, Fourth Session (June, 1949); ICAO Doc. 6029 LC/126, Fifth Session (Jan., 1950);

Later, the ICAO Legal Committee studied the question of aerial collisions as a separate subject. See Minutes and Documents in: ICAO Doc. 7601 LC/138, Tenth Session (Sept., 1954); ICAO Doc. 7921 LC/143-1-2, Eleventh Session (Sept., 1957); ICAO Doc. 8137 LC/147-1-2, Thirteenth Session (Sept., 1960). The draft convention prepared by the ICAO Subcommittee on Aerial Collisions in 1961 is found in pp. 7–12 of the subcommittee's *Report*, *supra* note 1.

For history of work done on developing a convention on aerial collisions see Bolla, *L'Abordage aérien* (Lausanne, 1947); G. F. FitzGerald, "The Development of International Liability Rules Concerning Aerial Collisions" (1954), 21 *J. Air L. & Com.* 203; de Rode Verschoor, "La responsabilité dans l'abordage entre des aéronefs" (1955), 18 *Revue Générale de l'Air* 279; ICAO Doc. 7601 LC/138, Tenth Session (Sept., 1954) Vol. I (Minutes), p. [xxiii].

[6]For a late list of parties to the Warsaw Convention, see The Carriage by Air (Parties to the Convention) Order (U.K.) 1961, S.I. 1961/834.

[7]Opened for signature in 1929. In 1955 it was amended by the Hague Protocol, which has not yet come into force. The convention provides for presumption of

regulated, for ten states only,[8] by the Rome Convention on Damage Caused by Foreign Aircraft to Third Parties on the Surface, 1952.[9] The completion and acceptance of a convention on aerial collisions would, accordingly, fill a gap in the expanding code of rules of liability relating to international aviation. Interestingly, though, there has not always been unanimity in ICAO on the need for such a convention. Some have denied the need on the ground that collisions are comparatively rare.[10] As early as 1954, however, the

---

the carrier's liability in case of damage during international carriage by air to passengers, baggage, and goods. The carrier can escape liability by proving that he or his agents took all necessary measures to avoid the damage or that it was impossible for him or them to take such measures. Another defence is the contributory negligence of the injured person. The carrier's liability is limited as follows: 125,000 gold francs (approx. $8,291.00 U.S.) for each passenger; 250 gold francs (approx. $16.58 U.S.) for each kg. of registered baggage and cargo; and 5,000 gold francs (approx. $331.67 U.S.) for objects of which the passenger himself takes charge. The passenger limit in the Hague Protocol is 250,000 gold francs (approx. $16,582.00 U.S.). The Hague limits for registered baggage, cargo, and hand baggage are the same as those in the convention. In the convention, no limitation is provided if the damage is caused by wilful misconduct of the carrier or by such default on his part as, according to the law of the court seized of the case, is considered to be equivalent to wilful misconduct. This formula has been changed in the Hague Protocol, which contains more detailed language on the point.

The convention was drawn up in the French language only. For the text of the English translation see The Carriage by Air Act, 22 & 23 Geo. V (U.K., 1932), c. 36, First Schedule; The Carriage by Air Act, 3 Geo. VI (Can., 1939), c. 12, First Schedule; R.S.C. 1952, c. 45; V. Hudson, *International Legislation*, Vol. V, p. 102; *League of Nations Treaty Series*, no. 137, p. 11; *British Treaty Series*, no. 11 (1933), Cmd. 4284. For the American translation, see *U.S. Treaty Series*, no. 876. For the text of the Hague Protocol, which was drawn up in English, French, and Spanish, see ICAO Doc. 7632 and Doc. 7686 LC/140, *International Conference on Private Air Law* (The Hague, Sept., 1955), Vol. II (Documents), p. 1; for English text only see (1955) 22 *J. Air L. & Com.* 460.

[8]These states are: Australia, Canada, Ceylon, Ecuador, Haiti, Honduras, Luxembourg, Pakistan, Spain, and United Arab Republic (Egypt).

[9]Signed at Rome on Oct. 7, 1952. It concerns extra-contractual relations between the aircraft operator who is the author of the damage and persons on the surface who suffer it. It imposes absolute liability on an operator of an aircraft which causes damage on the surface in the territory of a state other than its state of registry. The operator's liability is limited, such limitation being calculated in relation to the weight of the aircraft, with a special limit of 500,000 gold francs (approx. $33,164.00 U.S.) for loss of life or personal injury per person killed or injured. In some circumstances the operator loses the benefit of the limits. The Rome Convention was drawn up in English, French, and Spanish. For all three texts see ICAO Doc. 7364, and (1958) *U.N.T.S.* no. 310, p. 181; for English text see schedule to the Foreign Aircraft Third Party Damage Act, 3 & 4 Eliz. II (Can., 1955), c. 15; and (1952) 19 *J. Air L. & Com.* 447.

[10]Apart from the question of the frequency of collisions, a factor to be borne in mind in considering the need for a convention on aerial collisions is the ever-present danger of a collision with catastrophic consequences. For example, the

majority of the ICAO's Legal Committee thought otherwise. They were impressed by the fact that information then available showed an increasing number of collisions, and they thought that improvements in technique and procedures would not prevent collisions in the future, considering the increase in the volume of air traffic and the speed of aircraft. The majority was also mindful of the fact that if the convention could be applied to collisions involving military aircraft and not merely to those involving civil aircraft, it would have a wide application.[11] An International Air Transport Association resolution of 1958 called for a convention "outlining the rights and obligations of the owners of aircraft involved in such accidents vis-à-vis their passengers and shippers, third persons and property on the ground and to each other."[12] Since then the subject has been studied in ICAO legal circles,[13] although its priority has yet to be determined.[14]

SUMMARY OF THE PARIS DRAFT CONVENTION ON AERIAL COLLISIONS, 1961

THE DRAFT CONVENTION ON AERIAL COLLISIONS applies when damage contemplated by it results from a collision or interference between aircraft in flight in the territory of a contracting state, provided that at least one of the aircraft involved is registered in another contracting state; if two or more of the aircraft involved are registered in different contracting states, the convention applies irrespective of where the collision or interference occurs. The basic

collision between a United Air Lines DC-8 and a Trans-World Airlines Constellation in the New York City area on Dec. 16, 1960, caused the death of 134 persons, destruction of both aircraft, and extensive property damage on the surface.

[11] ICAO Doc. 7601 LC/138, Tenth Session (Sept., 1954), Vol. I (Minutes), p. [xxiv].

[12] For the complete text of the resolution see: ICAO A12-WP/32 LE/2 Assembly, Twelfth Session, Agenda Item no. 26.1, "Work Programme of the Legal Committee," p. 11.

[13] The subject was studied by a subcommittee of the ICAO Legal Committee at Paris in March-April, 1960, and March, 1961, as well as by the ICAO Legal Committee at Montreal in Sept., 1960.

[14] ICAO Doc. 8124 C/928, Action of the Council, Forty-first Session, Montreal, Sept. 29–Dec. 14, 1960, pp. 18–19.

rule is that the operator of each aircraft involved will be liable if it is proved that the collision or interference was caused by his fault or that of his servants or agents acting within the course of their employment or scope of authority. There is, however, a presumption of the operator's liability in certain cases. Claims governed by the draft are normally not to exceed stated amounts. Provision is made for apportioning damage among the operators according to a system which takes into account the degrees of their fault as well as cases where no operator has been at fault. Other provisions concern contributory negligence of the injured person, prohibitions against cumulation of claims, jurisdictions in which actions may be brought, limitation of actions, currency of compensation payments, and reservations. These and related items are discussed below.

SCOPE OF THE CONVENTION

The convention applies when damage results from a collision or interference between two or more aircraft in flight.[15] An aircraft is deemed to be in flight from the moment that power is applied for the purpose of actual take-off until the moment the landing run ends. For aircraft lighter than air, the expression "in flight" means the period between the moment that it becomes detached from the surface until the moment it becomes attached again.[16] The same definition is found in the Rome Convention.[17] Cases of collision or interference between aircraft moving on the surface otherwise than in flight are left for determination under applicable law. In this

[15]Art. 1(1). Unless otherwise indicated, references to articles in succeeding footnotes will be to articles of the Draft Convention on Aerial Collisions prepared at Paris in 1961.

[16]Art. 1(2).

[17]Rome Convention, art. 1(2). But the definition in the Rome Convention and in the draft on collisions is more restrictive than the definition of "flight time" found in Annex 6 (International Standards and Recommended Practices, Operation of Aircraft, International Commercial Air Transport) to the Convention on International Civil Aviation. (For the text of that convention, see sources indicated *infra* note 21.) The latter definition reads as follows: "*Flight time.* The total time from the moment an aircraft first moves under its own power for the purpose of taking off until the moment it comes to rest at the end of the flight. *Note*—Flight time as here defined is synonymous with the term 'block to block' time or 'chock to chock' time in general usage which is measured from the time the aircraft moves from the loading point until it stops at the unloading point."

respect the draft is narrower than an earlier text which applied to collisions between aircraft in movement, whether or not such movement was connected with flight.[18] In favour of the present draft's narrower reach it can be argued that an aircraft moving on the surface is more easily controlled by its crew than an aircraft committed to flight. On the other hand, given the oftentimes huge size and destructive capacity of an aircraft moving on the surface, and the fact that while moving about an airport it poses specialized risks to other machines, there is something to be said for the view that it should not be subject to the same régime of liability as that applicable to other surface vehicles.[19]

Many serious collisions involve military aircraft.[20] It has been thought, therefore, that states should be encouraged to bring military and other state aircraft within the convention's ambit. For purposes of the draft, aircraft used in military, customs, and police services are deemed to be state aircraft,[21] but aircraft engaged in carrying passengers, cargo, or mail for remuneration or hire are not deemed to be state aircraft.[22] An obvious difficulty here is that some

[18]A draft prepared by the ICAO Legal Committee in 1954: see ICAO Doc. 7601 LC/138, *supra* note 11, p. [xvii].

[19]For discussions about applying the draft to collisions between aircraft in movement under their own power, whether or not they are in flight, see ICAO Doc. 7601 LC/138, *supra* note 11, pp. [xxix], 11–21, and 45–51.

[20]For examples, see "Eastern Air Lines, DC-4 aircraft N-88727 and a P-39 collision when landing at Washington National Airport, Washington, D.C., on I November 1949," ICAO Circular 18-AN/15, *Aircraft Accident Digest*, no. 1 (1951), p. 60; "Trans-Canada Air Lines, Canadair C4-1, and an R.C.A.F. Harvard MK II involved in collision over outskirts of Moose Jaw, Saskatchewan, Canada, on 8 April 1954. Report on Board of Inquiry, Ref. AC-5-34, Department of Transport, Canada," ICAO Circular 47-AN/42 (1956), p. 93.

[21]Art. 16(3). See, in this regard, article 3(*b*) of the Convention on International Civil Aviation: *Canada Treaty Series*, no. 36 (1944), p. 34; *U.N.T.S.*, no. 15 (1948), p. 295. That article states that "Aircraft used in military, customs and police services shall be deemed to be state aircraft." The qualifying provision ("however, any aircraft engaged in the carriage of passengers, cargo or mail for remuneration or hire shall be subject to this Convention") in the Paris draft has been borrowed from the state aircraft definition in art. 1(3) of the Draft Convention on Offences and Certain Other Acts on Board Aircraft, Munich, 1959: ICAO Doc. 8111–LC/146-2, Twelfth Session (Aug.–Sept., 1959), Vol. II (Documents).

[22]Art. 16(3). As is evident from the definition of state aircraft, there is no question of exempting a state from the application of the convention when its aircraft are engaged in commerce. This principle has long been accepted because many commercial airlines are state-owned. For example, state-owned airlines are subject to the liability rules of the Warsaw Convention of 1929 provided the

states may be reluctant to subject all their state aircraft to he convention since they may not want to agree in advance to being impleaded in a foreign court in the case of collisions or interferences involving state aircraft. Accordingly, the convention provides that any state may, at any time, make either of the following reservations: (i) that the convention shall not apply to all or specified classes of its state aircraft, or (ii) that an action with respect to damage caused by its state aircraft shall be subject only to the jurisdiction of its own courts.[23] The fact that these reservations can be made at any time—rather than at the time of signature, ratification or adherence—gives states considerable latitude in the matter. A reservation is not irrevocable since it may be withdrawn at any time. The convention is not intended to apply to aircraft owned and operated by international organizations,[24] such as the United Nations, though this is a question which may have to be considered in the future.

carriage falls within the definition of "international carriage" contained in the treaty. For the similar position in the maritime field see the Brussels Convention of 1926 (Hudson, *supra* note 7, Vol. III, p. 1837), and Knauth's *Benedict on Admiralty* (7th ed.; 1957) Vol. VI, p. 239. Of particular interest on the draft's application to state aircraft is the Brussels position regarding collisions between warships and other vessels used exclusively on governmental and non-commercial service: claimants are given the right to taking proceedings in the courts of the state owning or operating the vessel, without that state being permitted to avail itself of its immunity. This accords with current thinking in some countries. For example, neither the Crown Proceedings Act, 10 & 11, Geo. VI. (U.K., 1947), c. 44, nor the Crown Liability Act, 1 & 2 Eliz. II (Can., 1952–3), c. 30 contemplates proceedings abroad against the Crown as shipowner. There are statutes which permit suits against the United States government in various aspects relating to shipping; however, as pointed out in Knauth, *supra*, p. 238, that government declines to be sued in any foreign court. Although the International Convention on Certain Rules Concerning Civil Jurisdiction in Matters of Collision (Brussels, May 10, 1952) specifies jurisdictions in which actions for maritime collisions might be brought, it nevertheless states in art. 6 that it does not "modify the rules of law now or hereafter in force in the various contracting states in regard to collisions involving warships or vessels owned by or in the service of a State." Such rules may be those of the Brussels Convention of 1926, if the state concerned is a party thereto. For the text of the 1952 convention, see Marsden, *Collisions at Sea* (10th ed.; 1953), p. 820 and *Knauth, supra*, p. 35.

[23]Art. 16(1).

[24]A specialized agency in relationship with the United Nations could own or operate an aircraft. For example, s. 11 of the Agreement between the International Civil Aviation Organization and the Government of Canada regarding the Headquarters of the organization (1951), *U.N.T.S.*, no. 96, p. 155, reads as follows: "(1) Any aircraft owned, operated or chartered by the Organization, by Representatives of Members or by officials of the Organization, when used on

As already stated, the draft concerns damage resulting from a collision or interference between two or more aircraft in flight. The words "collision" and "interference" are not defined. Nevertheless, the convention would seem to cover collisions involving physical contact of aircraft as well as aircraft manoeuvres which produce damage without physical contact. The convention, therefore, could apply to the case of an aircraft which crashed because it passed through the turbulent wake of a jet. Although the draft speaks of interference between aircraft, the use of the preposition "between" is not meant to imply that the text does not apply unless the interference has been mutual.

The convention applies if collision or interference occurs in the territory of a contracting state and at least one of the aircraft involved is registered in another contracting state, or if two or more of the aircraft involved are registered in different contracting states, irrespective of where the collision or interference occurs.[25] In the latter case, the convention applies even though collision occurs in a non-contracting state, over the high seas, or in other areas of unde-

---

official business or for or in connection with official meetings of the Organization, does not need prior permission for entry into or departure from Canadian territory, provided that notice be given to appropriate Canadian aeronautical authorities, and provided that any aircraft used will be subject to the standard Air Traffic Rules and Procedures and Air Regulations of Canada when operating within the territorial limits of Canada." See also, in regard to this agreement, Privileges and Immunities (United Nations) Act, R.S.C. 1952, c. 219, and Order in Council, P.C. 1954–1791, Nov. 18, 1954, Statutory Orders and Regulations, Vol. III, p. 2589.

[25]Art. 1(1). Examples of collisions between aircraft of different nationalities with disastrous results are: Nov. 1, 1949, Eastern Airlines DC-4 and Bolivian P-38 near Washington, D.C. (55 dead); April 25, 1951, Cuban aircraft and U.S. Navy aircraft near Key West, Florida (43 dead); Oct. 22, 1958, British European Airways Viscount and Italian F. 86 F in vicinity of Naples (31 dead); Feb. 25, 1960, DC-3 of R.E.A.I. and DC-6 of U.S. Navy above Guanabara Bay (65 dead).

Examples of a near miss between aricraft of different nationalities: "Capt. James Bell saved 136 lives by hurling his B.E.A. Viscount into a split-second dive under a giant Boeing jet on Thursday, the 11th August 1960, at Rome. The Viscount, with 44 passengers and five crew, was approaching Rome at 250 m.p.h.," in Aeronautical Society of India, *News Bulletin*, July-Sept., 1960.

Examples of collisions between aircraft of the same nationality with disastrous results are: April 8, 1954, Trans-Canada Air Lines C-4-1 and a R.C.A.F. Harvard MK II, Moosejaw, Saskatchewan (37 dead); Aug. 11, 1955, two transport aircraft of U.S. Army near Edelweiler, Germany (6 dead); Trans World Airlines L. 1049 and United Air Lines DC-7 above Grand Canyon (128 dead); Dec. 16, 1960, United Air Lines DC-8 jet and Trans World Airlines Constellation (134 dead).

termined sovereignty. The convention's application can be illustrated by the following table:[26]

TABLE I

State of Registry of Aircraft	Place of Accident			
	CSA	CSB	NCS	HS
CSA/CSA	No	Yes	No	No
CSA/NCS	No	Yes	No	No
CSB/CSB	Yes	No	No	No
CSB/NCS	Yes	No	No	No
CSA/CSB	Yes	Yes	Yes	Yes
NCS/NCS	No	No	No	No

CSA—Contracting State A; CSB—Contracting State B; NCS—Non-Contracting State; HS—High seas or area of undetermined sovereignty.

Peculiarly enough, the convention applies to the situation indicated in the first column of item CSB/CSB, not because the aircraft concerned are of different nationalities, but because collision or interference occurs outside the state of registry of the aircraft.

PRINCIPLES OF LIABILITY

SUBJECT to qualification, liability contemplated by the convention attaches to the aircraft operator.[27] The definition of the word "operator" is substantially the same as that in the Rome Convention, 1952. He is the person who was making use of the aircraft at the time that damage was caused. It is to be noted, however, that if navigational control of the aircraft was retained by the person from whom the right to make use of the machine was derived, whether directly or indirectly, that person is the operator.[28] A person is considered to be making use of an aircraft when he is using it personally or when his servants or agents are using it within the scope of their employment. The draft does not affect the liability, if any, of the owner of the aircraft,[29] if he is not also the operator, or of other

[26]The table is an adaptation of one prepared by Dr. Guldimann (Switzerland), Chairman of the ICAO Legal Subcommittee on Aerial Collisions.

[27]Art. 2(1).

[28]Art. 2(2).

[29]Unlike the Draft Convention on Aerial Collisions, the Rome Convention establishes a rebuttable presumption that the owner of an aircraft is its operator, art. 2(3).

persons, such as air traffic control agencies.[30] It does, however, protect the operator's servants or agents, in some measure, even though it does not establish a right of action against them.[31]

It could be argued that the owner should enjoy the same protection as the operator, since, otherwise, a claimant could circumvent the provisions limiting the operator's liability by suing the owner whenever a defect in the aircraft could be alleged as a cause of the accident.[32] On the other hand, it could be argued that the owner does not, unless he is also an operator, accept the aerial risk in the same way as the operator, and should not, therefore, have his liability limited.

The operator is subject to a dual system of liability in the case of a collision or interference. First, the operator of each aircraft involved will, if the claimant proves that collision or interference was caused by the operator's fault,[33] be liable for: (i) loss of or damage to any of the other aircraft involved, including equipment or accessories thereon;[34] (ii) loss, damage, or delay caused to any other property on that other aircraft and belonging to its operator;[35] (iii) loss of use of that aircraft; (iv) any amount the operator of the other aircraft has had to pay legally as compensation for damage caused by the collision or interference.[36] The operator's fault includes the fault of his servants or agents acting within the course of their employment or scope of authority.[37] Secondly, the operator of each aircraft will be presumed to be liable for damage due to: (i) death,

[30]Air traffic control agencies are discussed *infra*.

[31]Servants and agents are discussed *infra*.

[32]The Warsaw Convention does not mention the owner, but merely the carrier. The Rome Convention, 1952, is sparing in its references to the owner; see arts. 2, 3, 4, 9.

[33]As in the case of the Brussels Convention on collisions between vessels, 1910, the word "fault" rather than "negligence" is used. For the text of the Brussels Convention see 1913 Cmd. 5558; Martens, *N.R.G.* (3d ser.), Vol. VII, p. 711; Marsden, *supra* note 22, p. 810; Griffin, *American Law of Collision* (1949), p. 852; Temperley, *Merchant Shipping Acts* (5th ed.), p. 808; *Knauth, supra* note 22, p. 39. For a summary of the Convention, see Colombos, *International Law of the Sea* (3d ed.; 1954), p. 259.

[34]That is, equipment or accessories installed in the aircraft and used for operating purposes.

[35]The expression "property . . . belonging to its operator" includes spare parts and equipment carried on board in transit to a maintenance depot of the operator and not installed in the aircraft.

[36]Art. 4.

[37]Art. 9.

injury, or delay caused to a person on board another aircraft, and (ii) loss, damage, or delay caused to property on the other aircraft, except property belonging to the operator of the latter.[38] The main reason for having presumed liability in the cases just mentioned is that passengers or shippers involved therein would be considered to have accepted the risk[39] of collision or interference to a lesser extent than the plaintiff operator of the earlier cases who, being engaged full-time in aviation, with its attendant risk, could be required to prove fault of the defendant operator. The concept of presumed liability has been borrowed from the Warsaw Convention,[40] and, like the carrier under the Warsaw Convention, the defendant operator under the proposed draft can rebut that presumption by proving that he and his servants or agents took all necessary measures to avoid the damage or that it was impossible for him or them to do so.[41]

The convention does not cover all damage arising from collision or interference. Except, for example, in the case of recourse actions between the operator of an aircraft, his servants or agents, and the operator of another aircraft, his servants or agents, it does not apply to the liability of an operator, his servants or agents, in respect of persons or property on board his aircraft or of persons or property on the surface.[42] Direct actions brought in respect of passengers or property on board the operator's aircraft would, in the case of international carriage by air, normally be regulated by the Warsaw Convention, and direct actions in respect of damage to persons or property on the surface would, in theory, be regulated by the Rome Convention which, however, has been accepted by only ten states.[43] Where the two latter conventions do not apply, direct actions would be subject to the applicable system of national law.

The draft does not provide that suits may be brought against

[38]Art. 5.

[39]However, in the case of the Rome Convention on Damage Caused by Foreign Aircraft to Third Parties on the Surface, the operator is subject to absolute liability on the theory that persons suffering damage on the surface from falling aircraft will be comparative strangers to the aeronautical risk.

[40]Warsaw Convention, arts. 17, 18, 19, 20.

[41]Art. 5(2); see Warsaw Convention, art. 20(1).

[42]Art. 3.

[43]See *supra* note 8.

servants or agents of an operator. But, recognizing that actions may be brought apart from the convention, it provides that, in such cases, a servant or agent, if he proves that he acted within the scope of his employment, shall not be liable except upon proof of fault and shall also be entitled to avail himself of all the convention's provisions (including those limiting the operator's liability) which are applicable to the operator himself.[44] There is an important difference between suits brought against servants or agents and those brought against the operator himself. In the latter case, there is the dual system of fault or presumption of fault depending upon the type of damage involved; in the former, fault must be proved irrespective of the type of damage involved.

The provision on servants and agents mentioned above is intended not only to protect them, but also to prevent claimants from indirectly evading the limits of liability provided for the operator himself. For example, an operator might agree to indemnify a crew member for claims the crew member is obliged to meet. A claimant might then recover from the employee an amount exceeding the operator's liability. Under the indemnity clause, the employee might then seek to recoup his loss from the operator, who would be deprived, indirectly, of his limitation *vis-à-vis* the original claimant.

As already indicated, the draft does not seek to affect the liability of air traffic control agencies, though this question was discussed in the ICAO Legal Committee at some length.[45] The increasing impor-

[44]Art. 12.

[45]See ICAO Doc. 8137 LC/147-1, Thirteenth Session (Montreal, 1960), Vol. I (Minutes), pp. [xxvii] and 173–6; and Guldimann, "Responsabildad Civil de los Servicios de Control de la Circulación Aérea y el Proyecto de Convenio sobre Abordaje Aéreo" (1960), 1 *Revista Latino-americana de Derecho Aeronautico* (no. 2) 21–2. The exclusion of air traffic control agencies from the Convention on Aerial Collisions could lead to the following anomalous situation: "A claimant associated with one aircraft might, in a case where both the operator of the other aircraft and the air traffic control agency were at fault, find his action against the other operator subject to a limit, whilst the same claimant, in respect of the same damage, would be able to recover, if an action were available under national law against the air traffic control agencies, an amount without any limit." Doc. 8137 LC/147-1, *supra*, p. [xxix]. For a discussion of the liability of air traffic control agencies generally, see Eastman, "Liability of the Ground Control Operator for Negligence" (1950), 17 *J. Air L. & Com.*, 170; Chauveau, "La responsabilité des aides à la navigation" (1953), 16 *Rev. Gén. de l'Air* 214; Narx, "Government Tort Liability for Operation of Airports" (1958), 25 *J. Air L. & Com.* 173; Guerreri, *Governmental Liability in the Operation of Airport Control Towers in the United States* (Montreal, 1960).

tance of such agencies has been given as one reason why they should be covered by the treaty. In this regard, the following points are important: the speed of aircraft, the height at which they can fly, and the international aspect of air traffic control agencies, represented by the fact that, though located within a country, an agency controls aircraft outside the country.[46] On the other hand, it has been suggested that the liability of these agencies raises questions which are not confined to aerial collisions and that the problem must be studied in a broader context. Moreover, the argument continues, since many control agencies are operated by governments, the question of liability does not lend itself to regulation by convention. The general topic remains on the work programme of the ICAO Legal Committee.

The convention does not provide for direct actions for damage caused to persons or property as a result of collision or interference. During earlier stages of the draft's development it had been assumed that the Rome Convention would be widely accepted. Accordingly it was thought that the limits applicable to recourse actions for damage to persons and property on the surface due to aerial collision would be those of the Rome Convention.[47] However, because of lack of acceptance of that treaty,[48] subsequent thinking has been to this effect: to write into the Collisions Convention the limits of

[46]In this regard, attention is drawn to the "EUROCONTROL," International Convention Relating to Co-operation for the Safety of Air Navigation, signed at Brussels, Dec. 13, 1960. This convention establishes an international air traffic control organization called EUROCONTROL which will operate in respect of upper air space above the territories of several contracting parties. The expression "air traffic" includes civil aircraft and certain military, customs, and police aircraft. Provision is also made for the air traffic services for the whole or part of the lower air space of one of the contracting parties to be entrusted to the EUROCONTROL or to another contracting party.

[47]"Economic Aspects of the Liability Limits in the Proposed Aerial Collisions Convention—120th Report to Council by the Chairman of the Air Transport Committee," ICAO Doc. 7921 LC/143-2, Eleventh Session (Sept. 1957), Vol. II (Documents), pp. 187–99. In addition to containing limits calculated in relation to the weight of the aircraft causing damage on the surface, the Rome Convention provides for a sublimit of 500,000 francs (approx. $33,164.00 U.S.) in respect of loss of life or personal injury per person killed or injured.

[48]To date, only ten states have become parties to it. For the list of these states, see *supra* note 8. The effect of the lack of acceptance of the Rome Convention in relation to the preparation of a Convention on Aerial Collisions is discussed in ICAO Doc. 8137 LC/147-1 *supra* note 45, p. [xxviii].

the Rome treaty would, in a sense, pressure states which ratify or adhere to the former to accept, indirectly, the limits of the latter when they may have decided not to ratify or adhere to the Rome Convention at all. But the convention does not ignore the case of damage on the surface altogether. One operator, for example, may recover from another any amount paid under a legal obligation as compensation for damage on the surface caused by a collision or interference.[49]

The convention does not state who may claim compensation under its provisions. It follows that the owner of the damaged aircraft, or the holder of a legal right therein, if not its operator, is not excluded from claiming. With regard to loss of use of a damaged aircraft, a claim could be sustained by its operator or by any other person who has suffered damage which, in the judgment of the court, is not too remote. As to cargo, the person having a sufficient interest therein would be entitled to sue. It was suggested to the ICAO Legal Subcommittee on Aerial Collisions in 1961 that rules regarding remoteness of damages might vary among jurisdictions to such an extent that in some places even a theatre manager could sue successfully for loss of services of a singer who missed an engagement due to an aerial collision. The convention may require further clarification on this question of remoteness of damages if it is to effect unification on the matter. A point of particular interest in considering who may be a claimant is that the provision[50] which places on the operator a presumption of liability for damage due to death, injury or delay caused to a "person" does not define that word, which could, therefore, include a crew member or even a stowaway. Inclusion of the Warsaw Convention rule on a rebuttable presumption of liability calls logically for the inclusion of the Warsaw rule on contributory negligence in a suit against an operator of one of the aircraft involved in collision or interference by a person who is not an operator of one such aircraft. If, in such an action, the defendant operator proves that the damage was caused or contributed to by the negligence of the injured person,

[49]Art. 4(d).

[50]Art. 5(1)(*a*).

the court may, in accordance with its own law, exonerate the operator wholly or partly from liability.[51]

EXTENT OF LIABILITY

THE CONVENTION limits the operator's liability. The limits relate to claims over persons and property on board the other aircraft (excluding property belonging to its operator) as well as claims respecting the other aircraft, its equipment and accessories and any property thereon belonging to its operator, and the loss of use of such aircraft.

The ICAO Legal Committee has studied the question of whether there should be any limit at all to claims respecting passengers and property on the other aircraft.[52] It was submitted to the committee in 1960 that the answer turns largely on whether or not the international air transport industry was thought to have attained such economic strength as to make unnecessary continued protection by way of limitation of liability of operators.[53] In favour of limiting liability regarding claims over persons and property carried on one aircraft against the operator of the other aircraft involved in collision or interference, it can be argued that the claimant would be advantaged since he would not have to prove defendant's fault.[54] This is the familiar *quid pro quo* argument used in relation to the limitation of liability found in the Warsaw and Rome conventions.[55] Since the Warsaw Convention system of presumption of liability is applied to the operator of one aircraft involved in collision in respect of passengers and property on board the other aircraft, the ICAO Legal Committee decided that the limits applicable to related claims should be those of Warsaw as amended by the Hague Protocol. Therefore, the operator's liability is, respecting damage to persons or property on board another aircraft, subject to the following

[51]Art. 6; see Warsaw Convention, art. 21.

[52]ICAO Doc. 8137 LC/147-1, *supra* note 45, pp. [xxix]–[xxx].

[53]*Ibid*., p. [xxix].

[54]*Ibid*., p. [xxx].

[55]For summary of arguments for and against having a limitation of liability in air law conventions see Drion, *Limitation of Liabilities in International Air Law* (The Hague, 1954), paras. 14–42.

limits:[56] (i) for death, injury, or delay caused to a person on board, including a crew member or a stowaway, 250,000 francs[57] for each person; (ii) for all objects which a person on board had in his charge, 5,000 francs[58] per person; (iii) for loss, damage or delay caused to any other property, including mail or registered baggage, on board the aircraft not belonging to the operator of that aircraft, 250 francs per kilogram.[59]

The liability of the operator of one aircraft for damage caused to another aircraft is, in the case of loss of, or damage to, the latter aircraft, including equipment and accessories thereof, and any property thereon belonging to its operator, the proved value at the time of collision or interference or the cost of repairs or replacement, whichever is the least.[60] The expression "proved value" includes the market value attached to the aircraft immediately before collision or interference.[61] But in the case of some aircraft, particularly certain military aircraft or aircraft which are prototypes,[62] there may not necessarily be a market value. This accounts for the use of

[56]Art. 10(1) (*c*), (*d*) and (*e*).

[57]The limit of 250,000 francs is contained in the Hague Protocol of 1955 which doubled the liability of an air carrier in respect of death or injury of a passenger from 125,000 francs (approx. $8,291.00 U.S.) to 250,000 francs (approx. $16,582.00 U.S.). The Protocol will come into force upon ratification by thirty states. The franc is the Poincaré gold franc, a currency unit consisting of sixty-five half-milligrams of gold of millesimal fineness 900; it equals U.S. $0.066334.

[58]The limit of 5,000 francs (approx. $331.67 U.S.) is a Warsaw Convention limit which was left undisturbed by the Hague Protocol.

[59]The limit of 250 francs (approx. $16.58 U.S.) is a Warsaw Convention limit which was left undisturbed by the Hague Protocol.

[60]Art. 10(1)(*a*).

[61]Approximate new prices, as at Jan., 1960, of some of the more expensive aircraft are as follows: Boeing 707-320 Intercontinental, $5,350,000.00 U.S.; Douglas DC-8 Intercontinental, $5,650,000.00 U.S.; Vickers VC-10, $5,454,000.00 U.S.; Convair 600, $4,050,000.00 U.S.; Boeing 720, $3,750,000.00 U.S.; Convair 880, $3,650,000.00 U.S.; DH Comet 4, $3,190,000.00 U.S.; Bristol 175 Britannia 310, $3,050,000.00 U.S.; Canadair CL-44D, $3,500,000.00 U.S. These figures come from "The Technical, Economic and Social Consequences of the Introduction into Commercial Service of Supersonic Aircraft: A Preliminary Study," ICAO Doc. 8087-c/925 (Aug., 1960), p. 114. In the same document, it is indicated that "Various studies have estimated the initial purchase price of a supersonic airline at between $10–$20 million each for a Mach 3, 100-seat aircraft," *ibid.*, p. 35.

[62]Even in the case of a prototype, the developmental and other costs might be spread over a whole series of aircraft which followed the prototype, with the result that the claim for loss or damage thereto would not necessarily be too far beyond the market price of one of the series.

the expression "proved value." Property on board the other aircraft and belonging to the operator could include spare equipment not installed in the aircraft for operational purposes but being carried elsewhere for storage and eventual use for maintenance purposes. In the case of the loss of use[63] of the other aircraft, due to collision or interference, the defendant operator would not be liable for an amount in excess of 10 per cent of the value of that aircraft as determined above.[64]

The franc that is referred to in the convention is the so-called Poincaré gold franc.[65] The Warsaw and Rome conventions use the same franc. Like the Rome Convention, the draft provides that sums expressed therein may be converted into national currencies in round figures. In addition, conversion of sums into national currencies other than gold shall, in case of judicial proceedings, be made according to the gold value of such currencies at the date of the judgment.[66]

The convention contains no over-all limit on the operator's

[63]As to loss of use, see the remarks of the Air Transport Committee, in ICAO Doc. 7921 LC/143-2, *supra* note 47, at p. 194 where it is stated that: "Determination of the extent of consequential loss of this nature is a more difficult problem, and litigation may be expected to arise from it more frequently, especially since it is understood that in most cases the loss sustained will not be covered by insurance. No statistics are available on which any mathematical estimate of a suitable limit can be based, but exercising judgment the Committee concluded that the operator's liability for consequential loss should be limited to 10% of the market value attaching to the aircraft immediately prior to the collision."

The 10 per cent figure for loss of use could be justified, in part, on the assumption of early replacement of the aircraft concerned. If this assumption is correct, then, in the case of the projected supersonic aircraft, that figure may require some adjustment upward. After a collision or interference, a supersonic aircraft would hardly be replaced as quickly as a conventional type of aircraft, because of the length of time required to construct a new machine. Now if the period of loss of use where a supersonic aircraft has been destroyed is longer than in the case of the destruction of a conventional type of aircraft, then it is to be considered whether the percentage figure in the case of loss of use of a supersonic aircraft should be in excess of the 10 per cent figure given above. In relation to the foregoing, it is observed that, according to present thinking, the earning capacity of a supersonic aircraft would be comparable to that of other aircraft. In this regard, it is indicated in ICAO Doc. 8087-C/925, *supra* note 61, p. 38, that "If a Mach 3, 100-seat aircraft were to have fares averaging 3 cents per passenger-kilometre (4.8 cents per passenger-mile), it should be able to earn about $15.5 million per year, i.e., its earning power would be of the same order as its purchase price, which would make it comparable in this respect to most other aircraft."

[64]Art. 10(1)(*b*).

[65]See *supra* note 57.

[66]Art. 10(2).

liability for aerial collision.[67] In favour of including this limit is the argument that, if it were fixed at a fairly high level, operators would have a better estimate of the amount for which they should insure. A subsidiary argument is that, if within an over-all limit there were no limits on the categories of damage, there would be greater flexibility regarding settlement of the latter. On the other hand, since the convention includes no provisions on direct actions in cases of surface damage, there would be no limit to the amount recoverable in a recourse action where payment had to be made for such damage. Moreover, the ICAO Air Transport Committee recommended the exclusion of an over-all limit[68] and this recommendation was accepted by the ICAO Legal Committee as a basis for the draft.

The limits otherwise stipulated in the convention will not apply: (i) if it is proved that the damage resulted from an act or omission of the operator, his agents, or servants, done with intent to cause damage, or recklessly and with knowledge that damage would probably result, provided that in the case of such act or omission of an agent or servant, it is also proved that he was acting within the scope of his employment; or (ii) if the person liable has wrongfully taken and made use of the aircraft without the consent of a person entitled to permit its use.[69] The first situation is the same as that under which the limits of the Warsaw Convention, as amended by the Hague Protocol, may be breached.[70] The second situation has been borrowed from the Rome Convention of 1952.[71]

A claimant is not permitted by the draft to recover more than the maximum amounts specified above, regardless of whether his claim is against one or more of the operators liable.[72] Nor can several claimants suing one operator recover in the aggregate an amount exceeding the limits applicable in the case of a suit against that operator.[73] A claimant, moreover, cannot exceed the applicable limits by resorting to the device of suing an operator and separately suing his servants or agents.[74] As an additional safeguard the draft

[67]For discussion on this point, see ICAO Doc. 8137 LC/147-1, *supra* note 45, pp. [xxix] and 195 *et seq*.

[68]For the Air Transport Committee's view on the over-all limit, see ICAO Doc. 7921 LC/143-2, *supra* note 47, p. 195 *et seq*.

[69]Art. 11.

[70]See the Hague Protocol, art. XIII.

[71]See Rome Convention, art. 12(2).

[72]Art. 13(2).

[73]Art. 13(1).

[74]*Ibid.*

provides that the court trying a case against a defendant operator may require the claimant to provide such guarantees for observing the rule against cumulation as the court may consider necessary.[75]

APPORTIONMENT OF COMPENSATION

CLAIMS ARISING out of a collision or interference will ultimately have to be settled by the operators of the aircraft involved, whether through direct actions brought by non-operator claimants against the operators or by direct and recourse actions of the operators *inter se*. Accordingly, one of the prime purposes of the convention is to provide a mathematical basis for such settlement. This it does by establishing rules for apportioning compensation.

The basic rule is that if damage results from collision or interference caused by the fault of the operators of two or more aircraft, each operator will be liable to the other operators in proportion to the degrees of fault committed.[76] The same rule is found in Article 4 of the Brussels Convention, 1910,[77] and in section 648, subsection 1 of the Canada Shipping Act.[78] If degrees of fault cannot be ascertained, responsibility is shared equally by the operators involved.[79] The Brussels Convention, 1910,[80] and the Canada Shipping Act[81] contain the same rule. One argument against this rule is that a court can hardly hold that there has been fault without at the same time ascertaining degrees of fault. The convention also con-

[75]Art. 13(3).

[76]Art. 7(1).

[77]"If two or more vessels are in fault the liability of each vessel is in proportion to the degree of fault respectively committed." (First sentence.) For sources in which complete text of Brussels Convention (1910) may be found, see *supra* note 33.

[78]R.S.C. 1952, c. 29. The relevant text reads as follows: "(1) Where, by the fault of two or more vessels, damage or loss is caused to one or more of those vessels, to cargoes or freight, or to any property on board, the liability to make good the damage or loss shall be in proportion to the degree in which each vessel was in fault."

[79]Art. 7(1).

[80]Art. 4: ". . . Provided that if, having regard to the circumstances, it is not possible to establish the degree of the respective faults, or if it appears that the faults are equal, the liability is apportioned equally."

[81]S. 648(2): "Where, having regard to all the circumstances of the case, it is not possible to establish different degrees of fault, the liability shall be apportioned equally."

templates apportionment in cases where none of the operators has been at fault. In this situation the provision is that they bear equally all compensation which has been paid by any of them under a legal obligation for any damage caused by the collision or interference.[82] By way of contrast, the Brussels Convention rule is, in effect, that in these circumstances the damage lies where it falls,[83] while the Canada Shipping Act would operate to prevent a vessel from being liable "for any loss or damage to which her fault has not contributed."[84] The reason for the equal sharing rule in cases where no operator is at fault is that an innocent operator who has paid compensation because of strict liability, for example, in a direct action under the Rome Convention, should not have to bear more of the burden than the other innocent operator whom the original claimant did not choose to sue.[85] While the Brussels Convention provides that, if the cause of the collision is left in doubt, "the damages are borne by those who suffered them,"[86] the Convention on Aerial Collisions contains no such rule because such a case would seem to be included in the case where the fault of the operators was not proved or, to some extent, in the case where the degree of fault was not known.

The rules concerning apportionment are, however, subject to an important restriction. For example, an operator is not liable in any recourse action to pay any sum which would result in his liability's exceeding any applicable liability limit or in his being deprived of any defence or benefit to which he would be entitled in respect to persons or property on the surface or carried on his aircraft.[87]

[82]Art. 7(2).

[83]Art. 2 (in part): "If the collision is accidental, if it is caused by *force majeure*, or if the cause of the collision is left in doubt, the damages are borne by those who have suffered them."

[84]S. 648(3).

[85]This could happen, for example, under art. 7 of the Rome Convention on Damage Caused by Foreign Aircraft to Third Parties on the Surface, the text of art. 7 reading as follows: "When two or more aircraft have collided or interfered with each other in flight and damage for which a right to compensation as contemplated in Article 1 results, or when two or more aircraft have jointly caused such damage, each of the aircraft concerned shall be considered to have caused the damage and the operator of each aircraft shall be liable, each of them being bound under the provisions and within the limits of liability of this Convention."

[86]Art. 2. For relevant text, see *supra* note 33.

[87]Art. 8.

RULES OF PROCEDURE AND LIMITATION OF ACTIONS

LIKE THE Warsaw Convention,[88] the draft limits the number of jurisdictions in which actions may be brought. The plaintiff has the option of bringing his action in any contracting state in which the collision or interference occurred or in any contracting state in which the defendant operator has his domicile or principal place of business.[89] As claims could arise in respect of plaintiffs belonging to many states, one suggestion made to the ICAO Subcommittee on Aerial Collisions in 1961 was that claims might also be brought in the jurisdiction where the plaintiff was domiciled, provided the defendant is otherwise subject to that jurisdiction. This suggestion was not accepted.

In regard to fora, the draft is more flexible than the Rome Convention of 1952 which, unless the parties to the suit otherwise agree, provides as the only forum in which suit may be brought the courts of the contracting state where the damage occurred.[90] The main reason for accepting a single forum in the Rome Convention was the necessity of protecting the limits of the convention. Under the Rome scheme all claims would be consolidated in one place, thus permitting application of a scaling-down procedure provided by the treaty in order to prevent the limits being exceeded. But no over-all limit is provided in the Convention on Aerial Collisions and, in particular, no limits are imposed on recourse actions involving damage to persons and property on the surface. Therefore, the need to consolidate actions in a single forum has not been felt in the case of aerial collisions. Nevertheless, there is always the possibility that the plaintiff may sue different operators in various courts and, by a process of cumulation, evade the maximum limits specified in the draft. With a view to preventing this, the convention provides

[88] Art. 28 of the Warsaw Convention gives the plaintiff the option of bringing his action in the territory of one of the parties to the convention, "either before the court having jurisdiction where the carrier is ordinarily resident, or has his principal place of business, or has an establishment by which the contract has been made or before the court having jurisdiction at the place of destination."

[89] Art. 14.

[90] Art. 20(1).

that the court trying the case may oblige the claimant to provide such guarantees for ensuring observance of the rule against cumulation as that court may deem necessary.[91]

Like the Warsaw and Rome conventions, the draft provides for limitation of periods. Actions must be brought within two years from the date of the incident which caused the damage.[92] The law of the court trying the case determines what suspends or stops the running of the period. The right to start an action, however, is extinguished after three years from the date of the incident which caused the damage.[93] As has been seen earlier, many of the claims under the convention will be recourse actions and such an action cannot be brought by an operator until an original action has been brought against him. Therefore the periods just mentioned may be prolonged to allow a person desirous of bringing a recourse action a period of six months in which to do so, reckoned from the start of the original action against him.[94] The purpose of this provision is to assist an operator, who otherwise would have to wait until a judgment had been rendered on the action against him, by allowing him to bring his recourse action on the basis that a claim had been made against him respecting which he wishes to exercise a right of recourse.

CURRENCY PROVISIONS

IN REGARD to currency used for paying compensation, the convention stipulates that contracting states will, as far as possible, facilitate payment in the currency of the residence of the claimant, if he so desires.[95] The Rome Convention contains a similar provision.[96]

[91] Art. 13(3).
[92] Art. 15(1).
[93] Art. 15(2).
[94] Art. 15(3).
[95] Art. 17.
[96] Art. 27. The cautiously worded currency provisions of the Rome Convention and of the Draft Convention on Aerial Collisions seem to be based on the hypothesis of continued currency restrictions. But the International Law Association, at its Forty-ninth Conference (Hamburg, 1960), adopted a liberal régime which is contained in seven rules concerning money of account in case of damages resulting from collisions, whether such collisions occur on land, at sea, or in the air. See International Law Association, Hamburg Conference (1960), Resolution 4, and *Report of the Forty-eighth Conference* (New York, 1958), pp. 375–400.

CONCLUSIONS

THE DRAFT CONVENTION ON AERIAL COLLISIONS is intended to provide uniform solutions for liability problems which arise out of collisions occurring in a variety of places and involving aircraft, passengers and shippers of different nationalities. Not only does it stipulate the courts where claims may be litigated, but it also provides substantive rules for application therein. In preparing these rules, ICAO solicitors have attempted to combine certain elements—whether in original or modified form—which have proved useful in the maritime and aviation fields, and which seem to be applicable to aerial collisions. It is too soon to predict whether these combinations will be widely accepted. It is safe to say though that, even in its present form, the 1961 draft marks an important stage in the development of the legal side of international aviation.

The Quest For Impartiality in Legal Systems

By THOMAS M. FRANCK*

I. INTRODUCTION

THERE ARE three fundamental systems of order-creation or problem-solving known to the law. They may operate independently or successively or they may be integrated in a single process. The first system is distinguished by its power syndrome: the imposition of the will of one party on the rights or duties of another. Law or order achieved by military conquest, annexation, imposed treaties, as well as most legislation passed by the political majority over the objections of the opposition, are possible examples.

The second system is marked by a compromise syndrome: the reconciliation of contending claims which results in a rule of conduct allotting rights and duties to all parties in a manner mutually or universally acceptable. Law or order achieved by boards of conciliation in labour disputes, or by unanimous action in parliament as a result of a coalition of political parties, or the system of jury selection employed in most common law jurisdictions, exemplify this process. The system of compromise may simply involve two-party negotiation or it may call for complex mechanical devices as well as reference to other systems of decision-making. Take, for example, the ingenious scheme for the division by choice of eighty-seven art treasures left "equally" to the Metropolitan (N.Y.) and National (D.C.) Museums by the will of the late Mrs. Timken. The two directors first grouped the items into a series of artistic categories,

*Thomas F. Franck, S.J.D., Associate Professor of Law, School of Law, New York University. This paper is part of a forthcoming study on "Comparative Concepts of Impartiality."

then divided each category into two sections of roughly equivalent value. Thereafter, the directors wrote out, simultaneously, their first choice in each group. Each time both showed a preference for the same section of a particular category, a coin was flipped and the winner had first choice. The conciliation worked so successfully that litigation, which could have eaten away much of the devise, was avoided.[1]

The third system is marked by its impartiality syndrome: the resolution of disputes between two (or more) parties by reference to a neutral third party (or parties) for a binding decision. Examples of this range from the flipping of a coin—as in the Timken dispute—and chemical experiments in a laboratory, to decisions by judges in courts of law or tax officials passing on the validity of exemptions. The two men flipping a coin are referring their dispute to the metaphysical impartiality of fate;[2] conflicting chemical hypotheses are subject in the laboratory to the impersonal operation of scientific testing. Clearly, the perfect impartiality of fate or of chemical reactions cannot be emulated by human beings; nevertheless, parties contending before judges or administrators do expect a high degree of human impartiality. Consequently, the striving after this objective occupies, in most jurisdictions, an important role in the continuing process of legal reform. Moreover, the past decades have seen such a wide resort to third-party decision-making at the international level—especially in the expanding functions of the International Court of Justice and the United Nations Secretariat—that the problem of judicial and administrative impartiality takes on new urgency.

The search for human impartiality at the international level is just beginning, for the obvious reason that institutionalized third-party

[1]National Gallery of Art, News Release, May 8, 1960; *New York Times*, Monday, May 9, 1960; *New York Mirror*, May 15, 1960; Metropolitan Museum of Art, News Release, May 15, 1960.

[2]The Bible freely urges judges to relegate difficult problems to divine intercession. "... [T]he judgment (of the judges) is God's: and the cause that is too hard for you, bring it unto me, and I will hear it" (Deut. 1:17). "If there arise a matter too hard for thee in judgment ... then shalt thou arise and get thee up into the place which the Lord thy God shall choose" (Deut. 17:8).

decision-making is itself a relatively new experience in the international search for law and order. There has, of course, long been *ad hoc* third-party decision-making. It appears to have been used in disputes between Greek city states,[3] to have risen and fallen with the mediaeval papacy, and to have been revived in modern times by the Jay Treaty of 1794[4] and the Alabama Awards of 1872. Only in the last century, however, have efforts been made to create permanent machinery for the resolution of international disputes by impartial third parties. The first such efforts are evident in the British-French Treaty of Arbitration of 1903[5] and the Hague Convention for the Pacific Settlement of International Disputes of 1899[6] (revised in 1907) which set up the Permanent Court of International Arbitration. An additional step forward was taken by the creation, in 1921, of the Permanent Court of International Justice,[7] which has since become the International Court of Justice.

Yet there is by no means universal agreement among states, even today, as to whether third-party decision-making is entitled to recognition as a separate system of order-creation. Communism has traditionally regarded courts as little more than instruments of power. "The court is an agency of the Soviet Socialist State. The court may not serve any other cause but the cause of building up a socialist society, may not carry on any other policy but the policy of the Communist Party and the Soviet Government, may not carry

[3]See J. H. Ralston, *International Arbitration from Athens to Locarno* (1929), pp. 153–298. For a review of the history of arbitration see Julius Stone, *Legal Controls of International Conflict* (1954), chap. 4, and authorities cited therein. The term "arbitration" as used in most histories covers much of what would today be more appropriately regarded as conciliation.

[4]For a full discussion of the arbitrations under the Jay Treaty, see: J. B. Moore, *Digest of International Arbitrations* (1898), Vol. I, pp. 299–349. For treaty text see: W. M. Malloy, *Treaties, Conventions, International Acts, Protocols and Agreements* (1910), Vol. I, p. 590.

[5]"Agreement between Great Britain and France Providing for the Settlement by Arbitration of certain classes of questions which may arise between the two Governments," Oct. 14, 1903, *Hertslet's Commercial Treaties*, Vol. XXIII, p. 492.

[6]First Hague Peace Conference, Convention for the Pacific Settlement of International Disputes, Malloy, *supra* note 4, Vol. II, p. 2016; and Second Hague Peace Conference, Convention for Pacific Settlement of Disputes, *ibid.*, p. 2220.

[7]The Statute of the Court, which entered into force on August 20, 1921, may be found in M. O. Hudson, *International Legislation* (1931), Vol. I, no. 37a, p. 530.

out any will but the will of the Soviet people."[8] In 1946, Mr. Vyshinsky similarly argued before the General Assembly of the United Nations that a question of interpreting the scope of the Charter, although admittedly legal, should not be referred to the International Court of Justice. The proponents of such a suggestion, he said, "having been defeated on the political, the moral-political plane . . . [are] trying to transfer the dispute, the whole question, to the juridical plane . . . anticipating, not without reason, that if the matter is referred to a court, even the International Court, . . . it may easily be submerged, as legal soil is very marshy. But I personally do not want the whole matter to be submerged. . . . The Soviet delegation considers that justice must indeed be secured and that it should be secured by an international court; *but this international court is here, it is yourselves, it is all of us. . . .*"[9] The issue was the right of the General Assembly to pass resolutions about the treatment of Indians in South Africa, in the light of article 2(7) of the Charter prohibiting "intervention in matters essentially within the domestic jurisdiction of any state." Soviet equation of the ultra-partisan General Assembly with a court indicates as little appreciation of impartiality, the essence of third-party decision-making, on the international as on the national plane. Most recently, the effort by Premier Khrushchev to transform the office of the Secretary General of the United Nations into a partisan triumvirate indicates a continuing preference for political solutions based on systems of power and conciliation. Nevertheless, there are indications that this Soviet philosophy is becoming less dogmatic and that the independence of Soviet tribunals is growing.[10] Whether this is a genuine change of attitude toward impartiality and whether it will be

[8]Quoted in Gsovski and Grzybowski, *Government, Law and Courts in the Soviet Union and Eastern Europe* (1957), Vol. I, p. 521. Compare the recent statement by a distinguished judge of the United States Supreme Court: "Respect and prestige do not grow suddenly; they are the products of time and experience. But they flourish when judges are independent and courageous. The court that raises its hand against the mob may be temporarily unpopular; but it soon wins the confidence of the nation." William O. Douglas, *We The Judges* (1956), p. 445.

[9]GAOR I, 2, Plenary, pp. 7–8, Dec., 1946 [emphasis added].

[10]See H. Berman, "Soviet Law and Government" (1958), 21 *Modern L. Rev.* 19, at pp. 23 ff. See also: K. Grzybowski, "Soviet Criminal Law Reform of 1958" (1960), 35 *Ind. L. J.* 125.

reflected in Soviet international policy remains to be seen.[11] Communist theoreticians are the equals of common law judges in disguising important policy changes under a thin veil of dogmatic consistency.

In any event, the search for human impartiality is a historical stream the flow of which is scarcely affected by temporary diversions. The Bible repeatedly offers stern instructions to preserve the impartiality of judges: "Thou shalt not respect persons, neither take any gift: for a gift doth blind the eyes of the wise. . . ." "Ye shall hear the small as well as the great; ye shall not be afraid of the face of man. . . ."[12] "Ye shall do no unrighteousness in judgment; thou shalt not scorn the person of the poor nor honour the person of the mighty: but in righteousness shalt thou judge thy neighbour."[13] The Codex of Justinian (3. 1. 14) provides: "Even when the judge was appointed by the Emperor, for the reason that we have set our hearts upon all suits being conducted without any suspicion or unfairness, the party who thinks that a judge is liable to suspicion can reject him and have recourse to another."[14] It is in this tradition also that the Book of Common Prayer enjoins the congregation to pray for those "who truly and *indifferently* minister justice," and that the American settlers charged in the Declaration of Independence that the British King "has made judges dependent on his will alone, for the tenure of the offices and the amount, and payment of their salaries."

It is the purpose of this paper to examine the emerging problem of maximizing the human impartiality of the international judiciary and administration in the light of the long experience of the common law. In further research it is hoped to draw on the historical experiences of other communities and legal systems.

[11]"While there are neutral countries, there are no neutral men. You would not accept a Communist administrator and I cannot accept a non-Communist administrator. I will never entrust the security of the Soviet Union to any foreigner. We cannot have another Hammarskjold, no matter where he comes from among the neutral countries." Prime Minister Khrushchev, interviewed by Walter Lippmann, *New York Herald Tribune*, April 17, 1961, p. 2, cols. 5–6.

[12]Deut. 16:19 and 1:17.

[13]Levit. 19:15.

[14]Quoted in Scott, *The Civil Law: A Translation of Enactments of Justinian*, Vol. XII.

II. HYPOTHESIS: JUDICIAL INVOLVEMENT AND JUDICIAL IMPARTIALITY

OVER A PERIOD of eight centuries the experience of the common law has grown to constitute an impressive record of the striving towards human impartiality. One approach to a classification and appreciation of this record is in terms of the principal assumptions around which the experience has developed.

One fundamental assumption is that the expectation of human impartiality is not met if the third party making the decision has, or appears to have, a personal interest in the outcome of the dispute. The roots of this assumption reach down to the general sense of the community, from which it draws sustenance and vitality. Nevertheless, the record blossoms with dissents and dialectics, not over the validity of the assumption, but over its application in specific cases. This is hardly surprising: the broader the generalization, the more general its appeal, but the more contentious its application. The essence of the hypothesis stated above has been incorporated in a United States federal statute[15] which states that: "Whenever a party to any proceeding in a district court makes and files a timely and sufficient affidavit that the judge before whom the matter is pending has a personal bias or prejudice either against him or in favor of any adverse party, such judge shall proceed no further therein, but another judge shall be assigned to hear such proceeding. . . . A party may file only one such affidavit in any case. . . ."[16]

[15]28 U.S.C. §144 (1958). The federal law is to a greater or lesser degree complemented by the laws of the various states. The New York Judicial Law, §14, provides that, "A judge shall not sit as such in, or take any part in the decision of an action, claim, matter, motion or proceeding to which he is a party or in which he has been attorney or counsel, *or in which he is interested*, or if he is related by consanguinity of the sixth degree . . ." [emphasis added]. For a discussion of state practice see: J. M. Godman, "Disqualification for Bias of Judicial and Administrative Officers" (1948), 23 *N.Y.U.L.Q.Rev.* 109; R. Slovenko, "Je Recuse: The Disqualification of a Judge" (1959), 19 *La. L. Rev.* 644.

[16]The statute applies only to federal district courts: *Millslagle* v. *Olson* (1942), 128 F.2d 1015 (8th Cir.). It is not applicable to federal courts of appeals or state courts.

The problem of applying this generalization to specifics has produced extensive litigation, and an even larger body of customary law has emerged from the voluntary, non-litigious, action of judges who have recused themselves from cases which they thought they could not hear impartially. The reasons for voluntary recusations are generally not apparent in the case reports. In *Public Utilities Commission of the District of Columbia* v. *Pollack*[17] the United States Supreme Court had to rule on the constitutionality of the fearsome practice of broadcasting music and advertising over loudspeakers to the "captive" audience in the vehicles of the District of Columbia street railway company. Mr. Justice Frankfurter recused himself for the privately stated reason that, as the only member of the court to commute regularly by bus, he had developed such intense feelings about the practice as to believe himself to be incapable of judicial impartiality. Again, in *Hoag* v. *New Jersey*[18] Mr. Justice Brennan refused to participate in a case which he had previously encountered as a judge in New Jersey.[19]

Where demands for recusation have been resisted and litigation followed, the decisions have turned on two aspects of the law: (i) who determines the truth of the facts set out in the affidavit alleging bias; and, (ii) who determines whether those facts, if true, constitute a "sufficiency of evidence" to warrant drawing the deduction of probable personal bias?

The answer to the first question has been given by the United States Supreme Court in *Berger* v. *U.S.*:[20] the facts set out in the affidavit must be accepted as true by the judge against whom the allegations are made. Though this may seem overly generous to the litigant, it is balanced by the provision that each litigant is allowed only one challenge and that barristers filing perjured affidavits may be subject to disbarment. The concession to the litigant is also justified by the undesirability of alternative solutions, namely, that the question of fact be tried by the judge against whom the allega-

17(1952) 343 U.S. 451.
18(1958) 356 U.S. 464.
19*State* v. *Hoag* (1956), 122 A.2d 628 (N.J.). Mr. Justice Brennan dissented.
20(1921) 255 U.S. 22, at p. 36.

tion is made, with or without a jury, or by a brother-judge. Either alternative would be subject to additional suspicion of prejudice and prolonged waste of judicial time.

The *Berger Case* went on, however, to say that the presiding judge (subject, of course, to appeal) does have the right to determine whether the facts alleged against him, and assumed to be true, are sufficient to establish personal bias. The judge must accept the figures given, but he is allowed to do his own arithmetic. What test should be used to establish this "sufficiency"? The Supreme Court in the *Berger Case* was unavoidably vague: the affidavit must "give fair support to the charge of a bent mind that may prevent or impede impartiality of judgment" and indicate an "objectionable inclination or disposition."[21] A more precise definition has to be sought in the specific decisions. These fall, generally, into three categories: (i) those involving the personal feelings of a judge towards the litigant; (ii) those involving a prejudgment of the merits; and, (iii) those involving a prior connection between the judge and one of the parties.[22]

It is a fair deduction from the American cases that prejudice about the law or the merits of a case does not disqualify, whereas personal prejudice against a litigant does. Inevitably, men form opinions about their work, and judges develop attitudes to the law or even to the merits of cases pending before them—opinions which are formed before or outside the litigation. Such prejudices are subject, however, to questioning by way of courtroom evidence and argumentation. The same is not true of personal prejudice, which generally concerns matters not openly at issue in the litigation. The judge's personal prejudice is therefore likely to remain unchallenged during the proceedings.

The *Berger Case* is the classic example to fall within the first classification. Here Judge Landis, who had been chosen to try a case of alleged espionage by a German-American, was quoted as

[21] *Ibid.*, at pp. 33–5.

[22] For this classification and for many of the references in this part of the paper, the author is indebted to Professor Bernard Schwartz, and particularly to his article "Disqualification for Bias in the Federal Courts" (1950), 11 *U. Pitt. L, Rev.* 415; Note (1941), 51 *Yale L. J.* 169.

saying: "One must have a very judicial mind, indeed, not to be prejudiced against the German-Americans in the country. Their hearts are reeking with disloyalty." Such a remark, the court held, indicated strong personal feelings against the class to which the defendant belonged and was sufficient to require Landis' recusation. The case is unusual, however, because its facts project so clear an image of a judge in the grip of that element of personal animosity prohibited by the statute, although the intent of the drafter appears to have been rather broader.[23] Where the prejudice is less evidently personal, the courts have given the judge the benefit of very considerable doubts. In *Henry* v. *Speer*,[24] for example, a judge who had allegedly given an opinion to the newspapers "in which practically every issue is prejudged and determined," was held to be prejudiced only over the litigious merits and therefore was allowed to conduct the case.

Politically charged litigation has involved particularly difficult questions of drawing the line between personal bias and legal precommitment. In *Loew's Inc.* v. *Cole*[25] the federal district judge had remarked at a private social gathering that there was no legal ground for an employer's refusal to pay the contractual salary of an employee merely because of the employee's refusal to testify before the House Committee on Un-American Activities. This very issue happened to be pending before him. Such a preconceived idea as to the law, not being a personal prejudice, was again held not to disqualify.[26] On the other hand, in the recent *Connelly Case*[27] the trial judge, before whom Connelly was indicted for participating in a Communist conspiracy against constitutional government, was compelled by the Court of Appeal to recuse himself on a showing that, before his appointment, he had said in a speech to the Los Angeles Lions Club that Communist leaders were "hiding behind the Bill of Rights and the Constitution" only to "destroy that very document and the government that rests upon it."[28] Also, while

[23]See Schwartz, *ibid.*, at pp. 420 and 424–5.
[24](1913) 201 Fed. 869 (5th Cir.).
[25](1950) 185 F.2d 641 (9th Cir.) Certiorari denied, 340 U.S. 954.
[26]See also *U.S.* v. *Lattimore* (1954), 125 F. Supp. 295 (D.D.C.).
[27]*Connelly* v. *U.S. Dist. Cit.* (1951), 191 F.2d 692.
[28]*Ibid.*, at pp. 694–5.

the trial was pending, he had stopped Connelly's lawyer in the courthouse and said: "I am sorry to see you getting mixed up with the Commies, Dan. They're just trying to use you."[29]

The difficulty of distinguishing the pre-trial comments in the *Berger*, *Cole*, and *Connelly* cases suggests how very thin is the line between personal prejudice and litigious preconceptions in cases involving ethnic or political "group" crimes—for the obvious reason that many such crimes of association are themselves little more than the legislative enactments of widely held personal prejudices.

Another difficult determination must be made in cases where the judge has been directly or indirectly injured by one of the parties before the litigation came before him. Does such an injury raise a presumption of biasing anger? In *Price* v. *Johnson*[30] it was held that a judge who was a director of the bank for the robbery of which the defendant was being tried need not recuse himself. The facts were not "sufficient" to establish a likelihood of personal animosity; according to the appellate court, they only charged "an impersonal prejudice, and go to the judge's background and associations rather than his appraisal of the defendant personally."[31] Where the injury is more direct, however, the presumption of bias may disqualify. Thus, where the judge is a close personal friend of the person allegedly murdered by the accused[32] or where the defendant in a motor vehicle case narrowly avoided striking the judge with his automobile,[33] another magistrate must conduct the trial.[34] On the other hand, where the injury is caused after the litigation comes before the magistrate, the defendant is not permitted to use the injury as a device to elect another judge. For example, a defendant who starts a legal action against the judge before whom his case is

[29]*Ibid.*, at p. 694. Another case of judicial *ex cathedra*-ism in court-house corridors is found in *U.S.* v. *16,000 Acres of Land* (1942), 49 F. Supp. 645, at p. 654, where the judge remarked to petitioner that he was "a pettifogger." This was held insufficient to disqualify.

[30](1942) 125 F.2d 806 (9th Cir.).

[31]*Ibid.*, at p. 811.

[32]*McKay* v. *Superior Court* (1950), 220 P. (2d) 945 (Cal.).

[33]*State* v. *Muraski* (1949), 69 A.2d 745 (N.J.).

[34]The complex subject of contempt proceedings constitutes one possible exception to this rule. Cf. *Bisignano* v. *Municipal Court of Des Moines*, 23 N.W. (2d) 523, where a judge who had been physically attacked by defendant was neverthe-

being heard may not thereby demand the judge's recusation.[35] Conversely, a judge need not recuse himself merely because one of the parties has at some time in the past done him a favour which could cause him to "lean over backwards" to prove his independence.[36] (It would be different, of course, if the effect of the favour were to give the judge a stake in the outcome of the litigation.)

Though a judge who attacks or is attacked by a party to litigation before it comes to trial obviously has established a form of prior connection with the case, the third category of personal bias situations only concerns those in which a judge has some significant prior professional nexus with the cause before him. The leading American cases on the subject are *Eisler* v. *United States*[37] and the *Connelly Case*.[38] Eisler, a self-admitted Communist, was an Austrian national resident in the United States. He was indicted for contempt of the House Un-American Activities Committee and tried before Federal District Judge Holtzoff. In his affidavit Eisler asked for Holtzoff's recusation because the Judge: (i) had previously served as Special Assistant to the Attorney General of the United States; (ii) had directly assisted "in an important capacity in advising and aiding and determining the policy, nature, scope and objectives of the investigations directed against aliens and communists which necessarily included myself"; (iii) was a close personal friend of the Director of the F.B.I.; and, (iv) had, in connection with previous duties, sponsored legislation for the deportation of alien Communists. Said the Court of Appeal: "Upon review of such an affidavit we do not hesitate to uphold the ruling of the court below that the affidavit should be stricken, for it does not establish bias and prejudice in the personal sense contemplated by the statute . . . impersonal prejudice resulting from a judge's

less allowed to preside over the contempt proceedings. Note, however, that the court suggests that the judge might properly have recused himself, even though his failure to do so was not held a fatal defect.

[35]*Allen* v. *DuPont* (1948), 75 F. Supp. 546 (D. Del.).

[36]*Green* v. *Murphy* (1958), 259 F.2d 591 (3rd Cir.).

[37](1948) 170 F.2d 273 (D.C. Cir.).

[38](1951) 191 F.2d 692 (9th Cir.).

background or experience is not, in our opinion, within the purview of the statute."[39]

This decision is based on logic which, for reasons already discussed, is tenable when employed in reference to the ordinary prejudice of an opinionated judge; it is quite inapplicable, however, to the judge whose prejudgment of the law is due to a vested professional interest in the case. The judge who has previously been involved actively in the litigation before him on behalf of one of the parties cannot be equated to the judge whose prejudices are acquired from reading the newspapers or intellectual reflection. The appearance, if not the substance, of commitment is far greater in the former instance. In the words of Judge Prettyman's dissent: "Many able and conscientious lawyers and judges—and the trial judge here involved is certainly both—have a deep and abiding conviction of their own abilities to prosecute impersonally and to judge impersonally, and to do both in the same case. But such psychological detachment is not so well established that a belief to the contrary is unreasonable. That a judge has been the prosecutor in the early stages of a particular case against a particular individual is a fact 'from which a sane and reasonable mind might fairly infer personal bias or prejudice on the part of the judge.' "[40]

A short time later, the *Connelly Case*, involving an alleged Communist conspiracy, saw Federal District Judge Carter disqualified by the Court of Appeals because among other things he had previously, as a United States attorney, helped to prosecute some of Connelly's alleged co-conspirators for contempt of Congress. The decision distinguishes the *Eisler Case* by limiting it to facts which minimize Judge Holtzoff's role in those matters connected with Eisler's prosecution. Nevertheless, the sense of justice is better satisfied by the *Connelly Case* than by the *Eisler Case*. It is also more in harmony with American practice, which frowns equally on judges' associations with one of the parties or with counsel to the parties. The United States Supreme Court bars former law clerks from appearing before the court for two years after they leave a judge's employ—a reasonable cooling off period for possible influential

[39]*Eisler* v. *U.S.*, *supra* note 37, at p. 278. [40]*Ibid.*, at pp. 282–3.

impact.[41] Similarly, judges of many state and federal circuits do occasionally disqualify themselves because of close friendship with a party or with counsel.[42] More clearly non-discretionary, however, is the rule, frequently found in state statutes, that when a judge has previously had contact with a client and his case "disqualification is universal for the obvious, but seldom articulated, reason that a judge would seldom have an open mind under such circumstances, and to sit would invite charges of corruption."[43]

If the rule is applicable to judges who previously served one of the parties as practising attorney, it is even more apposite for judges who previously served the government as departmental counsel or state's attorney: the ordinary lawyer, once he becomes a judge, is beyond the reach of his former clients; a judge may be largely, but never entirely, insulated from governmental favour or displeasure. Thus a survey of American state and federal district practice shows that "prosecutors who become judges almost invariably disqualify themselves in these situations,"[44] where the role of the prosecutor necessarily constituted an actual, and not a merely formal nexus.[45]

Mining the more modest lode of British cases reveals a basic similarity in practice as regards the three categories. The gradual broadening down from precedent to precedent has had its effect. Blackstone did not believe that a judge could ever be presumed to be partial and therefore rejected all recusation for cause.[46] British practice, however, bypassed Blackstone. As early as 1610 it was held in *Dr. Bonham's Case*[47] that judicial officers "cannot be judges, ministers and parties; judges to give sentence and judgment; ministers to make summons; and parties to have the moiety of the

[41]See J. P. Frank's excellent survey: "Disqualification of Judges" (1947), 56 *Yale L. J.* 605, at p. 621.

[42]*Ibid.*, at pp. 622 and 639.

[43]*Ibid.*, at p. 622 and statutes cited therein.

[44]*Ibid.*, at pp. 623–4. Cf. *Wilson* v. *State* (1925), 153 Tenn. 206.

[45]*Ibid.*, at p. 625. Frank points out that a U.S. Attorney General is nominally responsible for every prosecution in every federal district court but that he does not generally recuse himself if such a case reaches him after his elevation to the bench. Under such circumstances, former Attorney General Murphy did not hesitate to vote in *Schneiderman* v. *U.S.* (1943), 320 U.S. 118 and to vote *against* the department which had launched the case at a time when he headed it.

[46]Cf. *Blackstone's Comm.* Vol. III, p. 361.

[47](1610) 8 Co. Rep. 113(b), at p. 118(a); 77 E.R. 646, at p. 652.

forfeiture, and one cannot be judge and attorney for one of the parties." However, Coke's view in *Bonham's Case* was far from universally shared. Lord Ellesmere's commentary complains that the Chief Justice spoke "having no precedent for him, but many judgments against him" and that the case "possesseth a better room in the press than it deserved."[48]

By the nineteenth century English cases had firmly established the principle that "precludes a justice, who is interested in the subject matter of a dispute, from acting as a justice therein."[49] Of course, as in the American courts, there has been difficulty in measuring "interest" so as to determine when it impairs impartiality.[50] Accordingly to Lord Esher in *Eckersley* v. *Mersey Docks and Harbour Board*,[51] the rule applicable to all judges is that, "not only must they be not biassed, but that, even though it be demonstrated that they would not be biassed, they ought not to act as judges in a matter where the circumstances are such that people—not necessarily reasonable people, but many people—would suspect them of being biassed."

In *The King* v. *Sussex Justices; Ex p. McCarthy*,[52] Lord Hewart said that it is "of fundamental importance that justice should not only be done, but should manifestly and undoubtedly be seen to be done." By 1954, a British court felt constrained to warn the public and the bar that this dictum "is being urged as a warrant for quashing convictions or invalidating orders upon quite unsubstantial grounds, and, indeed, in some cases upon the flimsiest pretexts of bias. Whilst endorsing and fully maintaining the integrity of the principle reasserted by Lord Hewart, this court feels that the con-

[48]Few prognosticators could have been more wrong. Dr. Bonham's case did no less than lay the foundation for recusation *and* judicial review. Lord Ellesmere's observations are reprinted under the text in 77 E.R. at p. 652.

[49]Halsbury, *Laws of England* (3rd ed.; 1958), Vol. XXV, at p. 131.

[50]In Britain as in the United States a direct *pecuniary* interest, no matter how small, always constitutes a ground for recusation. The problem is not dealt with here because it constitutes an aspect of "interest" which is unlikely to arise in international courts and is therefore irrelevant to the analogy being attempted in this paper. See, however, *Dimes* v. *Grand Junction Canal (No. 1.)* (1852), 3 H.L. Cas. 759, 88 Rev. Rep. 330; *Reg.* v. *The Justices of Hertfordshire* (1845), 6 Q.B. 753; 66 Rev. Rep. 556.

[51][1894] 2 Q.B. 667 (C.A.), at p. 671.

[52][1924] 1 K.B. 256, at p. 259.

tinued citation of it in cases to which it is not applicable may lead to the erroneous impression that it is more important that justice should appear to be done than that it should in fact be done."[53]

Perhaps because contemporary Britain has been happily free of litigation based on ethnic or political association, there is a paucity of case law on recusation for personal, political, or ethnic bias. There are, moreover, few instances of judges "talking out of court" so as to reveal other forms of pre-judgment. In *The Queen* v. *Farrant*[54] a justice, who was also a physician, treated the victim of an assault, and tried to act as intermediary between the parties to prevent a charge being laid. He appears to have done his best to urge the parties to reach an amicable settlement. The assaulted party alleged that the judge also had predicted that he could not win in litigation. These facts are not unlike those in *Loew's, Inc.* v. *Cole*, and *Henry* v. *Speer*, discussed above, and the court, while not drawing a distinction between a personal prejudice and one going to the litigious issue, came to the same conclusion by finding no "substantial interest" on the part of Judge Farrant which would "make it likely that he would have a real bias."[55]

The British courts have also applied the same principles as those in the United States in determining whether a judge who has been injured or attacked by a party to litigation before him must be withdrawn from the case;[56] and follow an even stricter rule of excluding judges from hearing cases with which they have formed a prior professional nexus. As regards the latter category, the case of *King* v. *Essex Justices; Ex p. Perkins*[57] is something of a high-water mark. Here the judges were served by a law clerk who, being a practising solicitor, himself employed a law clerk for his firm. It was the clerk's clerk who, unknown to his principal, briefly served a client in a matter which subsequently, in the hands of another firm of solicitors, came to litigation before the justices. The court held that the justices' decision in the matter was invalid, approving, in

[53]*Reg.* v. *Camborne Justices; Ex. p. Pearce*, [1955] 1 Q.B. 41, at p. 52.
[54](1887) 20 Q.B.D. 58.
[55]*Ibid.*, at p. 61.
[56]Cf. *Price* v. *Johnston* (1942), 125 F.2d 806 (9th Cir.) with *King* v. *Justices of County Tyrone*, [1909] 2 I.R. 762.
[57][1927] 2 K.B. 475.

effect, the legal fiction that in courts, as in the feudal hierarchy, my servant's servant is my servant.[58] Moreover, where a nexus is shown, the fact that a "contaminated" judge may have been only one member of a unanimous and otherwise "uncontaminated" bench, and took no part in conducting the case or in discussing it with his fellow-judges, will not save the validity of the judgment.[59]

III. INTERNATIONAL LEGAL IMPLICATIONS OF THE COMMON LAW EXPERIENCE

THE FOREGOING analysis suggests some of the prevalent attitudes of English-speaking peoples towards the problem of human impartiality in third-party decision-making. These attitudes are far from irrelevant to international decision-making and may be summarized as follows: (1). Impartiality does not require the decision-maker to be free of revealed prejudices or opinions about the law or the issues in dispute. For example, Judge Jessup of the International Court is not—any more than Judge Frankfurter—disqualified because of the partisanship of his legal writings prior to becoming a judge. (2). Impartiality does, however, demand that the decision-maker be free of personal prejudice or hostility towards one of the parties to the dispute. Political, religious, social, economic, and cultural antagonisms fall within this classification. (3). Impartiality requires the recusation of decision-makers who previously served one of the parties to the litigation or who have established a nexus with the case. A former foreign office legal adviser should not hear cases in which he previously took a professional interest, neither should a former lawyer hear cases involving his former clients.[60] (4). Attacks

[58]See also *The King* v. *Justices of Sunderland*, [1901] 2 K.B. 357 (C.A.).

[59]*Queen* v. *Meyer* (1875), 1 Q.B. 173.

[60]Judge Jessup has, for this very reason, recused himself in proceedings before the International Court involving the Temple of Preah Vihar (*Thailand* v. *Cambodia*) with which he was previously connected as counsel. The Statute of the Court states: "No member may participate in the decision of any case in which he has previously taken part as agent, counsel, or advocate for one of the parties, . . . or in any other capacity. Any doubt on this point shall be settled by the decision of the Court." (Art. 17.) This hardly exhausts the possible grounds for recusation suggested by the common law but it raises problems of construction familiar to it.

on, or abuse of, a decision-maker by a party to the dispute do not constitute grounds for requiring him to recuse himself if they are begun after the commencement of his role. If, however, there is a record or cause of hostility between a party and a decision-maker which precedes the initiation of the process of settlement, it may require the selection of another judge. Thus, a long-standing feud between a Dayal (who frequently exercises quasi-adjudicative functions) and a Kasavubu should disqualify the former from acting in a case involving the rights of the latter; but once a Dayal has assumed his role without objection he should not be subject to disqualification by attacks on him begun at the discretion of the latter.

IV. CONCLUSION

THE DEDUCTIONS drawn from common law experience and applicable to international legal practice are necessarily modest because the common law represents no more than one of the pools of human experience from which international jurisprudence can usefully draw. A more ambitious statement is warranted only after a comparative study. Moreover, the hypothesis here analysed represents but one facet of the experience of the common law. Lacking is an examination of other assumptions about impartiality, which also grow out of the general sense of the community and are refined and specified by the cases. The experience of administrative decision-making has barely been touched. "Breadth of Standard and Administrative Impartiality"; "Security of Tenure and Impartiality"; "Varying Demands on Impartiality Imposed by Fact Determinations and Determinations of Law"—these all suggest areas where the common law has stored its riches of experience, awaiting the adventurous microscope and spade.

*Obstacles To Private Foreign Investment in Underdeveloped Countries**

By A. A. FATOUROS**

ECONOMIC DEVELOPMENT AND PRIVATE FOREIGN INVESTMENT

INTENSE CONCERN for the economic development of the world's backward areas is a phenomenon of recent date. It is founded on the universal desire of improving one's condition, a desire which is as old as humanity. But the modern advances in technology, the spread of communications, and the prevailing international political atmosphere have given to this age-old desire a new form and a new vitality. The underdeveloped countries' drive for economic development cannot realistically be dissociated from their recent political evolution which has resulted in the emergence of several new independent states. National independence provides the poorer countries with the practical means for pursuing their economic aims, on the national as well as the international scene. In fact, the desire for economic development and the related movement toward political independence go deeper. They are both manifestations of the same driving force, the same powerful desire of self-realization. National independence has been won but economic development remains to be achieved. Indeed, the full realization of the former,

*The main body of this article constitutes an expanded version of the third chapter of a study on state guarantees to foreign investors, submitted as a doctoral dissertation to the Columbia University School of Law and to be published by Columbia University Press early in 1962.

**A. A. Fatouros, U. Dipl., M.C.L., LL.M., Lecturer in Law, University of Western Ontario.

if the substance of the matter is to be considered, depends inextricably on the outcome of the drive for the latter.

Despite the close interdependence of the two movements, their secondary effects and manifestations may, and do, clash. There exist certain contradictions, some superficial, others less so, between the desire for economic development and that for national independence. Most of the present article is devoted to an examination of one set of such contradictions, namely that between the desire for economic independence, as manifested in the control and regulation of national economic affairs and the limitation of the role of foreigners in them, and the need for private foreign capital to assist in the process of development.

The availability of capital is one of the fundamental prerequisites for economic development. It is true that it is not the sole condition of development, not even the most important one. The fundamental condition is probably psychological in character: a "desire of change,"[1] a determination to achieve a higher standard of living and a willingness to alter the existing economic and social structures when they hinder economic growth. In addition to this basic condition, several other factors, beside capital, affect the rate and mode of development. In spite of such necessary qualifications, capital remains all-important.[2] Even though its availability will not by itself assure rapid economic development, its lack will certainly impede it.

In view of their poverty, the underdeveloped countries can provide by themselves only a small part of the capital which they need. An important part of their capital requirements will have to be met by the importation of capital from the developed countries. Foreign capital has played an important role in the development of several,

[1]J. K. Galbraith, "Conditions for Economic Change in Underdeveloped Countries" (1951), 33 *J. Farm Econ.* 689, at p. 694. See also D. McCord Wright, "Closing the Production Gap," in J. Daniel (ed.), *Private Investment: the Key to International Industrial Development* (New York, 1958) 39, at p. 43; C. Furtado, "Capital Formation and Economic Development" (1954), 4 *Internat. Econ. Papers* 124, reprinted in A. N. Agarwala and S. P. Singh (eds.), *The Economics of Underdevelopment* (Bombay, 1958), p. 308, at p. 315.

[2]See P. T. Bauer and B. S. Yamey, *The Economics of Underdeveloped Countries*, (Cambridge, 1957), p. 127 *et seq.*; R. Nurkse, *Problems of Capital Formation in Under-developed Countries* (Oxford, 1953), pp. 155–7; C. Kindleberger, *Economic Development* (New York, 1958), pp. 33–55.

though by no means all, of the now economically advanced countries. In the past, such capital came exclusively from private sources. Though governments had an active part in assisting the process of development, the international movements of public capital were negligible and were chiefly related to war needs. The bulk of foreign capital was invested in securities; "direct" investment played but a minor role.[3] Today, the picture has changed significantly.

Public capital, that is, capital provided to governments or private persons by foreign governments or by international agencies in the form of loans or grants,[4] plays now a most important role. In the first postwar years, public capital accounted for almost the whole of international capital movements.[5] Since then, its absolute size and its relative importance have somewhat diminished, but its over-all significance can still hardly be exaggerated. In the fiscal year ending in 1959, about $2.7 billion in loans and grants were given to underdeveloped countries by the capital-exporting countries of the non-Communist world.[6]

Private foreign investment, on the other hand, was of negligible proportions during the first postwar years, but it has been increasing in importance ever since. Up to 1955, the average annual volume of

[3]Direct investment (i.e., investment involving managerial control of the enterprise) constituted in 1913 less than 20 per cent of total British foreign investment. See Nurkse, "International Investment To-Day in the Light of Nineteenth-Century Experience" (1954), 64 *Econ. J.* 744; H. Feis, *Europe The World's Banker 1870–1914* (New Haven, 1930), pp. 22–4; A. K. Cairncross, *Home and Foreign Investment 1870–1913* (London, 1953), p. 183 *et seq.* See also United Nations, Department of Economic Affairs, *International Capital Movements During the Inter-War Period* (1949).

[4]The dichotomy of international capital into public and private is, of course, an oversimplification. In fact, three parties are normally involved: the original source of the funds, the intermediary, and the user of the funds. Each of them may be public or private. For a discussion of the related problems, see F. Pazos, "Private versus Public Foreign Investment in Under-Developed Areas," in H. S. Ellis and H. C. Wallich (eds.), *Economic Development for Latin America* (New York, 1961), p. 201.

[5]Total net export of public capital from the United States in the period 1946–52 amounted to over $34 billion, while total net private capital export amounted to about $8 billion; J. Barnérias, "International Movements of Public Long-Term Capital and Grant, 1951–1952" (1956), 5 *International Monetary Fund Staff Papers* 108, at p. 110; UN, Dept. of Economic Affairs, *The International Flow of Private Capital 1946–1952* (1954), p. 3.

[6]See, UN, Dept. of Economic and Social Affairs, *International Economic Assistance to the Less Developed Countries* (1961), p. 14 (Table II).

such investment was less than $2 billion.[7] It rose to an average of $4 billion yearly in 1955–8, and, in 1958–9, it exceeded $5 billion yearly.[8] Not all of this capital goes to the underdeveloped countries; indeed, more than half is directed to already developed countries, such as Canada or Australia. In 1958–9, for instance, only about $2 billion a year were invested in underdeveloped areas.[9] Investments in such areas are predominantly direct in form. Indirect or portfolio investment plays today a far less important role than it did in the past. Such investment, moreover, is directed chiefly to the developed countries; at the end of 1957, Canadian and western European securities accounted for over 75 per cent of total United States private portfolio.[10] Direct investment in underdeveloped countries is heavily concentrated in the extractive industries.[11] Manufacturing is second in importance; very little capital is invested in public utilities or other such basic industries.

The total of foreign, private and public, capital invested in the underdeveloped countries is insufficient to assure their development. It has been estimated that these countries will need in the next few years an additional sum of $3 to $4 billion yearly in order to achieve a minimum rate of growth.[12] Part of this sum, indeed the major part, will have to consist of public capital.[13] But it would be very

[7]See "Financing of Economic Development—The International Flow of Private Capital 1953–1955," UN Doc. E/2901, June 21, 1956, p. 7.

[8]See, UN, Dept. of Economic and Social Affairs, *The International Flow of Private Capital 1956–1958* (1959), p. 9; "Economic Development of Under-Developed Countries—International Flow of Private Capital 1959–1960," UN Doc. E/3513, June 14, 1961, (mimeo.) p. 10.

[9]See, UN Doc. E/3513, *supra* note 8, at p. 19.

[10]UN, Dept. of Economic and Social Affairs, *supra* note 8, p. 51.

[11]In 1959, total United States direct investment in underdeveloped areas amounted to about $11.2 billion, out of which over $5.3 billion (or about 47 per cent) constituted investments in the petroleum industry and about $1.6 billion (or over 14 per cent) were investments in mining and smelting. See S. Pizer and F. Cutler, *U.S. Business Investments in Foreign Countries* (U.S. Dept. of Commerce, 1960), p. 89 (Table I).

[12]For a summary of several calculations, reaching similar conclusions, see R. Asher, *Grants, Loans and Local Currencies—Their Role in Foreign Aid* (Washington, D.C., 1961), pp. 116–18. See also P. N. Rosenstein-Rodan, "International Aid for Underdeveloped Countries" (1961), 43 *Rev. Econ. & Stat.* 107, summarized in M. F. Millikan and D. L. M. Blackmer (eds.), *The Emerging Nations—Their Growth and United States Policy* (Boston, 1961), pp. 149–59.

[13]See also *infra*, text to note 148.

helpful, not only to the capital-importing countries but also to the capital-exporting states and to the international agencies faced with the task of raising the above mentioned sum, if as large as possible a part of it were contributed by private investors.

However, businessmen in the developed countries have generally shown themselves unwilling to invest in the underdeveloped areas. It is mostly a small number of large companies which invest capital in such areas. Ten corporations account for over 40 per cent of United States foreign investment, and sixty-two corporations for over 70 per cent.[14] The great majority of potential investors seem reluctant to enter the international field. The causes of this attitude are numerous and complex; no complete list or comprehensive classification is possible.[15] The countries involved differ widely from each other in culture and political conditions, as well as in the present stage and future possibilities of development. The factors limiting private foreign investment in these countries are of diverse character: economic, legal, social, and cultural. They follow no fixed hierarchical order of importance and they are largely cumulative in their effects. The total or partial elimination of a number of these limiting factors may or may not improve the rate of the flow of private capital; the remaining obstacles may in each case be sufficient to keep it at its present level. Elimination of one or more impediments is therefore a necessary but not an adequate condition for the increase of private foreign investment in the underdeveloped areas.

[14]S. Surrey, "Current Issues in the Taxation of Corporate Foreign Investment" (1956), 56 *Colum. L. Rev.* 814, at pp. 851–2, citing E. R. Barlow and I. T. Wender, *Foreign Investment and Taxation* (1955).

[15]For descriptions and discussions, see League of Nations, Special Joint Committee on Private Foreign Investment, *Conditions of Private Foreign Investment* (1946); C. Lewis, *The United States and Foreign Investment Problems* (Washington, 1948), pp. 141–67; Comment, "Point Four: A Re-examination of Ends and Means" (1950), 59 *Yale L. J.* 1277, at pp. 1286–92; M. Brandon, "Legal Deterrents and Incentives to Private Foreign Investments" (1957), 43 *Grotius Soc. Trans.* 39; B. H. Higgins, *Economic Development—Principles, Problems and Policies* (New York, 1959), pp. 572–8. See also the major surveys in this field: J. F. Gaston (ed.), *Obstacles to Direct Foreign Investment* (National Industrial Conference Board, 1951); U. S., Dept. of Commerce, *Factors Limiting U.S. Investment Abroad,* Part I: *Survey of Factors in Foreign Countries* (1953), Part II: *Business Views on the U.S. Government's Role* (1954); [Canadian] Advisory Committee on Overseas Investment, *Report* (Ottawa, 1951).

The present study deals with a few only of the factors involved. It examines in detail only one category of those factors, namely, that relating to legal regulation or measures affecting foreign business. A first section, however, deals briefly with some economic and other factors whose role cannot be ignored in a study of the present topic.

THE ECONOMIC AND SOCIAL BACKGROUND

ONE VERY IMPORTANT obstacle to private foreign investment in underdeveloped countries is the presence of competing opportunities for highly profitable investments in the already developed countries. This has been considered by some authorities as the most important single cause of the shortage in private international investment in underdeveloped areas.[16] It is evident that any businessman will prefer to invest at home or in a country similar to his own whose economic conditions and play of market forces he understands. He will invest in a country differing from his own in culture and economic structure only if he considers the difference between the local rate of profit and the one prevalent in the country in question important enough to warrant the additional efforts and risks. During the postwar period, with the exception of relatively short and rare deflationary periods, the rates of profit in most developed countries have been consistently high. Indeed, the rates of return in such countries have been so high that, combined with the financial stability and virtual absence of non-business risks which prevail there, they have attracted investors even from the underdeveloped regions.[17]

[16]Cf., e.g., Higgins, *supra* note 15, at pp. 571–2, 579–82; W. Diamond, "Economic Problems of Foreign Trade and Investment in Underdeveloped Countries" (1956), 17 *Ohio St. L. J.* 254, at p. 256. See also Nurkse, *supra* note 3, at pp. 753–4; N. S. Buchanan and H. S. Ellis, *Approaches to Economic Development* (New York, 1955), p. 345; W. Y. Elliot *et al.*, *The Political Economy of American Foreign Policy* (1955), pp. 332–3; G. Myrdal, *An International Economy* (New York, 1956), p. 110.

[17]The "capital flight" from the underdeveloped areas to the developed countries, Switzerland and the United States in particular, is a common feature of the post-war international scene. See A. I. Bloomfield, *Speculative and Flight Movements of Capital in Postwar International Finance* (Princeton, 1954); Myrdal, *Economic Theory and Underdeveloped Regions* (London, 1957), pp. 53–4.

It is true, however, that the rates of return of foreign investment during that same period have been, equally consistently, higher than those of domestic investment. The average annual rate of return for American direct foreign investment from 1946 to 1953 was 15 per cent of book value; the corresponding rate of return for domestic investments was about 10.5 per cent.[18] Considerable variations among industries may be noted. In the petroleum industry, the yield on investments abroad was, in 1951, over 24 per cent of the investments' value, while that on domestic investments was about 11.5 per cent.[19] In that same year, the return on foreign investments in manufacturing was 16 per cent, compared to about 10 per cent for domestic investments.[20] On the other hand, foreign investment in public utilities had a lower rate of return than its domestic counterpart.[21] The relative lack of response on the part of American businessmen indicates that, with the notable exception of petroleum enterprises, the existing difference between rates of return was not considered as sufficiently high.

Another important factor, which limits the amount of capital invested in underdeveloped areas and determines the particular form of the investment, is the absence of sizeable markets in such areas.[22] This phenomenon is chiefly due to the prevailing great poverty, the very small personal incomes, corresponding to low productivity and low national income; other structural factors, such as the high proportion of production for self-consumption and the absence of transportation and other facilities, as well as social and

[18]S. H. Axilrod, "Yield on U.S. Foreign Investment, 1920–1953" (1956), 38 *Rev. Econ. & Stat.* 331, at p. 333 (Table II). Similar figures, for the periods 1946–55 and 1950–5, respectively, are given by J. H. Adler, Statement in U.S. Congress, Joint Committee on the Economic Report (84th Cong., 1st Sess.), *Hearings before the Subcommittee on Foreign Economic Policy* (1955), p. 456, at pp. 458–9 and R. F. Mikesell, *Promoting United States Private Investment Abroad* (Washington, D.C., 1957), pp. 21–2. Cf. also J. F. Rippy, *Globe and Hemisphere—Latin America's Place in the Postwar Foreign Relations of the United States* (1958), pp. 73–7.

[19]Axilrod, *supra* note 18, at p. 333 (Table III).

[20]*Ibid.*

[21]Three per cent, as compared to 5.4 per cent; *ibid.*

[22]For a masterful analysis of this factor, see Nurkse, *supra* note 2, pp. 6 *et seq.*, *passim.* See also Diamond, *supra* note 6, at pp. 257–9; G. M. Meier and R. E. Baldwin, *Economic Development-Theory, History, Policy* (New York, 1957), pp. 316–18.

cultural factors, are also of importance in this connection. The effect on the size of foreign investment is evident. Prospective foreign investors will not attempt to invest in any industry producing for the local market, if the latter is too small to permit an initial industry of reasonable size as well as future expansion. The industries which can develop on the basis of existing market conditions will necessarily be of fairly small size and they probably will not be of any interest to foreign investors. Under such conditions, it may even be inappropriate to establish certain kinds of industries. Another equally important consequence is the trend toward investment in industries producing for the export market. In view of the local market's small size, foreign investors may prefer to avoid investments in manufacturing industries producing for local consumption and concentrate on extractive industries, such as mining or petroleum extraction, or on certain export-directed agricultural enterprises, such as plantations of coffee, tea, or cocoa.[23]

A third serious impediment to private foreign investment in underdeveloped countries is the lack of certain basic facilities, such as railways, roads, or electric power.[24] This is the cause of major bottlenecks in such economies. Lack of the means of transportation results in insufficient communication between regions of the same country or between neighbouring countries and, ultimately, in economic as well as cultural stagnation.[25] The lack of electrical power and other kinds of energy, due to the inadequate develop-

[23]The description applies to the initial static conditions. In fact, however, conditions change and markets do expand; this may be considered as the chief characteristic of a developing economy. Under such conditions and with the possible added inducement of government measures, foreign investors might well find it profitable to invest in manufacturing for the local market.

[24]Cf. the data and observations in V. V. Bhatt, "Employment and Capital Formation in Underdeveloped Economies" (1958), 11 *Economia Internazionale* 121, at pp. 124–6.

[25]It is highly significant that in most regions of recent settlement the industries which attracted large amounts of foreign capital and which thus grew rapidly at the very start of the regions' development were those related to transportation, especially the railways. See L. H. Jenks, "Railroads as an Economic Force in American Development" (1944), 4 *J. Econ. Hist.* 1, reprinted in F. C. Lane and J. C. Riemersma (eds.), *Enterprise and Secular Change* (Homewood, Ill., 1953), p. 161. But the railroad did not have the same effect everywhere, e.g., in India; cf. Jenks, "British Experience with Foreign Investments" (1944), 4 *J. Econ. Hist. Supp.* 68, at pp. 75–6. And cf. Nurkse, *supra* note 16, at pp. 749–50; Feis, *supra* note 3, at pp. 27–8.

ment of existing sources, is another bottleneck of the same order.[26] The absence of such facilities means to the investor an important increase in the overhead cost of his operations, since he has to provide for himself many of the basic facilities he needs.

Other problems in underdeveloped regions are related to the lack of some categories of personnel whose direct or indirect co-operation is essential for the effective operation of the foreign investor's enterprise. There is a general scarcity of skilled labour and there are few trained persons who can be used in higher managerial positions,[27] while the use of aliens, even apart from possible legal difficulties, is not always possible or appropriate. The state of public administration, on whose smooth and efficient functioning depends the development of both the private and the public sectors of the economy, is also in most cases far from satisfactory. The administrative machinery in underdeveloped countries often functions on the basis of outdated principles, too rigid in some respects and too loose in others. It is generally inefficient and sometimes, though not as frequently as it is often believed in advanced countries, open to bribery and the exercise of influence. Banking and credit facilities are often inadequate, too, and the related institutions are not always adequately developed.

Political instability is another impediment of major importance.[28] The political situation of poverty-ridden countries in Southeast Asia, Latin America, or the Middle East is a function of their economic and social condition. Several of these countries have only

[26]For some interesting studies of the possible economic effects of the development of new sources of energy, such as atomic energy and solar or geothermic energy, see UN, Dept. of Economic and Social Affairs, *New Sources of Energy and Economic Development* (1957); *ibid., Economic Applications of Atomic Energy: Power Generation and Industrial and Agricultural Uses* (1957); B. C. Netschert and S. H. Schurr, *Atomic Energy Applications with Reference to Underdeveloped Countries* (Baltimore, 1957).

[27]On this point, see UN, Economic Commission for Asia and the Far East, "Fields of Economic Development Handicapped by Lack of Trained Personnel in ECAFE Countries" (1950), 1 *Econ. Bull. for Asia & the Far East* 40; UN, Dept. of Economic and Social Affairs, *Management of Industrial Enterprises in Under-Developed Countries* (1958).

[28]Cf. the recent study of J. J. Spengler, "Economic Development: Political Preconditions and Political Consequences" (1960), 22 *J. Politics* 387. For a recent general survey and interpretation, see G. A. Almond and J. S. Coleman (eds.) *The Politics of the Developing Areas* (Princeton, 1960).

recently acquired their independence. Others, while nominally independent for a longer period, have until recently been ruled by totalitarian factions, often subservient to foreign interests. Their politics are governed by a reaction against their previous condition. But they have not yet found the form and substance of their political régimes and their peoples have yet to learn the techniques and limitations of self-government. Their emergence as political units coincided with the deep division of the world into opposed "blocs"; the "cold war" has contributed to the political difficulties and confusion already existing in these states. As a consequence, the political climate in underdeveloped countries is today stormy and unpredictable. Not only governments and parties but political régimes as well are rapidly changing with consequent effects on the legal regulation of these countries' economic affairs. Economic underdevelopment greatly contributes to the persistence of political instability though it is not the sole factor affecting it.

Closely related to their political instability and partly due to the same causes is the underdeveloped countries' economic and financial instability. It is chiefly a consequence of their underdevelopment, of their political situation, and of world economic and financial conditions.[29] Its importance as a deterrent of foreign investment is evident. Financial instability in the capital-importing countries is the main reason for the predominance of direct investment, since portfolio investment is dependent on stable financial conditions. The low levels of direct investment, as well, are in large part due to the persistence of such instability. We shall deal later with one of its most important effects, namely the imposition of exchange control and restrictions.

[29]Especially their dependence on the export of primary products, whose prices are subject to wide fluctuations. Cf. J. Viner, "Stability and Progress: The Poorer Countries' Problem," in D. Hague (ed.), *Stability and Progress in the World Economy* (1958), p. 41, at p. 59 *et seq.*; Diamond, *supra* note 16, at p. 262; R. Blough, "The Role of Government in Promoting Economic Stability," in L. D. White (ed.) *The State of the Social Sciences* (Chicago, 1956), p. 353, at pp. 360–1. See also UN, Dept. of Economic Affairs studies, *Relative Prices of Exports and Imports of Underdeveloped Countries* (1949); *Instability in Export Markets of Underdeveloped Countries* (1952); *Commodity Trade and Economic Development* (1954), and *World Economic Survey 1958*, pp. 17–176 (1959). But see the critical comments of S. May, "Folklore and Fact About Underdeveloped Areas" (1955), 33 *Foreign Affairs* 212.

Finally, a major impediment which underlies many minor ones is the cultural difference between the prospective investors and the peoples of the underdeveloped areas. It has been noted that "foreign business investment is not always a happy form of encounter between different civilizations."[30] The cultural patterns in most underdeveloped countries are, in varying degrees, dissimilar to the western European pattern, which prevails in the developed countries. On the other hand, a strong western influence has been felt in virtually all non-western countries, ever since their first contacts with the West, intensified by their extensive colonization by it and their contemporary drive for economic development.[31] Still, adjustment to an environment significantly foreign to western mentality remains a difficult task for the average foreign investor who is, after all, but the average western businessman.[32]

One can do little more than enumerate these obstacles. Their main common characteristic is that they do not relate specifically to private foreign investment. They affect it to the same extent, more or less, that they influence other manifestations of the economic and political life in the underdeveloped countries. Generally, these obstacles are not due to direct governmental action. They are manifestations of the conditions prevailing there and of the very fact of economic underdevelopment.

It is difficult to propose any concrete measures for elimination of such problems. The average foreign investor can affect them only to a small extent. He may adapt his products and techniques to local conditions, when this is possible; he may provide himself with the necessary basic facilities for the operation of his enterprise, if his investment is important or profitable enough. Governments, espe-

[30]Nurkse, *supra* note 16, at p. 752. See also W. G. Friedmann and G. Kalmanoff (eds.), *Joint International Business Ventures* (New York, 1961), pp. 274–7.

[31]Cf. the interesting observations of N. R. Keddie, "Western Rule versus Western Values" (1959), *Diogenes* no. 26, 71. See also S. P. Hayes, "Personality and Culture Problems of Point IV," in B. F. Hoselitz (ed.) *The Progress of Underdeveloped Areas* (Chicago, 1952), p. 203, at pp. 224–5.

[32]The predominance of the corporate form in foreign investment does not significantly change this picture. Corporate enterprises may even be more rigid than natural persons in their reactions to unfamiliar conditions. It is certainly true, on the other hand, that large corporations are in a position to employ people familiar with the countries to which they direct their investments.

cially those of the capital-importing countries, can be more effective. They can offer tax exemptions or other arrangements, thus effectively raising the investment's profit rate; they can improve their own administrative services and provide training for skilled workers and technicians; and they can affect, through their fiscal policies, their countries' financial situation, though not to the point of total control. In most cases, economic development itself constitutes the only really effective solution. We are thus confronted with another vicious circle, or rather a group of vicious circles. Each of them separately may be broken by governmental or other action. How to break all of them at the same time, as is necessary, constitutes the main problem not only of foreign private investment but of economic development itself.

THE INVESTMENT CLIMATE IN UNDERDEVELOPED COUNTRIES

A SECOND CATEGORY of obstacles to private foreign investment in the underdeveloped countries consists of those sometimes classified under the general heading of "investment climate."[33] For present purposes, this term should be understood as referring to the general attitude in a given country toward foreign investment, chiefly as expressed in the relevant legal regulations. Many elements of diverse character contribute to the formation of a country's investment climate. The use, however, of a single term is more than a matter of convenience. It suggests the underlying unity in the origin and functions of these various elements.

A country's investment climate depends closely, though not solely, on positive or negative action on the part of the governments of capital-importing states. Governmental interference in a country's economy is not a new idea, nor is it a practice confined to under-

[33]The term is commonly employed in a number of related meanings, differing from each other in their inclusiveness. The meaning here adopted includes all factors affecting foreign investors chiefly in a legal form and neither purely economic nor purely psychological in character. For similar use of the term, see Diamond, *supra* note 16, at p. 263; M. Brandon, *supra* note 15, at pp. 39, 41, and *passim.*

developed areas. In fact, the question of state interference is one of degree only. It is true, nonetheless, that, in the non-Communist world, there is a stronger tendency toward extensive interference by the state in the underdeveloped than in most of the developed countries. This should be attributed to the very fact of their underdevelopment. Economic history is quite instructive in this connection. In all the now developed countries, governments had to intervene extensively in the economy during the initial stages of their economic development, precisely in order to make such development possible.[34]

Thus, the conditions today prevailing in the underdeveloped countries make it necessary for their governments to undertake a wide range of functions. They have to provide the lacking basic facilities, to substitute for reluctant or missing entrepreneurs in founding new industries,[35] and to protect the weaker classes from exploitation. In the developed countries, some of the corresponding functions belong to the private sector, while others are exercised by the government through indirect measures, which cannot be very effective in less developed economies.

The ultimate synthesis of all state measures of interference in a given country is the national plan, which provides a classification of particular measures and partial objectives. Far from being a peculiarity of underdeveloped countries, national planning is to be

[34]For a theoretical statement of the wider issues involved, see J. Stone, "The Myths of Planning and Laissez-Faire: A Re-orientation" (1949), 18 *Geo. Wash. L. Rev.* 1. See also the historical and theoretical studies in H. G. H. Aitken (ed.), *The State and Economic Growth* (New York, 1959). And cf. J. B. Brebner, "Laissez Faire and State Intervention in Nineteenth-Century Britain" (1948), 8 *J. Econ. Hist. Supp.* 59; H. G. Aubrey, "The Role of the State in Economic Development" (1951), 41 *Amer. Econ. Rev. Papers & Proceedings* 266–9; A. Gerschenkron, "Economic Backwardness in Historical Perspective," in Hoselitz, *supra* note 31, p. 3; W. T. Easterbrook, "State Control and Free Enterprise in Their Impact on Economic Growth," *ibid.*, at p. 60; J. Baster, "Development and the Free Economy—Some Typical Dilemmas" (1954), 7 *Kyklos* 1; Spengler, *supra* note 28.

[35]The weakness of the private sector in many underdeveloped economies is one of the chief reasons for the high degree of state intervention. Cf. Baster, *supra* note 34; D. Krivine, "Private Enterprise in an Underdeveloped Economy" (1959), 30 *Polit. Q.* 379; R. S. Bhambri, "Myth and Reality About Private Enterprise in India" (1960), 12 *World Politics* 186; and cf. *contra*, Bauer and Yamey, *supra* note 2, at pp. 82–112. For an interesting description of the conditions prevailing in some underdeveloped areas see, S. Tax, *Penny Capitalism* (Smithsonian Institution Publ.; Washington, D.C., 1953).

found, with wide variations as to the form and extent of the related measures, in most modern states. Indeed, its main tools, such as the national accounts, the national budget, or the input-output analysis, have been created and perfected in the developed countries of the non-Communist world. The necessity of planning for the underdeveloped countries can hardly be disputed. It is based on the need for rational allocation of the scarce resources available, on the basis of as precise as possible an estimate of existing needs and possibilities and the establishment of priorities. Planning is an essential prerequisite for the rapid development to which all poorer nations aspire today.[36] Its importance as such is now well recognized by the developed countries. Most recently, in the comprehensive programme of economic assistance for international development presented by the Kennedy administration in the United States, it is provided that the formulation of a development programme by the capital-receiving country will be a condition for assistance. Other direct and indirect methods are also to be used to promote development of responsible programming.[37]

State measures affecting private foreign investment are taken in response to a number of causes which will be examined in more detail when each particular variety of measures is studied. At this point, two general categories of such measures may be distinguished on the basis of the relation of their objectives to foreign investment. The first one consists of measures relating specifically to foreign investors, whose activities they are intended to control or regulate; such is the case of screening requirements, or of restrictions on the ownership of enterprises. This is also the case with measures which are directly discriminatory against the foreign investor. The second category is composed of measures whose objectives are general, that is, relate to both foreign and domestic investors, but which either affect foreign investors more than domestic ones (as in the case of exchange restrictions) or affect both to the same extent but are of

[36]Cf. the strong argumentation in the same sense in Myrdal's *Beyond the Welfare State* (New Haven, 1960), p. 121 and *passim*. See also, J. A. Mayobre, "Global Programming as an Instrument of Economic Development Policy," in Ellis and Wallich, *supra* note 4, at p. 29.

[37]See U.S., Dept. of State, *An Act for International Development* (Dept. of State Publ. 7205; June, 1961), p. 12.

vital importance to all investors (as in the case of expropriation or of taxation measures).

It does not seem likely that state interference by itself is the chief cause of an unfavourable investment climate. State interference can work both ways and few investors have ever been heard to complain about interference favourable to their interests. It is rather the particular quality of state interference today that prospective foreign investors find objectionable. The chief cause for this quality lies in the general attitude of the peoples in underdeveloped countries toward foreign interference in their political and economic affairs. The countries in question were, until very recently, under western domination. Many of them, in particular those in Asia and Africa, were colonial dependencies of western powers. Even where national independence nominally existed, western interests clearly dominated in the economic sphere and, indirectly, in the political one as well.

Since the first decade of our century, gradually, at first, and then, especially after the Second World War, with increasing speed, what has been called a "great awakening" has taken place. Its chief manifestation has been the emergence of a great number of new states into political independence. On a deeper level, it is expressed by a desire for liberation from foreign influences and the assertion of national autonomy in the economic, political, and even cultural spheres. This movement is usually referred to by the name of "nationalism," but one should be careful not to confuse it with the "nationalism" of European states in the nineteenth century. The contemporary brand of nationalism is much more openly economic in its origin and manifestations than its western counterpart. Moreover, it expresses a strong feeling of resentment; it is a reaction against earlier situations and conditions. It may be that the reaction is excessive, and that it is directed against certain features which are now declining in the western countries. Still, it is an attitude which one cannot condemn offhand as unjustified. Furthermore, such nationalism is not solely (and even not chiefly) a negative attitude. At present, it is the strongest of the integrating forces operative in the underdeveloped countries. The success of their development policies depends upon it as much as that of their struggles for liberation did. Nationalist feelings may thus provide some of the incentives and other conditions for economic development, which are inadequate or lacking in the underdeveloped countries today.[38]

Nationalism is generally expressed by the distrust of foreign investors. Foreign investment has often been associated in the past with political and economic control of the capital-importing state.[39] Sometimes investors actively contributed to the creation of these conditions, though, in most instances, they only took advantage of the existing situation.[40] However changed the situation might be today, past experience cannot easily be forgotten or ignored. Even under present-day conditions, the size and power of some of the internationally operating modern corporations, as well as the open support afforded to them by their governments, strengthen the distrust and suspicion already present in the minds of the peoples and governments of the underdeveloped countries.

A final observation should be made at this point. The conditions we are studying constitute, for the foreign investors, "non-business-risks," that is to say, risks far beyond those which the average businessman regards as normal. This qualification does not add

[38]This idea has been stated in a variety of ways by several writers, but it has yet to receive an appropriately thorough and extensive treatment. See, e.g., Wallich, "Some Notes Towards a Theory of Derived Development," Paper presented at the Third Meeting of Central Bank Technicians of the American Continent, (1952), reprinted in Agarwala and Singh (eds.), *supra* note 1, p. 189, at p. 191; H. W. Singer, "Obstacles to Economic Development" (1953), 20 *Social Research* 10, at p. 22; H. Myint, "An Interpretation of Economic Backwardness" (1954), 7 *Oxford Econ. Papers* 132, reprinted in Agarwala and Singh (eds.), *supra* note 1, p. 93, at pp. 131–2; M. J. Levy, "Some Social Obstacles to 'Capital Formation' in 'Underdeveloped Areas,'" in M. Abramovits (ed.), *Capital Formation and Economic Growth* (Princeton, 1955), p. 441, at pp. 483–4; A. Bonné, "Towards a Theory of Implanted Development in Underdeveloped Countries" (1959), 9 *Kyklos* 1, at p. 17; R. Bendix, "A Study of Managerial Ideologies" (1957), 5 *Econ. Devel. & Cultural Change* 118, at p. 128; W. H. Nicholls, "Accommodating Economic Change in Underdeveloped Countries" (1959), 49 *Amer. Econ. Rev. Papers & Proceedings* 156–8. And cf. Myrdal, *supra* note 36, at pp. 200–25.

[39]For a recent survey of past and present conditions, see J. P. Nichols, "Hazards of American Private Investment in Underdeveloped Countries" (1960), 4 *Orbis* 174.

[40]Myrdal, *supra* note 17, at p. 55 *et seq.* makes the valid point that the increase of international inequalities brought about by colonial "exploitation" was not due to any "sinister design" on the part of foreign investors or colonial administrators. According to him, "colonialism meant primarily only a strengthening of all the forces in the markets which anyhow were working towards internal and international inequalities." *Ibid.*, p. 60. See also Higgins, *supra* note 15, at pp. 345–83.

anything to our picture of the factors themselves; it does give us, however, an insight into the prospective investors' mentality. The investors' criteria are generally the habits and conventions of their own economies. Extensive interference and an unfriendly public attitude are risks which the investors are not willing to undertake without added inducement. However correct or realistic, this is a point of view which should be kept in mind when discussing the investors' opinions on their own interests and on the problems of foreign investment.

THE "SCREENING" OF FOREIGN INVESTMENT

ONE OF THE SITUATIONS sometimes cited as constituting an obstacle to private foreign investment in underdeveloped countries is the imposition by these countries of restrictions or conditions on the entry of foreign capital. Typically, such restrictions take the form of "screening":[41] in order to import his capital, the prospective investor needs the prior approval of the competent government body to which he submits his plans and which reaches its decision on the basis of considerations of general economic policy. Lately, this practice has assumed in many countries a slightly different form, closely related to the granting of legal guarantees to foreign investors. In these countries the importation of foreign capital is left nominally free and no approval of the capital-receiving state's government is mandatory. On the other hand, if such approval is granted, certain legal guarantees and/or privileges regarding such matters as taxation and exchange restrictions are granted along with it. Thus, the approval of the capital-importing state becomes necessary in substance, even if not in form.

The requirement of approval, in whatever form, is founded on a number of considerations of economic policy. Perhaps the most important and certainly the most widely found is the concern over the condition of the capital-importing country's balance of pay-

[41]For a recent survey of screening procedures and criteria, see UN Doc. A/AC.97/5/Rev. 1, Dec. 27, 1960, pp. 46–60.

ments.[42] The governments of such countries seek to assure themselves that the foreign capital to be imported will not ultimately have an adverse effect on their balance-of-payments position. They tend to favour the establishment of enterprises contributing to an expansion of exports or to the limitation of imports and they pay particular attention to the amount of foreign exchange required in the future for the remittance of interest and dividends and for possible repatriation of the capital invested or for imports necessary to the enterprise's operation. A second objective of screening relates to the avoidance of excessive concentration of foreign investment in a few fields. Such concentration of productive capital within a poor and capital-hungry economy might well create difficult long-range problems.[43] More generally, control over the entry and direction of capital is an indispensable condition for the operation of national economic planning. Finally, screening may be used to exclude foreign investors from certain fields of the economy,[44] to avoid the possible inflationary effects of foreign investment, or to pursue any other objectives deemed appropriate by the capital-importing country's government. The desirability of such objectives cannot, of course, be evaluated in the abstract, since it depends on the conditions obtaining in each particular country.

The practice of screening has sometimes been blamed by prospective investors for contributing seriously to the shortage of private international investment. Its removal has been advocated as a necessary precondition for the increase of such investments.[45] The extent,

[42]Balance-of-payments difficulties also account in large part for another important obstacle to private foreign investment, namely, exchange control, on which see *infra.*

[43]See, H. W. Singer, "The Distribution of Gains between Investing and Borrowing Countries" (1950), 40 *Amer. Econ. Rev. Papers & Proceedings* 473. See also Nurkse, *supra* note 2, at pp. 24–31; Myrdal, *supra* note 16, at p. 99 *et seq.*; P. A. Baran, *The Political Economy of Growth* (New York, 1957), p. 178 *et seq.*; Mayobre, *supra* note 36, at p. 30. The matter is in dispute; cf. *contra,* E. G. Collado, "Private U.S. Direct Investment Abroad," in *International Banking and Foreign Trade* (1956), p. 180, at p. 183 *et seq.*; and, by direct implication, S. Pizer and F. Cutler, *U.S. Investments in the Latin American Economy* (U.S. Dept. of Commerce, 1957), pp. 3–26 and *passim.* See also *infra,* text to note 146.

[44]Cf. *infra.*

[45]See, e.g., International Chamber of Commerce, *Fair Treatment for International Investments. International Code* (I.C.C. Brochure no. 129; 1949) Appendix, p. 19; Collado, *supra* note 43, at p. 191; Brandon, *supra* note 33, at p. 51.

however, to which screening affects the volume of foreign capital invested in underdeveloped areas is open to grave doubts. It is true that in some cases the criteria in effect express not only excessive nationalistic attitudes but also a desire to protect existing uneconomic or privileged domestic industries. Furthermore, screening sometimes results in the establishment of a governmental bureaucracy which may be to some extent antagonistic to foreign investors. The latter complain that screening authorities are generally rigid and sometimes arbitrary in their application of the relevant regulations; their inquiries into the projected enterprises' plans and prospects are detailed to the point of absurdity and their standards of valuation of such capital assets as machinery and patents are arbitrary and detrimental to the investors' interests.[46] There is a familiar ring to these complaints, for they are voiced in many instances of contact between private business and regulatory public authorities. Even though such charges may in several instances be justified, they indicate the need for improving rather than totally eliminating the practice of screening.[47]

From a legal viewpoint, the practice's lawfulness in international law cannot be contested.[48] Furthermore, screening has generally no adverse effects on the individual investors' interests. Before its admission into a country, foreign capital is not committed in any way; once it is admitted, it generally ceases to be affected by the conditions of its entry.[49] "Rejected" capital suffers no loss from its

[46]See, e.g., L. Cutler, Address, in American Society of International Law, *First Investment Law Conference* (mimeo.; 1956), p. 10, at pp. 12–18.

[47]Note, however, that the two demands are partly contradictory: more "flexibility" of the administrative authorities might well be construed as a grant of arbitrary powers, while the provision of special procedures to eliminate the element of arbitrariness may result in increased "rigidity."

[48]Screening may be considered as coming under the general rules allowing states to impose any restrictions they see fit on the entry and residence of aliens; C. C. Hyde, *International Law* (rev. ed.; Boston, 1945), Vol. I, p. 216 *et seq*.; G. Hackworth, *Digest of International Law* (1942), Vol. III, pp. 549–52, 732–4; and cf. Brandon, *supra* note 33, at p. 51. A. Roth, *The Minimum Standard of International Law Applied to Aliens* (Leiden, 1949), p. 46, holds that "excessive use of the discretionary power of a state in this matter" would constitute an "act against international comity," but he does not give any indication as to the concrete legal effects.

[49]Screening may however be harmful to the investors when it relates to the entry of additional capital to be invested in an already established enterprise. Denial of entry in such a case may be highly damaging to the enterprise. This is a special case and special provision can be made for it in the relevant regulations.

rejection, except perhaps for the minor expenses of preliminary surveys. There is then considerable substance to the argument that screening is "probably desirable from the standpoint of the foreign investor," since it carries with it the assurance that the investor has successfully met the capital-importing country's public policy requirements as well as certain safeguards and possibly privileges.[50]

RESTRICTIONS ON THE ENTRY OF FOREIGN CAPITAL

THE PRACTICE of screening is as a rule closely related to the imposition of restrictions on the entry of foreign capital, either into certain specified fields of the economy or into the country as a whole. Such restrictions are usually imposed by legislation, but they sometimes may result indirectly from the consistent policies of screening authorities. Some of these restrictions are imposed for reasons of national security and have little to do with foreign investment. For instance, in many states the acquisition of real property near the state's borders or coasts is forbidden to aliens.[51] This restriction may affect foreign investors only if they are exploiting or intend to exploit natural resources located in such territories. Such restrictions scarcely, if at all, affect the country's investment climate.

In most underdeveloped countries—as well as in most developed ones, though we are not dealing with them here—there exist today certain additional restrictions which are directed specifically against foreign investment. In large part such restrictions express the deep distrust toward foreign investors which, as we have noted, prevails in many such countries. Control over a country's key industries entails a significant measure of influence over the operations of its whole economy. It is understandable that this may be found inadmissible by governments which, while valuing highly their country's independence, still feel rather insecure about it. Moreover, certain industries, such as public utilities, offer ample opportunities for

[50]Mikesell, *supra* note 18, at p. 45.

[51]This is the case, for instance, in Greece, Japan, and several Latin American states; see UN Doc., *supra* note 41, at pp. 156, 166. See also *ibid.*, at pp. 150–61, for an elaborate survey of restrictions and exclusions relating to land and to natural resources.

exploitation of the public, under the conditions obtaining in underdeveloped countries. Governments, therefore, may wish to exclude foreign investors from such industries, since they often cannot exercise the same measure of control over aliens that they can over their own nationals.

Such restrictions, however, often seek to achieve not the total exclusion of aliens but the increased participation of local capital in foreign-financed enterprises. Such participation is useful to the capital-importing country, because it facilitates the full integration of such enterprises in the local economy and it promotes more effectively the transmission of technical and managerial skill and know-how.[52] These purposes are deemed by the capital-importing countries important enough to offset certain possible disadvantages of local participation in ownership.

The lawfulness of restrictions of this type under international law is well-settled.[52] It is well accepted in international law that a state has exclusive competence to regulate all matters pertaining to the acquisition and transfer of property within its territory as well as to determine the conditions for the exercise in it of the natural or legal persons' economic activities. It is not unlawful for it to require that no foreign-owned enterprises operate in certain industries or that certain pursuits are open to its nationals only. *A fortiori*, it may require that nationals own a part of such enterprises.

In most instances, the ownership of a minority share by nationals is accepted as sufficient to permit the establishment of a foreign-financed enterprise. In India, where a government policy statement of 1948 provides that, with respect to all industrial undertakings, "as a rule, the major interest in ownership and effective control should always be in Indian hands," it is further provided that "power will be taken to deal with exceptional cases in a manner calculated to serve the national interest."[54] In fact, several enter-

[52]See League of Nations Special Joint Committee on Private Foreign Investment, *supra* note 15, at p. 14; and see now, Friedmann and Kalmanoff, *supra* note 30, at pp. 129–32 and *passim*. A thorough survey of measures requiring or encouraging such participation is found in UN Doc., *supra* note 41, at pp. 76–95.

[53]Cf., e.g., Hyde, *supra* note 48, at p. 650 *et seq.*; Hackworth, *supra* note 48, at pp. 612–19; Brandon, *supra* note 33, at p. 51.

[54]Government of India Resolution on Industrial Policy, of April 6, 1948; UN, Dept. of Economic Affairs, *Foreign Investment Laws and Regulations of the Countries of Asia and the Far East* (hereinafter cited UN, *Investment Laws*)

prises in which aliens own a majority share have been allowed to operate.[55] In Pakistan, a policy statement in 1948 provided that local nationals "should ordinarily be given the option to subscribe at least 51 per cent of all classes of share capital and debentures" in a number of specified industries, while "with regard to other industries, an opportunity should normally be given to Pakistan nationals to subscribe at least 30 per cent of all classes of share capital and debentures."[56] From 1947 to June, 1949, thirty-four foreign companies were allowed to issue capital in Pakistan; in twenty-three of them no Pakistani capital participated and only in three out of the remaining eleven had Pakistani capital a majority share.[57] Since 1954, foreign investors are permitted to own up to 60 per cent of enterprises operating in the more restricted category of industries.[58] Government policies favouring the participation of local nationals in the ownership of foreign-controlled enterprises have resulted in the creation of jointly-owned undertakings in several other countries, such as Burma, Turkey, and Chile.[59]

Regardless of the existence of general requirements on participation of nationals in the ownership of local enterprises, there exist in most countries restrictions on the entry of aliens and foreign capital in a number of particular fields, mainly those of mining and petroleum extraction,[60] transportation, public utilities, and banking and insurance.[61] In Columbia, for instance, aliens may have only a

(1951), p. 15; U.S., Dept. of Commerce, *Investment in India* (1953), p. 107; R. A. Narayanan, "India," in W. G. Friedmann and R. C. Pugh (eds.), *Legal Aspects of Foreign Investment* (hereinafter cited *Legal Aspects*) (Boston, 1959), p. 249, at pp. 256–7.

55See, Friedmann and Kalmanoff, *supra* note 30, at p. 194.

56The Government of Pakistan Statement of Industrial Policy of April 2, 1948; UN, *Investment Laws*, p. 56. The regulations were amended in 1954; cf. *infra* note 58.

57UN, *Investment Laws*, p. 57; U.S., Dept. of Commerce, *Investment in Pakistan* (1954), pp. 54–5.

58See, UN Doc. E/2901, June 21, 1956, Appendix 17; K. M. Ishaque, "Pakistan," in *Legal Aspects*, p. 397, at p. 404.

59See, Friedmann and Kalmanoff, *supra* note 30, at pp. 195–6, 197; UN, Dept. of Economic and Social Affairs, *Foreign Capital in Latin America* (hereinafter cited as UN, *Foreign Capital*) (1955), p. 65.

60For a thorough survey and analysis of restrictions in these fields, see UN, Office of Legal Affairs, *Survey of Mining Legislation with Special Reference to Asia and the Far East* (Bangkok, 1957).

61For a general discussion and description of such measures, see UN Doc., *supra* note 41, at pp. 150–61.

minority share in the ownership of enterprises engaged in air transport or coastal shipping.[62] In Burma, the participation of foreign investors in public utilities or in enterprises engaged in the exploitation of the country's natural resources is limited by the constitution to a minority share.[63] Finally, in several countries, certain fields are controlled by the state and the entry of private investors, domestic as well as foreign, in them is severely limited.[64] In several of the Latin American states, for instance, there exist state petroleum monopolies of varying strictness; this is the case, for example, in Chile,[65] in Bolivia,[66] in Brazil,[67] and in Mexico.[68] In India, shipbuilding, banking, mining, petroleum extraction, coastal shipping, and several other industries are under government control, though private investors, domestic or foreign, may be admitted under certain conditions.[69] In Korea, as well, by virtue of the constitution of 1948, extensive areas of the economy are under state control.[70]

It is now possible to assess more clearly the importance of restrictions on the ownership of enterprises by aliens as a deterrent to private foreign investment. Provisions of this sort may affect unfavourably the interests of foreign investors when they require majority participation or effective control of the enterprise by local nationals. Even then, several foreign investors have found it profitable to operate in underdeveloped countries under such conditions, relying either on the continuing need for the services they provide

[62]See UN, *Foreign Capital*, p. 71; U.S. Dept. of Commerce, *Investment in Colombia* (1953), p. 13; G. Kalmanoff and R. Bernal Salamanca, "Colombia," in *Legal Aspects*, p. 169, at pp. 174–5.

[63]Exceptions are possible when provided by statute. See, U Than Aung, "Burma," in *Legal Aspects*, pp. 93–4; UN, *Investment Laws*, pp. 1–2; UN Doc., *supra* note 58, Appendix 11–12.

[64]For a survey, see UN Doc., *supra* note 41, at pp. 161–66.

[65]O. Aramayo, "Chile," in *Legal Aspects*, p. 135, at p. 150; UN, *Foreign Capital*, p. 67.

[66]UN, *Foreign Capital*, p. 46.

[67]F. E. Nattier, "Brazil," in *Legal Aspects*, p. 77, at p. 82; UN, *Foreign Capital*, pp. 19, 57.

[68]E. Hidalgo, "Mexico," in *Legal Aspects*, p. 355, at pp. 356–7; UN, *Foreign Capital*, pp. 19, 115–17.

[69]See, Government of India Resolution on Industrial Policy, of April 6, 1948, and statement of the Prime Minister on the participation of foreign capital in industry, of April 6, 1949.

[70]See, K. L. Koh, "Korea," in *Legal Aspects*, p. 334, at pp. 335–41.

or on a number of legal arrangements, such as management contracts, which permit them to retain effective control over the operation of the enterprise.[71] As has been noted, however, majority participation of nationals is not often required in fact; when it is, special arrangements and individual exceptions are often allowed.

Requirements for minority participation are more common, but it is highly doubtful whether they should be regarded as major deterrents to foreign investment. Foreign investors sometimes tend to exaggerate the importance of the disadvantages of local participation in ownership, pointing to the possibility of friction between the partners and the undesirability of sharing the enterprise's profits. It is true that, in certain cases, collaboration with local businessmen may be inadvisable, because of the political climate in the particular country or the character of the industry involved. In many other cases, however, such collaboration offers distinct advantages to the foreign investor. The amount of capital which he risks is decreased and he is assured of better knowledge of local economic, political, and other conditions. There may also be important effects on the enterprise's popularity, in view of the nationalistic feelings prevailing in the countries of investment. Often enough the collaboration of local businessmen makes possible the use of political or social connections to further the interests of the enterprise. In the last few years, a great number of joint international business ventures have been established. Better than any theoretical argument, this fact indicates the possible advantages of co-operation between foreign and local capital.[72]

RESTRICTIONS ON THE EMPLOYMENT OF ALIENS

SIMILAR PROBLEMS arise with regard to the requirements found in the labour legislation of several states concerning the obligatory

[71]See the several cases of profitable foreign minority participation described in Friedmann and Kalmanoff, *supra* note 30, at pp. 329 *et seq.*, 356 *et seq.*, 374 *et seq.*, 442 *et seq.* See also *ibid.*, pp. 220–1, 266–8, for a more general discussion on this point.

[72]The whole question is now thoroughly treated in Friedmann and Kalmanoff, *ibid.*, on which the present brief discussion is in part based.

employment of their nationals by all enterprises operating therein. Under such legislation, a certain proportion of the personnel of all enterprises must consist of nationals of the country in which they are operating. An additional or alternative requirement is sometimes imposed to the effect that a minimum percentage of the enterprises' payroll must be paid to local nationals. The fixed proportions vary from country to country.[73] In Brazil, two-thirds of any enterprise's personnel must be Brazilians or long-time alien residents; two-thirds of the total payroll must also be paid to Brazilians.[74] In Colombia, the corresponding percentages are 90 and 80 per cent respectively,[75] while in Chile the proportion is 85 per cent in both cases.[76] Seventy-five per cent of all employees of enterprises operating in Saudi Arabia must be local nationals and at least 45 per cent of the total payroll must be paid to such nationals.[77] There exist further variations, apart from those in the proportion of nationals employed. In the case of branches of foreign companies operating in the United Arab Republic, at least 90 per cent of the workmen, receiving at least 80 per cent of the pay, must be local nationals.[78] The investment law of Iraq, on the other hand, promises certain advantages to enterprises employing over 90 per cent of local nationals.[79]

Similar requirements may be imposed with respect to certain specified industries only. This seems to be the practice in some Latin American states.[80] Other countries impose requirements for the training of the locally recruited personnel of foreign enterprises.[81] Limitation on the employment of aliens may also be imposed indirectly by means of administrative regulations concerning the

[73]For a general survey, see UN Doc. *supra* note 41, at pp. 96–104.

[74]UN, *Foreign Capital*, p. 56.

[75]*Ibid.*, p. 72.

[76]*Ibid.*, p. 65.

[77]Regulation for the Investment of Foreign Capital, May 23, 1957, as reported in UN Doc., *supra* note 41, at p. 102.

[78]United Arab Republic, Company Law, Law no. 26 of Jan., 1954, as reported in *ibid.*, at p. 103, and by S. Habachy, "United Arab Republic," in *Legal Aspects*, p. 562, at p. 568. According to the latter, however, this requirement applies to all corporations operating in the United Arab Republic; *ibid.*, at p. 573.

[79]Iraq, Industrial Undertakings Encouragement Law, Law no. 43 of 1950, as reported in UN Doc., *supra* note 41, at p. 103.

[80]Such as Honduras and Uruguay; see UN, *Foreign Capital*, pp. 107–8, 141.

[81]Such requirements are found in several states, including Burma, Ceylon, Ecuador, India, and Iran; UN Doc., *supra* note 41, at pp. 103–4.

entry, residence, and work permits of aliens. Their legality in international law is unquestionable, since they rest on the uncontested right of each state to control the entry of aliens in its territory and to regulate their economic activities therein.[82]

Limitations on the employment of aliens are a direct consequence of the labour situation in underdeveloped countries. They are calculated to contribute to a raising of the general level of employment and to reduce the existing shortage of local skilled labour.[83] They also have a psychological significance in that the employment of aliens tends to emphasize the "foreignness" of the enterprises concerned, while the salaries paid to them, usually much higher than those of local personnel, constitute an easy source of popular dissatisfaction.[84]

Such regulations and, more generally, the state of labour legislation in many underdeveloped countries today, may serve as an illustration of the basic contradiction in their present situation, namely, the contradiction between a backward economy and the modern demands for nationalism, democracy, and social welfare. In attempting to establish certain standards of "social justice" labour law in these countries tends to add new elements of rigidity to those already present in the underdeveloped economies. Legislation relating to minimum wages or to workmen's compensation may contribute to the existing high levels of unemployment, for instance, by making the employment of seasonal labour uneconomic. Im-

[82]Such limitations may, however, be illegal according to the municipal law of a particular country. Such is the case in the United States, where it has been held that the right of aliens "to work for a living in the common occupations of the community" is protected from state interference by the Fourteenth Amendment to the U.S. Constitution; *Truax et al.* v. *Raich* (1915), 239 U.S. 33. Cf. Hackworth, *supra* note 48, at pp. 612–14; E. Corwin (ed.), *The Constitution of the U.S.A.: Analysis and Interpretation*, (Washington, D.C., 1953), pp. 1157–8; B. O'Connor, "Constitutional Protection of the Alien's Right to Work" (1941), 18 *N. Y. U. L. Q. Rev.* 483.

[83]This is of particular importance with respect to managerial personnel, whose training largely depends on practical experience; cf. W. A. Lewis, *The Theory of Economic Growth* (1955), p. 258.

[84]The high levels of the salaries paid to foreign personnel are, in the great majority of cases, justifiable on economic grounds, in view of the higher wage rates prevailing in the advanced countries and the need for additional inducement for service abroad. Popular psychological reactions, however, tend not to take such factors into consideration.

provements in productivity may be impeded by strict regulation of the hiring or dismissal of employees.[85] On the other hand, regulation designed to protect labour, is more needed, in terms of immediate human welfare, in underdeveloped countries than in the developed ones. Though it is necessary for these countries to keep welfare legislation at a minimum level,[86] this level will certainly have to be far above that of, say, the European equivalent in the beginnings of the industrial revolution.

With respect to unskilled labour, no serious problem seems to arise, since in the great majority of cases there exist obvious economic reasons in favour of the employment of local labour. It is true that in a few cases the importation of cheap foreign labour might be practically possible and economically profitable to the individual investor, but the social, political, and economic consequences of such a practice to the capital-importing country as a whole are such that its limitation is generally indicated.

More serious problems are raised by the limitations on the employment of skilled personnel in technical or managerial capacities. Foreign investors tend to emphasize the complications and inefficiency likely to arise because of the presence of inexperienced and unqualified persons among the higher-level personnel. They stress the need of their having the freedom to employ foreign technical and managerial personnel in order to ensure the efficient operation of their enterprises. Such fears and demands are to some extent justified, but the needs of the capital-importing states' economy must necessarily take precedence over the mere convenience of foreign investors. Moreover, a chief argument of the supporters of private foreign investment is that such investment always brings along with it into the capital-receiving countries the technical and managerial skills and "know-how" which are needed there, while

[85]For discussions of related conditions, see M. A. Borges, "Labor Relations in Latin America" (1959), 17 *Ohio St. L. J.* 290; UN, *Foreign Capital*, pp. 20–1, 72, 82, and *passim*; Friedmann and Pugh, "Comparative Analysis," in *Legal Aspects*, p. 734, at pp. 744–5.

[86]See, in this sense, Spengler, *supra* note 28, at p. 414; Myrdal, *supra* note 17, at p. 82. And see, in a more general context, Millikan and Blackmer, *supra* note 12, at pp. 38–42.

public investment can only provide money and equipment.[87] Indiscriminate attacks on all labour legislation of the type discussed here would seem to contradict this basic thesis.

On the other hand, there is no doubt that such legislation should be elastic enough to admit of exceptions whenever the employment of foreign personnel is essential for the efficient operation of the enterprise. As a matter of fact, the relevant legislation in most underdeveloped countries makes special provision for such exceptions, though wide variations exist as between states. In some cases, special proportions are determined with respect to high-level or trained personnel, differing from the proportions applicable to unskilled labour. In Burma, only 25 per cent of skilled personnel must consist of Burmese nationals,[88] while in Nepal[89] and Pakistan,[90] the required proportion is 50 per cent. In Colombia, aliens may constitute up to 20 per cent of trained personnel, while they may represent only 10 per cent of unskilled labour.[91] The labour legislation in several other states admits exceptions to the general rules requiring set proportions of nationals in the enterprises' personnel, in cases where the aliens involved are specially qualified and no local persons correspondingly qualified are available.[92] Such provisions are, of course, interpreted and applied with varying degrees of strictness. A related problem is that of the effect of exchange restrictions on the remittances of foreign personnel.[93]

[87]Cf., e.g., A. Coudert and A. Lans, "Direct Foreign Investment in Underdeveloped Countries: Some Practical Problems" (1946), 11 *Law & Contemp. Prob.* 741, at pp. 744–5; E. G. Collado and J. F. Bennett, "Private Investment and Economic Development" (1957), 35 *Foreign Affairs* 631, at pp. 635–6; U.S. Congress, Joint Committee on the Economic Report, *Report on Foreign Economic Policy*, Sen. Rep. no. 1312 (Jan., 1956), p. 22.

[88]See, UN, *Investment Laws*, pp. 2–3.

[89]*Ibid.*, p. 52.

[90]With respect to certain industries only and with a gradual increase in the proportion of nationals employed; *ibid.*, pp. 57–8; U.S., Dept. of Commerce, *supra* note 57, at pp. 54, 187.

[91]See, UN, *Foreign Capital*, p. 72; Kalmanoff and Bernal Salamanca, *supra* note 62, at p. 175. And see the general survey in UN Doc. *supra* note 41, at pp. 96–104.

[92]This is, for instance, the case in Brazil, Chile, Mexico, and Uruguay; UN, *Foreign Capital*, pp. 56, 65, 115, 141. Also in Ceylon and India; UN, *Investment Laws*, pp. 8, 14; Narayanan, *supra* note 54, at p. 261.

[93]See *infra* p. 222 ff.

Requirements of this sort are sometimes also imposed with respect to the members of the boards of directors or equivalent bodies of domestic corporations. In the United Arab Republic, for instance, the majority of the members of any company's board of directors must be citizens of the Republic.[94] In Portugal, similar requirements are in effect with respect to a number of industries.[95] In most instances, such provisions require that company directors be residents, and not necessarily citizens, of the country. Thus, in Iran, all members of a corporation's board of directors must be permanent residents.[96] The same requirement is in effect in Brazil,[97] while in Mexico a similar legislative provision is construed as applying to managing directors only.[98] Several capital-importing countries do not impose such requirements,[99] but in some cases similar demands are made as a matter of policy rather than statute, on the basis of the consistent practice of the competent administrative authorities.

Such requirements do not in fact relate to employment of aliens or to labour legislation but rather to ownership of enterprises and to company law. They are an effective indirect (though fairly obvious) means of achieving participation of local nationals in the ownership and control of enterprises established by foreign investors.[100] As such, they are subject to the considerations advanced in the previous section.

EXCHANGE CONTROL AND RESTRICTIONS

FOREIGN EXCHANGE CONTROL has a long history but, like other mercantilist policies, it had disappeared from the peacetime practice of states in the nineteenth and early twentieth centuries. It made its

94Decree of Aug. 12, 1958; cf. Habachy, in *Legal Aspects*, at p. 572.

95See, C. Fernandes, "Portugal," *ibid.*, p. 445, at pp. 449–50. And cf. also W. J. Wijnberg, "Indonesia," *ibid.*, p. 265, at p. 271.

96See, M. Nasr, "Iran," *ibid.*, p. 280, at p. 285.

97See, Nattier, *ibid.*, at p. 81.

98See, Hidalgo, *ibid.*, at pp. 365–6.

99Cf., e.g., Kalmanoff and Bernal Salamanca, *ibid.*, at p. 175; Koh, *ibid.*, at p. 345; W. J. Gibbons, "Venezuela," *ibid.*, p. 647, at p. 652.

100See, in this sense, Friedmann and Kalmanoff, *supra* note 30, at pp. 199–202.

appearance again in the interwar period and has been extensively used since the end of World War II. In recent years, its dominance has begun to decrease[101] but it still incontestably constitutes an all-important feature of the international financial scene.

In its typical form, exchange control involves a monopoly of all foreign exchange by a central agency, which handles all imports and exports of foreign currencies. In allocating the available foreign exchange, the control agency is in a position to choose among requests and thus discriminate against or in favour of certain persons, countries, or categories of goods. Exchange restrictions may also involve the use of multiple exchange rates, that is to say, different currency rates for different categories of transactions.

The basic purpose of exchange control is the protection of a country's balance-of-payments position through the limitation of effective demand for foreign exchange and the full utilization of available foreign currency. Its original objective, in the early thirties, was the limitation of outward movements of capital in times of financial crisis. Such control involves restrictions on capital outflows only, without any limitation on current transactions.[102] This form of control is still permitted, under the provisions of the IMF Agreement.[103] However, in view of the continuing national and international financial difficulties, of the necessities of its operation, and of its suitability as a tool of economic policy, exchange control soon spread over all international transactions. It also came to serve a variety of subsidiary purposes: protection of currency parities, pro-

[101]The most significant manifestation of this trend has been the adoption of convertibility by several European countries at the end of 1958. For a statement of its importance, see P. Jacobsson, "Toward More Stable Money" (1959), 37 *Foreign Affairs* 378 and cf. International Monetary Fund, *Tenth Annual Report on Exchange Restrictions 1959*, pp. 1–9; M. D. Goldstein, "Progress in Currency Convertibility and Its Significance for Trade and Investment," in Southwestern Legal Foundation, *Proceedings of the 1959 Institute on Private Investment Abroad* (New York, 1959), p. 165.

[102]Transfers and payments for "current transactions" are defined in the IMF Agreement, Article XIX(i), as payments due in connection with foreign trade and other current business, normal short-term banking and credit facilities, interest and amortization on loans, net income from and depreciation on direct investments and remittances for family living expenses. The list is not exhaustive; the term includes all "payments which are not for the purpose of transferring capital."

[103]IMF Agreement, Article VI(3).

vision of public revenue, or support of domestic industries. Exchange control seems to be most effective when used to curb the outflow of capital. As a more general measure, it is apparently successful in the short run, when imposed in times of exceptional balance-of-payments difficulties. In the long run, a country's balance of payments can be improved only through internal adjustments; exchange control tends to perpetuate the conditions which made necessary its initial imposition.[104]

Foreign exchange control is of particular importance to the underdeveloped countries. The fluctuations in the prices of primary products, which are these countries' principal exports, constitute a constant source of balance-of-payments instability.[105] The effort to industrialize places great strains on their balances of payments. Developing countries need foreign exchange to buy the capital equipment for the establishment of new industries and the raw materials necessary for their operation. Their other expenditures before and during such operation will probably also be used in part, directly or indirectly, for imports.[106] Furthermore, such countries are vulnerable to the adverse effects of movements of capital, particularly since these movements tend to occur in times of financial difficulties. Besides being needed to protect their balance-of-payments position, exchange control constitutes today one of the main tools of the underdeveloped countries' economic development policies.[107] It is thus used to protect their balance of payments from inflationary pressures, to encourage imports of productive capital equipment, or to protect existing domestic industries. Again, however, we note that exchange control by itself, even if it achieves its

[104]Obviously, this is an oversimplified exposition of an all too complicated issue. For brief discussions of this topic, see Nurkse, *International Currency Experience* (League of Nations, 1944), pp. 183–9; Mikesell, *Foreign Exchange in the Postwar World* (New York, 1954), p. 423 *et seq*.

[105]See UN, Dept. of Economic Affairs, *Instability in Export Markets of Under-Developed Countries*; Mikesell, *supra* note 104, at pp. 441–4; Jacobsson, *supra* note 101, at pp. 382–3. And cf. the studies cited *supra* note 29.

[106]For a survey of balance-of-payments problems of industrialization, see UN, Dept. of Economic and Social Affairs, *Processes and Problems of Industrialization* (New York, 1955), p. 58 *et seq*.

[107]See the survey of related policies in *ibid.*, at pp. 60–5, and the critique in Mikesell, *supra* note 104, at pp. 444–9.

own particular objectives, will be of little use to the economy as a whole if it is not supplemented by other measures leading to internal adjustment.[108]

Originally set up by municipal legislation, exchange control led necessarily to the conclusion of numerous bilateral arrangements between countries ("payment agreements"). Later, certain multilateral conventions were also concluded, the most general and most important of which is that instituting the International Monetary Fund.[109] The fund's members undertook not to impose exchange restrictions on current transactions, to furnish certain information to the fund regarding their financial condition and to abide by its decisions or suggestions. At the same time, the fund disposes of reserves which its members may use to weather temporary difficulties.[110]

Despite the development of treaty law on the matter, customary international law has evolved no special rules regarding exchange control. The general principle applicable is that a state has exclusive competence to regulate monetary matters. Consequently, the imposition of exchange control and restrictions is in no way unlawful in international law.[111] It is sometimes held that exchange control is internationally unlawful when "discriminatory."[112] This thesis can be defended meaningfully only in the sense that, in administering its exchange controls, a state must not discriminate against the citizens of another state and favour its own nationals or

[108]For instance, exchange (or import) control may effectively restrict the importation of luxury goods. In the absence, however, of any supplementary measures (e.g. taxation) the income not spent on such goods will probably be spent on similar goods of domestic origin and might even induce investment for the domestic production of such good. This hardly is the intended effect. See, Nurkse, *supra* note 2, p. 109 *et seq.*; UN, *supra* note 106, at pp. 61–2.

[109]Cf. F. A. Mann, *The Legal Aspect of Money* (2d ed.; London, 1953), pp. 339–40, 378–87; A. Nussbaum, *Money in the Law, National and International* (2d ed.; Brooklyn, 1950), pp. 513–46.

[110]On the Fund's role in assisting the United Kingdom during the Suez crisis, see Jacobsson, *Towards a Modern Monetary Standard* (London, 1959), pp. 18–19. And cf., more generally, Jacobsson, *supra* note 101, at pp. 389–93.

[111]See, Hyde, *supra* note 48, at pp. 690–2; Mann, *supra* note 109, at pp. 419–23.

[112]Cf., Hyde, *supra* note 48, at pp. 690–2; Hackworth, *supra* note 48, Vol. II, pp. 68–70.

aliens of other nationalities, when other considerations are equal, that is, when the same currency, the same goods, and even the same country of exportation are involved. For it would be meaningless to ask for an exchange control not discriminating against a certain currency. "Allocation of scarce currency" means, in fact, discrimination against it.[113] "National treatment," moreover, is an unsatisfactory standard with respect to exchange control, for the alien's dependence on and need of foreign exchange is as a rule much greater than any national's.

The existence, or possibility of future imposition, of exchange control constitutes a major obstacle to foreign private investment.[114] Foreign investors have, at best, to submit to various requirements, formalities, and delays whenever they wish to transfer their earnings or their capital outside the country of investment. At worst, they may not be allowed to take such funds out of the country, or they may be permitted to take out only a fraction. It is true that, as a matter of business practice, the profits of a successful foreign enterprise are often reinvested in the country in which it is operating. Investors, however, want to have the choice as to whether they will reinvest the enterprise's profits and to what proportion. Again, though capital is brought into a country to stay, at least for a time, investors tend to place a high value on its availability in case of special need on their part or of any general crisis. Exchange control also affects foreign enterprises in that it renders difficult the employment of foreign technical or managerial personnel, in view of the limitations on the transfer of their salaries abroad.

The problem is not an easy one to solve. Under present conditions, the underdeveloped countries cannot be expected to eliminate all measures of exchange control or to guarantee that none will be imposed in the future. And foreign investors are justified in pre-

[113]See, Nussbaum, *supra* note 109, at pp. 475–6; Mann, *supra* note 109, at pp. 424–5.

[114]According to a 1951 survey, measures of exchange control were the most frequently mentioned of the conditions regarded by American businessmen as constituting obstacles to private investment abroad; see Gaston, *supra* note 15, at p. 8. A Canadian survey reached, around the same time, similar conclusions, though with certain important differences in emphasis: see, Advisory Committee on Overseas Investment, *Report* (1951), pp. 42–4, 64–5, 69, 73.

ferring to invest their capital in stable advanced countries or in industries less affected by exchange control.[115] Any improvement in the investment climate of capital-importing countries will then have to be a compromise between the two extreme positions. The measures to be taken fall mostly within the competence of the capital-importing countries' governments; they should limit the effects of exchange control on foreign investment without necessarily eliminating it altogether.

A first requirement would be the elimination of uncertainty: the relevant regulations should be as clear and well organized as possible and they should not be subject to frequent alterations. They should provide for the possibility of transfer abroad of the foreign enterprises' earnings as well as of those of their foreign employees, within reasonable limits and with the minimum of delay and special formalities. They may provide for the limitation of capital movements, though not for their total prohibition. Finally, the exchange control regulations in force in capital-receiving countries may provide for a general limitation of payments in foreign currency in the event of exceptionally adverse balance-of-payments conditions. Such conditions, however, would have to be defined as clearly as possible and care should be taken to allow for absolutely necessary payments and to give the transfer of earnings by foreign enterprises a good rank of priority.

THE FEAR OF EXPROPRIATION

THE STRONGEST POSSIBLE MEASURE against an investor's interests is the taking of his property with inadequate or no compensation. Accordingly, the fear of expropriation constitutes a serious deterrent to private foreign investment in underdeveloped countries.

The problem of expropriation is in itself but one aspect of the more general question of the status of private property in the present national and international social setting. It is not possible to deal

[115]The presence of exchange restrictions is an additional cause for the predominance of foreign investment in industries producing primary goods for export. Their receipts being usually in foreign currency, it is easier to have them transferred to the investors' own currency, despite certain possible limitations and other difficulties.

adequately with such a problem in the present context. In broad terms, it is correct to state that the right of private property has never been an absolute one, in the sense that it has always been determined, and thereby limited, by law. In the last century, special emphasis was placed on the rights of property owners rather than on their corresponding obligations. In our times, the emphasis has changed. The limitations imposed on private property by the laws in effect in the various states have greatly expanded in scope as well as in number. The "social function" of property and the consequent duties of property owners are now stressed.[116] The extent, however, to which this trend has affected the law in every state varies greatly. There exists no well-established general consensus on the matter, as it existed during the later half of the nineteenth century.

State action often affects private property indirectly, through measures regulating the exercise of property rights. But direct action by the state, resulting in the deprivation of individuals of their property, is also possible. The state's right to expropriate the property of its subjects has been well-established for a long time, both in positive law and in legal theory.[117] However, the manner in which this right is exercised and, ultimately, the whole conception of expropriation have changed radically in our days. During the nineteenth century, expropriations were generally rare, but since the end of the First World War,[118] the picture has changed: a great number of expropriations have occurred in a great number of states.[119] Today, expropriations are generally associated with social, political, and economic reforms. They are large-scale operations and

[116]For some descriptions and comments, see Friedmann, *Law in a Changing Society* (London, 1959), pp. 65–89; R. Pound, *Jurisprudence* (1959), Vol. III, pp. 135–40; Vol. V, pp. 123–5. A survey of developments from the socialist viewpoint is found in K. Katzarov, *Théorie de la Nationalisation* (hereinafter cited Katzarov, *Nationalisation*) (Paris, 1960), pp. 153–95.

[117]See the excellent historical survey in F. A. Mann, "Outlines of a History of Expropriation" (1959), 75 *L. Q. Rev.* 188. It is our submission, however, that the learned writer minimizes unduly the effects of twentieth century developments.

[118]For a discussion of certain earlier manifestations, indicative of present trends, see Katzarov, *Nationalisation*, pp. 27–32.

[119]The most systematic survey seems to be Katzarov's, *Nationalisation*, pp. 32–131. See also S. Friedman, *Expropriation in International Law* (hereinafter cited Friedman *Expropriation*) (London, 1953), pp. 12–66; I. Foighel, *Nationalization* (London, 1957), pp. 56–69. Several detailed studies have been published, covering particular countries (especially the Western European ones). Cf., e.g.,

they assume a variety of forms, the most important of which is "nationalization," that is, the taking over by the state of the ownership and operation of whole sectors of the economy.[120] The requirements for their validity in the various states have also changed. But there is today little uniformity in the matter, from which general rules could be deduced.[121]

The effect of these radical changes upon international law has yet to be ascertained with any precision. The "classical" theory of international law was largely founded on the nineteenth-century Western European conception of private property. There is wide disagreement today, among states as well as among scholars, as to the extent to which modern conceptions of private property have been adopted in international law.[122] The same is true with respect to questions of expropriation or nationalization. Despite several recent attempts to formulate the law on the matter,[123] there are relatively few points which may be considered as settled.

Expropriation becomes a problem of international law when it involves the property of aliens. It is generally accepted that expropriation in violation of international commitments of the state is

on France, Julliot de la Morandière and M. Byé (eds.), *Les Nationalisations en France et à l'étranger*, Vol. I, *Les Nationalisations en France* (Paris, 1948); M. Einaudi, M. Byé, and E. Rossi, *Nationalization in France and Italy* (Ithaca, N.Y., 1955); on the United Kingdom, W. Robson (ed.), *Problems of Nationalized Industry* (London, 1952); and more generally, H. Puget (ed.), *Les Nationalisations en France et à l'étranger*; Vol II, *Les Nationalisations à l'étranger* (Paris, 1958).

120For a discussion of the meaning of "nationalization," see Foighel, *supra* note 119, at pp. 14–23. See also Katzarov, *Nationalisation*, pp. 21–7, 125–8.

121The constitutional and legislative provisions with respect to expropriation which are in effect in the various states are reviewed in detail in UN Doc., *supra* note 41, at pp. 125–32.

122The main difficulty, of course, is that conceptions vary widely as between the states of the world community. For a perceptive early statement of the problem, see F. Dunn, "International Law and Private Property Rights" (1928), 28 *Colum. L. Rev.* 166. A more recent discussion, from a socialist (though not orthodox Marxist) viewpoint, is found in Katzarov, *Nationalisation*, pp. 372–91, for an English version of which, see his "Private Property and Public International Law" (1957), 84 *Journal de Droit International* (Clunet) 6. Indications of a natural law approach to this issue may be found in B. A. Wortley, *Expropriation in Public International Law* (hereinafter cited Wortley, *Expropriation*) (Cambridge, 1959), p. 12 *et seq.*

123In addition to a considerable number of articles on the problem, four recent books have dealt with it; Friedman, *Expropriation* (1953); Foighel, *Nationalization* (1957); Wortley, *Expropriation* (1959); and Katzarov, *Nationalisation* (1960), pp. 392–483.

internationally unlawful. It is also accepted that discriminatory expropriation is unlawful; but the meaning of that term is not very clear. Expropriatory measures directed against aliens as such, which do not affect those of the host state's nationals who are in a similar condition, would probably be considered unlawful. In most cases, however, the situation is far more complex. It may be that the measures are not openly called expropriations by the state which takes them or that the latter bases the legality of its measures on the existence of a state of war or some other similar state of emergency. It may be also that the expropriation is nominally of general application although in fact it affects only aliens (because, for instance, the industries involved were owned by aliens). It would be very difficult to give a definitive answer applicable to all situations. The particular facts in each case will have to determine the outcome.

A direct consequence of the expropriation of alien property is the expropriating state's obligation to grant fair compensation to the aliens affected. Whether as a condition for the expropriation's legality or as an obligation arising out of the act of expropriation,[124] the payment of compensation is well established in modern state practice as well as in theory and judicial practice.[125]

The main field of controversy is the manner and the extent to which, in the absence of discrimination or violation of international commitments, a state may protect its national whose property has been taken by another state without compensation or with inadequate compensation. No general answer to this question (in the present context, at least) is possible, since the law on the matter is still developing and therefore uncertain.

[124]The matter is in dispute among the jurists; see, e.g., on the one side, K. S. Carlston, "Concession Agreements and Nationalization" (1958), 52 *Am. J. of Int'l L.* 260, at p. 267; Hyde, *supra* note 48, at pp. 710–17; L. T. Kissam and E. K. Leach, "Sovereign Expropriation of Property and Abrogation of Concession Contracts" (1959), 28 *Fordham L. Rev.* 177, at pp. 190–2; and, on the other side, S. J. Rubin, *Private Foreign Investment* (Baltimore, 1956), pp. 9–10; Foighel, *Nationalization*, p. 75; R. Bindschedler, "La Protection de la propriété privée en droit international public" (1956), 90 *Recueil des Cours* 173, at p. 246. The author's reasons for accepting the latter view are stated in chap. 10 of his forthcoming book, *State Guarantees to Foreign Investors* (1962).

[125]It is to be noted that in all recent cases of expropriation, some compensation was finally awarded to the aliens affected. The question is discussed in some detail, in the specific context of state contracts with aliens, *ibid.*

The expropriation of foreign property has special appeal for the peoples of the underdeveloped countries. This can be explained on several grounds. From a strictly economic viewpoint, there may be considerable profit to a country's economy from the partial or total confiscation of foreign holdings.[126] It is true that the profit may be offset by the reaction of the states affected by the measures and by certain limitations in the underdeveloped countries. Often these countries may be unable to operate profitably the industries seized, because they lack the necessary skilled personnel. The high degree of control which the major capital-exporting states and their nationals exercise over the distribution of several primary products is another limitation. However, this is not always the case; moreover, the existing division of the world into conflicting blocs serves to decrease significantly the probability and effectiveness of any reprisals against expropriating states. Psychological considerations are also important: the widely felt fear of, and resentment against, the erstwhile colonial powers account in part for the incidence of expropriations of the property of their nationals.[127] Finally, in some of the underdeveloped countries, private property has never had the "sacrosanct" character it had in the West in the nineteenth century. At the same time, the powers of the state in the non-western countries are often, either because of their tradition or because of the prevailing conditions, much wider—and more overt—than they are in the western countries.

It is easy enough to understand how the fear of expropriation operates as a deterrent of private foreign investment. It may be that its importance is sometimes overemphasized, at least as far as outright expropriation[128] is concerned. Existing surveys certainly do not

[126]Cf., M. Bronfenbrenner, "The Appeal of Confiscation in Economic Development" (1955), 3 *Econ. Devel. & Cultural Change* 201 reprinted in Agarwala and Singh *supra* note 1, at p. 472. The learned author's concluding suggestion of a "neoisolationist" policy seems, however, much less convincing than his main argument.

[127]Cf., Myrdal, *supra* note 36, at pp. 214–15, 259–60.

[128]In contradistinction to the so-called "creeping expropriation," that is, the gradual taking over of an enterprise through increasing economic controls, taxation, and other government measures, which may actually be more feared by foreign investors. For a discussion of the process of "creeping expropriation," see Rubin, *supra* note 124, at pp. 37–43.

indicate that businessmen consider expropriation one of the principal deterrents,[129] though recent events may have affected their attitude on this point. Whatever its exact rank, the fear of expropriation is a serious obstacle to foreign investment. The existence of an obligation to compensate on the part of the expropriating state is not sufficient assurance to the investors for they fear that such compensation may be inadequate or may be granted after a long time.

PROBLEMS OF TAXATION

TAXATION is the last of the elements of a country's investment climate to be discussed. Compared to the other elements which have been examined, it presents certain peculiarities of its own. In the first place, the capital-exporting country's policies and measures are in this connection as important as those of the capital-importing one. In the second place, taxation is usually considered as a normal business risk. It is only under exceptional conditions that it becomes a non-business risk. In the third place, taxation is the sole element of the investment climate which affects directly a basic economic factor, namely, the investment's rate of return: from the investor's viewpoint, any increase or decrease in the taxes which he would normally have to pay corresponds to a change in the profit rate of his investment. Finally, and in view of the preceding, taxation constitutes not only a possible deterrent but also a possible incentive to private foreign investment. Because of its peculiarities and also of the extent of its domain and the variety of possible measures and policies, the subject of taxation can only be treated summarily in the present context.[130]

[129] In the 1951 National Industrial Conference Board survey, *supra* note 114, the fear of expropriation ranked thirteenth among twenty-two possible obstacles to private foreign investment. Its rank was eighth with respect to investment in Europe (memory of the postwar nationalizations was still fresh), fourteenth with respect to investment in Asia and Latin America and nineteenth with regard to investment in Africa. The Canadian survey's conclusions were largely similar; cf. its *Report*, *supra* note 114, at pp. 40–1, 60.

[130] Cf. the work of the Harvard Law School International Program in Taxation and, especially, Barlow and Wender, *United States Tax Incentives to Direct Private Foreign Investment* (1954); Barlow and Wender, *supra* note 14.

Taxation is an obstacle to foreign investment chiefly in two ways. On the one hand, the foreign investor's income may be taxed both in his state of residence (that is, the capital-exporting state) and in the state of investment (the capital-importing one). Though lawful under international law,[131] "double taxation" is resented by the investor and undesirable from the viewpoint of the development of international trade and investment. Under certain conditions, its partial elimination may be achieved by unilateral action on the part of individual states.[132] It may be more effectively achieved by joint action on the part of capital-exporting and capital-importing states. A great number of related international agreements have been concluded to regulate interstate problems of taxation.[133] There is some variation among their provisions in the manner in which such problems are settled. In most cases, the state of investment is given priority in taxing the foreign investor's income. The state of residence may impose its own taxes afterwards, taking into account the taxes already paid to the other state, for example, treating them as deductions from the taxable income or granting a credit against its own taxes. Such a system does eliminate, or at least mitigate, double taxation and also has certain advantages for the capital-importing countries in that it allows them to collect fully their taxes. It does not, however, help in alleviating the investor's tax burden

[131] Cf., Hyde, *supra* note 48, at pp. 673–6; E. Allix, "La Condition des étrangers au point de vue fiscal" (1937), 61 *Recueil des Cours* 541, at p. 616 *et seq.*; M. Chrétien, *A la Recherche du droit international fiscal commun* (Paris, 1955), pp. 208–12.

[132] This is the case with the United States, whose income tax legislation provides for "foreign tax credit" and "tax deferral" on income earned abroad by American corporations, regardless of the conclusion or not of international agreements to that effect. See S. Surrey, "Current Issues in the Taxation of Corporate Foreign Investment" (1956), 56 *Colum. L. Rev.* 815, at pp. 817–38; Surrey, "The United States Taxation of Foreign Income" (1958), 1 *J. Law & Econ.* 72, at pp. 73–7, 84–5; and the studies cited *supra* note 130. The importance of the effect of such American policies is certainly due to the country's position as the chief capital-exporting state as well as to the high degree of stability of its economic and other policies.

[133] See the UN Dept. of Economic and Social Affairs series "International Tax Agreements," especially Vol. VIII, *World Guide to International Tax Agreements* (1958), and the publications of the International Bureau of Fiscal Documentation. On the related legal problems, see the earlier studies of J. P. Niboyet, "Les Doubles Impositions au point de vue juridique" (1930), *Recueil des Cours* 5, and O. Bühler, "Les Accords internationaux concernant la double imposition et l'évasion fiscale" (1936), 55 *ibid.*, 433.

and it does not assist the capital-importing country in providing tax incentives to foreign investors.

A second manner in which tax measures may unfavourably affect foreign investment relates to possible discrimination against aliens, to excessive taxation, and, especially, to the imperfect functioning of the capital-importing country's tax system and the consequent uncertainty and instability. Discrimination or excessive taxation should be avoided in view of their obvious adverse effect on prospective foreign investors. They cannot, however, be considered as unlawful in international law,[134] except perhaps if they become in fact confiscatory.[135] The achievement of a degree of stability and certainty in taxation, on the other hand, should be considered as a *conditio sine qua non*, not only of foreign investment, but of economic development itself. It should not be impossible for most underdeveloped countries to set up a fairly well-organized system of taxation, in accordance with accepted principles of public finance and with their own special needs and conditions.[136] As long as they can make fairly accurate predictions concerning its impact, businessmen all over the world are used to coping with taxation.

Taxation can play an important role as an incentive to foreign investment. Generally speaking, and apart from the question of double taxation, tax considerations favour investment in the underdeveloped countries, for the investor's tax burden there is, as a rule, less heavy than in the developed countries. Additional measures may also be taken, by capital-exporting as well as capital-importing countries, to render such investment more attractive to investors. Foreign investors may be exempted from some taxes or they may be granted special facilities. It is not possible to enumerate or study here the tax incentives which may be offered.[137] Nor can one deal

[134]Cf. Chrétien, *supra* note 131, at pp. 215–19; B. Grizioti, "L'imposition fiscale des étrangers" (1926), 13 *Recueil des Cours* 4, at pp. 64–7; Allix, *supra* note 131, at pp. 601, 603.

[135]Cf. Hyde, *supra* note 48, at p. 664; A. R. Albrecht, "Taxation of Aliens under International Law" (1952), 29 *Brit. Y. B. Int'l L.* 145, at pp. 170–1.

[136]See, e.g., Surrey, "Tax Administration in Underdeveloped Countries" (1958), 12 *U. Miami L. Rev.* 158; N. H. Jacoby, "Taxation in Laos: Policies for a New Country with an Underdeveloped Economy" (1961), 14 *Nat'l Tax J.* 145.

[137]For a recent survey of such incentives, see S. G. Ross, "Foreign Governments' Tax Incentives for Investment," in Southwestern Legal Foundation, *supra* note 101, at p. 285.

with the fundamental question of whether and to what extent tax incentives are in fact an effective tool for the promotion of a country's economic development.[138] All that can be done at this point is glance at the policy background of the measures in question.

On the part of capital-exporting states, the willingness to offer tax incentives, to the detriment of their public revenue, should be chiefly attributed to their general economic and political interest in the development of the underdeveloped areas. Certain more immediate economic considerations, such as the need for raw materials and the necessity to utilize their potentially excessive domestic savings,[139] also indicate the desirability of the expansion of foreign investment. State revenue from the taxation of such investment, moreover, is of relatively minor importance. The extent, therefore, to which tax relief may be granted in such states to enterprises investing abroad will chiefly depend on considerations of domestic and international policy as well as on the prevailing views as to the effectiveness of such relief as a means of increasing private foreign investment. Serious doubts have been expressed on this last point.[140]

The underdeveloped countries' economic interest in attracting foreign investors is certainly more immediate. Their offer of tax incentives represents the sacrifice of possible future revenue in view not only of the country's development but also of the increase of public revenue which is a necessary consequence of such development. Their chief criterion in granting tax relief will be the usefulness of the particular investment and its effect on the country's economy. It cannot be denied that, even if all private foreign investment benefits the country in which it is made, certain kinds of investment are of more (or more immediate) benefit to it. A capital-

138Note, however, that in view of the differences in needs and in taxation structures between developed and underdeveloped countries, different considerations may apply as to each category of countries. Cf., on this point, Surrey, *supra* note 132, at p. 90, n. 26.

139The latter consideration, it is true, may not be operative at all times; it has been of relatively minor importance in the postwar years. It does constitute, however, a significant factor which should not be left out of consideration.

140See, e.g., Surrey, "Current Issues in the Taxation of Foreign Corporate Investment" (1956), 56 *Colum. L. Rev.* 815, at pp. 838–57; Surrey, *supra* note 132, at p. 80 *et seq.*; N. Gordon, "Some Aspects of United States Policy in the Taxation of Foreign Income," in P. O. Proehl (ed.), *Legal Problems of International Trade* (Urbana, Ill., 1959), pp. 222, 225–8.

importing country may then, with justification, grant tax exemptions or other privileges to some investors only and not to all of them. Moreover, the offer of tax concessions may be limited in time. Exemptions or reductions may be granted for a specified number of years only (usually five to ten). In this manner, the foreign-owned enterprise is materially assisted during its critical first years in the country of investment, while the latter retains its right to tax it at the regular rates after the end of the prescribed period.

It should never be forgotten, on the other hand, that underdeveloped countries are not always able to act in pursuit of their long-run aims. Their revenue from the taxation of some large foreign enterprises may sometimes be of such immediate importance that they cannot afford to sacrifice it. With respect to taxation, and many other economic considerations, they have to effect a compromise between their long-range interests and their immediate needs.

Finally, important problems arise in the co-ordination of the tax policies of capital-importing and capital-exporting states. The "tax sparing" issue may serve as an illustration of the needs and difficulties in this field.[141] It has already been noted that, in several capital-exporting countries and, in particular, in the United States, the taxes paid by a foreign corporate investor to the country of investment are credited against the taxes which he has to pay in his country of residence.[142] To the extent that the tax rates in capital-importing countries are lower than those prevailing in the United States (and this is the usual case), this system results in cancelling any change in the tax burden imposed by the capital-importing country, since any taxes the investor will not pay in that country,

[141]For some discussions of the problem, see Surrey, *supra* note 140, at pp. 849–50, 854–957; Surrey, *supra* note 132, at pp. 84–90; Surrey, Statement in U.S. Congress (85th Cong., 2d Sess.), *Private Foreign Investment Hearings before the Subcommittee on Foreign Trade Policy of the House Committee on Ways and Means* (1958), p. 377, at pp. 381–3, 389–91; Gordon, *supra* note 140, at pp. 230–2; M. J. Kust, "United States Tax Concessions for American Private Enterprise Abroad," in Southwestern Legal Foundation, *supra* note 101, at pp. 145, 148–52; Friedmann and Kalmanoff, *supra* note 30, at pp. 232–5.

[142]Tax credit of this sort is applicable to income earned by branches of United States companies operating abroad. In the case of foreign subsidiaries of such companies, the income is not taxed until it is brought in the United States for distribution, i.e., they operate under a "tax deferral" system. See Surrey, *supra* note 140, at pp. 817–30. The distinction is of importance in the present context in that it limits the applicability of the "tax sparing" argument.

he will have to pay in the United States. The tax credit system, therefore, may well render meaningless any tax incentive offered by a capital-importing country.

It has been suggested that this effect could be avoided by the inclusion in the international tax agreements negotiated with underdeveloped countries of a clause to the effect that the taxes not paid by foreign investors as a result of the operation of tax incentive provisions in the country of investment should be treated by the country of residence as if they were paid, that is, they should be credited against the latter country's taxes. A provision to this effect was included in an agreement in 1957 between the United States and Pakistan, but it was removed before final ratification. A similar clause has been included in a more recent agreement between the United States and India and will probably be included in several other treaties now being negotiated.[143]

These suggestions have received strong criticism, chiefly on the grounds that they tend to establish a régime of inequality in taxation as between foreign and domestic investors. It has also been argued more cogently, from an international viewpoint, that the "cancellation effect" of tax credit policies is to the advantage of capital-importing states in that it relieves them from increased pressures to offer tax concessions and it encourages the re-investment of the earnings of foreign-owned corporations in the country of investment. There exist, moreover, several other possible methods to avoid the cancellation of tax incentives by means of certain devices which can be used by capital-exporting[144] or capital-importing countries.[145]

[143]See the then Under-Secretary of State Dillon's statement before the U.S. Senate Committee on Foreign Relations, in support of that treaty, in (1960) 43 *Dept. State Bull.* 111. And see Friedmann and Kalmanoff, *supra* note 30, at pp. 233–4.

[144]A device strongly supported by a number of American authorities on the matter, is that of the establishment of "foreign business corporations," i.e., of American corporations receiving income from foreign sources whose such income would be taxed only when distributed to their shareholders. Thus, such companies, while established in the United States, would have the "tax deferral" advantages of foreign subsidiaries of American companies. See Surrey, *supra* note 132, at pp. 94–5; Friedmann and Kalmanoff, *supra* note 30, at pp. 238–41. These proposals are modelled on the British "overseas trade corporations," on which see C. M. Schmitthoff and T. P. E. Curry (eds.), *Palmer's Company Law* (20th ed.), pp. 804–5.

[145]Cf., e.g., Professor Surrey's suggestion for the substitution of subsidies to tax incentives by capital-importing countries, *supra* note 140, at p. 857, n. 84.

It is not possible to offer here a solution of the problem, nor is it necessary to do so in the present context. It is, however, hoped that its mere statement has served to show some of the considerations which must be taken into account in attempting to effect a co-ordination of the tax policies of capital-exporting and capital-importing countries.

THE ROLE OF PRIVATE FOREIGN INVESTMENT IN UNDERDEVELOPED COUNTRIES

IT HAS been shown, it is hoped, that the conditions responsible for the present relative shortage in private foreign investment in underdeveloped countries are not accidental phenomena, nor are they due to the immorality or malevolence of either the foreign investors or the governments of the capital-importing countries. The shortage is due to a number of objective causes, which are, in part, outside the control of individual foreign investors and of the governments of particular states.

Apart from the shortage of private foreign investment, there exist certain definite limitations on the role which such investment can play in the underdeveloped regions of the world. The first limitation stems from the demand for an accelerated rate of economic development. Private foreign investment can certainly assist and probably, in the long run, assure a country's development, but it cannot do so within the time limits imposed by the contemporary "revolution of rising expectations."

The second limitation reinforces the effects of the first. It has been noted that nowadays direct investment prevails over indirect. The latter was, in the past, concentrated in public utilities and transportation, while the former is today directed to industries producing primary goods, for export or, at best, to industries producing consumer goods for the local market. The most pressing need in underdeveloped countries, however, is for industries of the former type, for the building of the infrastructure of the economy which is indispensable for any further development. Private investors can help little in this direction, partly because of the heavy initial outlays of capital needed, but mostly because of the low rates of return which such industries offer, owing to market conditions and to government price regulation.

Furthermore, the development of extractive and other primary-producing industries is, by itself, of limited usefulness to the country's economy as a whole.[146] The main contribution of such industries lies in the funds they provide to local governments, through taxes or royalties, the foreign exchange they bring into the country, and the employment of local labour. Industries of this sort often tend to remain separate from the rest of the economy, their high productivity little affecting that of other industries. Their excessive growth may render the country dependent on the market condition of a single primary product and consequently vulnerable to the fluctuation of its price. Important and useful as they are, therefore, such industries are not sufficient to effect the radical changes necessary for the start of the economic development process.

Out of this situation arises the need for public capital. A recent study of the capital needs of underdeveloped areas concludes that about $5.7 billion per year will be required in the next five years in order to keep a minimum rate of development in these areas. Only about 25 per cent of this sum (or $1.41 billion) is allocated to private investment; it is public capital that will provide the bulk of the capital needed.[147] A slight change in the proportions of public and private capital is estimated for the ten years after 1966.

The use of public capital entails certain definite advantages to the underdeveloped countries. In the first place, public capital can be used to provide the basic facilities which are scarce or lacking and which cannot be provided by private investors. Secondly, public capital is strictly controlled by the country's government and may

[146]See *supra* note 43. In calculating the foreign capital inflow required for the underdeveloped countries in the next few years, Professor Paul N. Rosenstein-Rodan counts oil and mineral investment at only half its amount. He justifies "this somewhat rough assumption" by invoking "the fact that—although such industries provide important tax and other revenues—their diffusion and complementarity effects are markedly smaller than those of other industries." "International Aid for Underdeveloped Countries" (1961), 43 *Rev. Econ. & Stat.* 107, at p. 110.

[147]*Ibid.*, at p. 137 (Table 5-A). In comparing this sum with the amounts already noted *supra* note 9, the assumption mentioned *supra* note 146 should be taken into account. See the discussion *ibid.*, at p. 116.

thus be used in accordance with an over-all plan to cover in a balanced manner the multiple needs of the economy. The development of particular industries can then be encouraged, either indirectly, through the financing or other support of private entrepreneurs, or directly, by the establishment by the state of such industries as local businessmen are reluctant to establish by themselves.

The extensive employment of public capital is not devoid of problems and difficulties.[148] Prevailing political conditions may often affect adversely its effective use. Furthermore, the condition of governmental administration in many underdeveloped countries is hardly promising of a rational and economic use of available capital and resources. Over-all plans are often lacking or they are the product of wishful thinking or of the influence of special interests rather than of objective study. Under such conditions, part of the available public capital might be wasted, contributing little to the country's economic development.

Acceptance of the need for public capital does not imply any disregard of the importance of private investment, domestic or foreign. Under present conditions, these two forms of financing are not exclusive of each other, but complementary. Ideological as well as practical considerations may be adduced to support this view.

Private foreign investment can play an important role in assisting the economic development of the poorer countries. Its role will depend in part on the form which it will assume. There is today great need for indirect investment, but it is improbable that portfolio investment in its early forms will revive to any considerable extent. New forms of indirect investment are, however, possible, perhaps through association with public capital or in other, as yet unexplored, ways.[149]

[148]See F. Deyrup, "Limits of Government Activity in Underdeveloped Countries" (1957), 24 *Social Research* 191; and, for a rather extreme view, limiting governmental activity to measures concerning education and public health, see T. W. Schultz, "The Role of Government in Promoting Economic Growth," in L. D. White (ed.), *The State of the Social Sciences* (Chicago, 1956), p. 372.

[149]"The difficulties in the way of again building up an international capital market are immense. Nevertheless, I feel that we must try to do it, if we do not want to see the collapse of all our hopes of a developing progressive welfare democracy in the world." Myrdal, *supra* note 36, p. 247.

Direct investment, on the other hand, can assist the backward countries' development through the establishment of new manufacturing and other industries producing goods for consumption or even of heavy industry, processing local raw materials or producing capital goods for the local market. Its contribution would lie in its providing the necessary capital and in assisting the transmission of technical and administrative skills. Before private foreign capital can engage in such activities on any increased scale, however, certain changes of attitude on both sides are necessary. Capital-importing countries have to admit that the investors' fear of economic and political instability is both well-founded and legitimate. They can help to diminish it, though probably not eliminate it altogether, by adjusting their own administrative procedures to render them more efficient and by undertaking, by themselves or in co-operation with the capital-exporting countries, to guarantee a certain minimum of security to the investor.[150] On the part of the foreign investors, some understanding is needed of the precarious economic conditions of most underdeveloped countries and of the powerful forces now at work in them. There should be a realization of the grave difficulties which the local governments are facing and of the need for co-operation with them. Some tolerance of (or perhaps resignation to) a certain amount of inefficiency in the operation of these countries' administrative machinery is also in order. What is basically needed on the investors' part is an awareness of the fact that their profits and the continuation of their enterprise's operation depend not on an initial "good bargain" but on a continuing contribution to the welfare of the country of investment. Whenever no community of interests exists between the investors and the host country, trouble is bound to start, even if it does not take the form of extreme or violent measures.

This may seem too ambitious a programme, too difficult a course to be followed consistently by either the foreign investors or the governments of capital-importing countries. It is so if one looks only

[150]For a summary review of such guarantees, see A. A. Fatouros, "Legal Security for International Investment," in *Legal Aspects*, p. 699. The topic is discussed in more detail in the author's forthcoming *State Guarantees to Foreign Investors*.

at the official pronouncements on either side; however, the practice in the last few years which has resulted in an increase in the amount of foreign capital invested in the underdeveloped countries, despite the existing difficulties, points to a different conclusion. Both the sides involved have in fact shown considerable flexibility and there is every indication that more flexibility is possible. One may conclude therefore on a note of definite, though qualified, hopefulness.

Controlling Narcotic Drug Addiction in Canada: RECENT DEVELOPMENTS

By R. ST. J. MACDONALD*

THE CONTINUED OUTPOURING of books,[1] monographs,[2] novels,[3] articles,[4] newspaper and magazine reports[5] about narcotic drug addiction in Canada and elsewhere evidences the persistence of the problem and its abiding interest for specialists and the public at

*R. St. J. Macdonald, B.A., LL.B., LL.M., Professor of Law, University of Toronto.

[1]T. T. Brown, *The Enigma of Drug Addiction* (Springfield, Ill., 1961); Marshall B. Clinard, *Sociology of Deviant Behaviour* (New York, 1960)—a very useful book on a wide range of related matters; ch. 10 deals with drug addiction; D. Abrahamsen, *The Psychology of Crime* (New York, 1960)—considers personality, family tension, and psychosomatic disorders in the derangement of the criminal; emphasizes rehabilitation and detention; pp. 293–5 deal with drug addiction, especially Detroit projects; M. L. Harvey and J. C. Cross, *The Informer in Law Enforcement* (Springfield, Ill., 1961)—deals mostly with narcotic law enforcement; Burke Shartel and Marcus Plant, *The Law of Medical Practice* (Springfield, Ill., 1959)—provides medical men with essential notions of the way U.S. law bears on their professional activities; pp. 304–24 deal helpfully with narcotics; L. Uhr and J. Miller (eds.), *Drugs and Behaviour* (New York, 1960)—collection of fifty-one essays; F. Sondern, *Brotherhood of Evil: The Mafia* (London, 1959)—on organized crime and the narcotics traffic in the U.S.

[2]Interim and Final Reports of the Joint Committee of the American Bar Association and the American Medical Association on Narcotic Drugs, *Drug Addiction: Crime or Disease* (Bloomington: Indiana U.P., 1961); State of California, Special Study Commission on Narcotics, *Interim Report*, Dec. 9, 1960 (Sacramento, 1960).

[3]Clarence L. Cooper, *The Scene* (London, 1960)—an ex-junkie shows not only the squalor, the fear, the pain, and the hunger of the addict but also his moments of ecstasy and, most important perhaps, the total moral vacuum in which his life is lived.

[4]D. P. Ausubel, "Controversial Issues in the Management of Drug Addiction; Legislation, Ambulatory Treatment and the British System" (1960), 44 *Mental Hygiene* 535; D. J. Cantor, "The Criminal Law and the Narcotic Problem" (1961), 51 *J. Crim. Law Criminology & Pol. Sc.* 512; J. David, "Hard Hearts and Heroin" (1960), 15 *Int. Crim. Pol. Rev.* 233; J. L. Harvey *et al.*, Symposium on drugs and modern society (1961), 6 *J. Forensic Sci.* 1–87; G. Nadeau and G. Subolewski, "Tolerance to Drugs, Especially to Morphine" (1960), 186 *Nature* 169; J. Nepote, "Drug Addiction and Traffic" (1960), 15 *Int. Crim. Pol. Rev.*

large. Yet it is encouraging to note that recent developments mark important advances in the fight against this social evil. In this regard a number of items may be referred to. There is, for example, the single convention on narcotics signed in New York on March 25, 1961;[6] the United Nations discovery of a new method for pinpointing the country, and the region within the country, from which opium is smuggled;[7] the tests that are being made in the United States on a new analgesic that is not liable to lead to addiction;[8] the claim by a Seattle researcher that a natural body chemical named DPN (diphosphopyridine nucleotide) has enabled addicts to stop using narcotics immediately and permanently, without experiencing withdrawal agonies or unfavourable side effects;[9] and the decline, which may eventually lead to non-use, in the employment of opium and its derivatives in medical practice. In Canada, however, the most important recent development in the narcotics field has been

198; M. Ploscowe, "Methods of Treatment of Drug Addiction," in G. O. W. Mueller (ed.), *Essays in Criminal Science* (London, 1961), p. 357; H. A. Rosenfeld, "On Drug Addiction" (1960), *Int. J. Psycho-Anal.* 467; E. M. Schur, "British Narcotics Policies" (1961), 51 *J. Crim. Law Criminology & Pol. Sc.* 619; E. M. Schur, "Drug Addiction in America and England" (1960), 30 *Commentary* 241–8, with a reply at p. 531 by M. L. Harvey, formerly of the Illinois Division of Narcotic Control, and at p. 532 by Stanley Budner, a member of the N.Y. State Psychiatric Institute, and a rejoinder by E. M. Schur at p. 534; R. L. Wolk and M. H. Diskind, "Personality Dynamics of Mothers and Wives of Drug Addicts" (1961), 7 *Crime and Delinquency* 148; G. Yates, "The Control of Narcotic Drugs" (1960), 14 *W. H. O. Chronicle* 309. Very extensive bibliographies appear in (1959) 11 *Bulletin on Narcotics*, no. 2, p. 30, and in no. 3, p. 30.

[5]There has been much concern recently in Ontario and B.C. about alleged increases in crime, corruption, labour racketeering, narcotics trafficking, and prostitution. R.C.M.P. Commissioner Clifford Harrison states in his 1961 report that international crime syndicates are active in Canada and that they pose "an extremely serious problem." Evidence of the gravity of the situation is the fact that in May, 1961, an international conference of police officials was held in Toronto to co-ordinate operations aimed at stamping out gambling and narcotics syndicates.

[6]See, for example, L. M. Goodrich, "New Trends in Narcotics Control" (1960), 530 *Int. Conciliation* 181; R. W. Gregg, "The Single Convention for Narcotic Drugs" (1961), 16 *Food Drug Cosm. L. J.* 187.

[7]The *New York Times*, Sunday, June 4, 1961, p. 3, col. 5.

[8]*Ibid.*, May 28, 1961, p. 2, col. 5, reporting on a paper delivered by Dr. L. B. Witkin of CIBA Pharmaceutical Products, Summit, N.J., to the American Societies for Experimental Biology.

[9]Paul O'Hollaren, "Diphosphopyridine Nucleotide in the Prevention, Diagnosis and Treatment of Drug Addiction: A Preliminary Report" (1961), 69 *Western J. Surgery, Obstet. & Gyn.* 213. Dr. O'Hollaren's research was conducted at the Shadel Hospital, Seattle, Wash.

the passage of the Narcotic Control Act[10] by the House of Commons on June 12, 1961. In addition to repealing the Opium and Narcotic Drug Act,[11] which was Canada's basic legislation in the area for over forty years, the new statute separates criminal enforcement from legal distribution aspects, introduces new offences and stiffer penalties, and, most significantly, substitutes for mere imprisonment the idea of committing addicts to custody for treatment in special centres. The statute eliminates archaic provisions that appeared in the old Act, such as those on opium pipes, brings forward a new definition of "narcotic addict," makes possession mean possession as defined in the Criminal Code, and encourages enactment of provincial legislation under which non-criminal addicts can submit voluntarily to the federal committal procedure, thereby securing the benefit of treatment. The legislation puts at rest, temporarily at least, the extensive debates that have been raging over what Canada's policy on the matter should be;[12] and though many months must pass before the statute's effectiveness can be evaluated, there is no doubt that the thinking behind it represents an improvement over what we have had in the past. The Act incidentally is an interesting example of the impact that the Canadian Bill of Rights[13] can have on legislation which touches sensitive areas of personal freedom. The object of the following remarks is simply to describe the above-mentioned changes in the light of the writer's discussion of addiction in this series last year.[14] It may be helpful at the outset to point out that the basis of the new statute was analysed during a series of especially valuable

[10]In force as of Sept. 15, 1961, *excepting ss. 15–19 inclusive*: *Canada Gazette*, Saturday, Aug. 26, 1961, p. 2953.

[11]R.S.C. 1952, c. 201, amended 2 & 3 Eliz. II, c. 38 (Can., 1954).

[12]A special committee of the Anglican Church of Canada reported on the matter regularly and in an excellent final report, the result of five years' study, urged establishment of treatment centres: *Narcotic Addiction, A Report Prepared by the General Synod Committee on Narcotics* (Toronto, 1960). The Catholic Women's League have debated the topic off and on, and now favour treatment centres: *Canadian Register*, Sept. 24, 1960, p. 3, as does the National Council of Jewish Women, which recommends that such institutions be situated in metropolitan areas: *Montreal Gazette*, Tuesday, June 6, 1961, p. 9, col. 3.

[13]Stat. Can. 1960, c. 44.

[14]R. St. J. Macdonald, "Narcotic Drug Addiction in Canada" in *Current Law and Social Problems* Vol. I (1960), p. 162.

debates in the House of Commons in May-June, 1961, and that the Minister of Justice, Hon. E. D. Fulton, and the Minister of National Health and Welfare, Hon. J. W. Monteith, at that time made full submissions on governmental thinking about narcotic problems generally.[15] The writer has turned enthusiastically to these sources when the words of the Act have been found not to carry their own explanation on their face.

I

THE ORIGIN of the new legislation is the Senate Report of 1955.[16] It will be remembered that a special committee of the Senate made an investigation into the narcotic drug traffic in Canada and problems related thereto, and that, on June 23, 1955, the committee handed down a comprehensive report which contained a number of recommendations for suppressing the illicit traffic. In 1957 a measure described as Bill D, an Act to provide for the Control of Narcotic Drugs, was introduced in the Senate to implement these recommendations.[17] This bill was passed in the Senate and was given first reading in the Commons before Parliament dissolved in the spring of 1957. Its reintroduction was delayed, however, because there was need for further study of the problem,[18] particularly of measures for treating addicts, and because federal elections took place in 1957 and 1958. Hence it was not until January 24, 1961, that the Minister of Justice was able to announce, in an important policy statement,[19] that the government had approved a new approach to drug addiction in Canada. The Narcotic Control Act

[15] *House of Commons Debates*, CV, Wednesday, June 7, 1961, pp. 5977–6007; Monday, June 12, 1961, pp. 6203–19. See too the address by Hon. J. W. Monteith to the Canadian Arthritis and Rheumatism Society in Toronto on April 14, 1961 (mimeo.).

[16] *Proceedings of the Special Committee on the Traffic in Narcotic Drugs in Canada* (Ottawa, 1955).

[17] *Debates of the Senate*, CIV, Jan. 9, 1957, p. 5 (first reading); March 6, 1957, pp. 317–22 (second reading); March 7, 1957, p. 330 (report of committee); March 12, 1957, p. 348 (third reading).

[18] See *House of Commons Debates*, CII, Jan. 9, 1958, pp. 3102–5, 3107–10, esp. statement by Mr. Fulton at p. 3108. There was an inconclusive debate on the topic in the Senate on July 3 and 10, 1958: *Debates of the Senate*, CVI, pp. 256–9, 307–9.

[19] *House of Commons Debates*, CV, Tuesday, Jan. 24, 1961, p. 1344.

followed four months later and is thus seen to be based upon the Senate Report and Bill D, as revised in the light of experience acquired in the intervening years.

The statute is divided into two parts. Part I, entitled Offences and Enforcement, comprises sections 3–14 inclusive, and is the responsibility of the Minister of National Health and Welfare. Part II, entitled Preventive Detention and Custody for Treatment, includes sections 12–21, and attracts the primary responsibility of the Minister of Justice. Narcotic legislation has traditionally been the responsibility of the health ministry but the responsibility of the Minister of Justice arises in connection with the enforcement of the control measures, the apprehension and detention of those who break the law, and the custody and treatment of those who are convicted of such offences. It will be convenient to start with the particular offences enumerated in Part I. Sections 3–6 inclusive set out the following five particular offences: unauthorized possession of narcotics, trafficking, possession for the purpose of trafficking, illegal importation or exportation, and cultivation of opium or marihuana without authority.

II

Possession

Simple possession of a narcotic in any form except as authorized by the Act or regulations continues to be an indictable offence under section 3. Every person guilty of the offence is liable to imprisonment for seven years. This maximum is the same as that provided previously by the old Opium and Narcotic Drug Act,[20] but the new statute drops the old mandatory minimum of six months' imprisonment.[21] Except as provided for proven addicts under Part II, as will be mentioned presently, no mandatory minimum is imposed. It will now be possible for the court to suspend sentence for a non-addict found in simple possession. This is a small though certainly not unimportant advance over the corresponding provision in the old statute.

[20]R.S.C. 1952, c. 201, s. 4(1)(d), s. 4(1)(g)(i).
[21]*Ibid.*, s. 4(1)(g)(ii).

Trafficking and Possession for Purposes of Trafficking

Section 4(1) provides that no person shall traffic in a narcotic or any substance represented or held out by him to be a narcotic. Section 4(2) provides that no person shall have in his possession any narcotic for the purpose of trafficking. There are thus the separate offences of trafficking and possession for the purpose of trafficking. Trafficking is defined to include the unauthorized selling, giving, administering, delivering, or distributing of narcotics,[22] and it follows that possession for that purpose is related to trafficking, with some procedural differences that will be noted regarding its proof. It is obvious that in the charge of possession for the purpose of trafficking an important element is the quantity of narcotics found and the circumstances in which it was found: this substantially has been the criterion in narcotic enforcement. Every person who violates either subsection (1) or (2) of section 4 is guilty of an indictable offence and is liable to imprisonment for life.[23] This is a significant increase in the severity of the penalty, especially for first offenders, and carries forward a "get tough" policy inaugurated some years ago. The Senate Report recommended that trafficking, regardless of purpose, should be made a costly and hazardous undertaking in terms of penalty. It also advised that there be mandatory minimums for second or subsequent trafficking offences. In 1952 the penalty for trafficking was seven years maximum, upon indictment.[24] In 1954 the statute was amended to make the trafficker liable upon conviction to imprisonment for a term not exceeding fourteen years and, at the judge's discretion, to be whipped.[25] No sentence of more than fourteen years could be imposed upon a second or subsequent conviction. Probation could be granted to first offenders. By contrast, the new Act now provides for life imprisonment as the maximum punishment. The court has thus been given an almost complete discretion to impose, within the maximum, whatever penalty is most appropriate in the individual case. Probation continues to be available in

[22] S. 2(i).
[23] S. 4(3).
[24] *Ibid.*, s. 4(1)(f).
[25] 2 & 3 Eliz. II, c. 38 (Can. 1954), s. 3.

proper cases for first offenders. And, since, as will be mentioned, Part II controls section 4, a person convicted for trafficking for the second time will be sentenced to detention for an indeterminate period, during which period he could be committed for treatment. Whether or not there should be a minimum sentence for a first trafficking offence remains to be seen. It might be argued that would-be traffickers should be given very clear notice that there is a heavy minimum and that they could not expect release until its elapse. On the other hand, wiser policy probably declares that the courts be allowed the wide discretion they now enjoy, and that they take a reasonable time to work out the strengths and weaknesses of the new legislation. More important perhaps is the fact that, since professional peddlers frequently use adolescents as pushers, it would be unduly harsh, and not strike at the root of the problem, to impose a heavy minimum upon these young people.

The object of increasing the trafficking penalty is to deter and punish: "to indicate to the courts, the country as a whole and the traffickers themselves the detestation in which this crime is held and to provide the courts with sufficient means of ordering detention in the case of these offences."[26] There was not unanimous agreement, however, that the change went far enough. During debate on second reading, and later in committee, Mr. John Drysdale, the Progressive Conservative member for Burnaby-Richmond, argued that the provision for life imprisonment was insufficient and that, especially in the case of a trafficker who is not a user himself, the death sentence should have been included as an alternative.[27] In urging that "we have here the most obvious case for the maximum deterrent," he adopted the following language of Mr. Harold Winch, C.C.F. member for Vancouver-East: "A murderer kills and that is it. But one who traffics in drugs, who brings a person to addiction, to that insatiable craziness, makes an absolute hourly and daily hell for life for the addict. I, therefore, have no sympathy for him. . . ."[28] Mr. Drysdale also said that he took the position he did

[26]*House of Commons Debates*, CV, June 12, 1961, p. 6216 (statement of Hon. E. D. Fulton).

[27]*Ibid.*, p. 6214.

[28]*Ibid.*, p. 6214.

"because I am unable to see the necessity or justification for the state maintaining that type of individual at a cost of $2,000 per year which, if applied to a life sentence of 10 or 20 years, would amount to $20,000 or $40,000 respectively."[29] In supporting the Drysdale amendment, which was rejected by a vote of 44-7, the Conservative member for Vancouver-Kingsway, Mr. J. F. Browne, suggested that since the House had previously accepted the idea that capital punishment should be retained in Canada as a unique deterrent, consistency required that this deterrent be applied to trafficking.[30] Mr. Fulton, however, expressing the Government's view, said that during the debate on capital punishment the House approved "that generally speaking the grounds for capital punishment should be restricted rather than enlarged. I know that it is still a potential penalty for those guilty of treason or piracy but broadly speaking capital punishment is now restricted to those who kill as a result of planning and deliberation. We think it would be completely inconsistent with that principle to enlarge the types of crimes to which capital punishment is now applicable so as to include trafficking in narcotics."[31] He went on to remind the committee that a person convicted of trafficking on a second or any subsequent offence is liable to an indeterminate sentence under Part II, the effect being that he would be under supervision for life even if he should be paroled.[32] Discussion of the (for Canada) revolutionary point that traffickers may be eligible for treatment will be postponed until we come to section 17(1) under Part II of the Act.

The important procedure that must be followed in prosecuting traffickers is set out in section 8, which reproduces the substance of the old section 4(4). It is now provided that in any prosecution for violating section 4(2)—possession for the purpose of trafficking—if the accused does not plead guilty, the trial shall proceed as if it were a prosecution for simple possession under section 3, and after the close of the prosecutor's case and the accused's defence, the court shall determine whether the accused was in possession contrary to

[29]*Ibid.*, June 7, 1961, p. 6000.
[30]*Ibid.*, June 12, 1961, p. 6215.
[31]*Ibid.*, p. 6216.
[32]*Ibid.*, p. 6216.

section 3; if he was not, he shall be acquitted; but if he was in possession contrary to section 3 he shall be given an opportunity to establish that he was not in possession for the purpose of trafficking, and thereafter the prosecutor shall be given an opportunity to prove the contrary; if the accused proves that he was not in possession for the purpose of trafficking he shall be acquitted of the offence charged but shall be convicted under section 3; if he fails so to prove he shall be convicted under section 4(2) and sentenced accordingly. Additionally, section 7(2) provides that in any prosecution under the Act the burden is on the accused to prove that an exemption or qualification prescribed by law operates in his favour. During debate on the bill in committee, Hon. Paul Martin, former Liberal Minister of National Health and Welfare, raised the question whether these provisions violate section 2(f) of the Canadian Bill of Rights, which provides for retention of the common law principle of presumption of innocence. He argued that when the accused is found to be in simple possession the effect of section 8 is to establish a presumption of guilt, which is contrary to the Bill of Rights. He insisted that in cases where the accused is found to be in possession the onus continues to rest on the Crown, and he suggested a reference to the Supreme Court of Canada to test the presumption's constitutional validity.[33] Mr. Martin's explanation was widely reported in the press, much to the chagrin of Mr. Fulton, who thought that a perverse interpretation of technical law was being exploited for partisan political purposes.

Though many solicitors seem to share Mr. Martin's view there really does not appear to be anything more novel than the familiar rebuttal presumption in section 8, nor, as will be shown, can it be said now that the statute containing the presumption is unconstitutional as offensive to the Bill of Rights. The disputable presumption is an old and necessary device in the law of evidence, its reach including, as here, the possession of property which is normally

[33]*Ibid.*, p. 6218. This was the second time that Mr. Martin had raised the point. He first raised it in connection with the "goofball" legislation (an Act to amend the Food and Drugs Act, Bill C–99, proclaimed Saturday, Aug. 26, 1961, in force Sept. 15, 1961: *Canada Gazette*, Saturday, Aug. 26, 1961, p. 2952), and his main argument may be found in *House of Commons Debates*, CV, Tuesday, May 30, 1961, p. 5621 ff.

possessed or acquired unlawfully, the possession of which is made presumptive evidence of unlawful acquisition. Such devices define the amount of evidence necessary to support a particular allegation, but are open to rebuttal by countervailing evidence, and often are said to be conclusive in the absence of such evidence.[34] Mr. Fulton, moreover, was able to call in aid the case of *R.* v. *Guertin*,[35] where the Ontario Court of Appeal denied that section 80 of the Criminal Code (possession of explosives) infringes the presumption of innocence preserved by the Bill of Rights, and he assured the committee that he had the bill in mind when section 8 was drafted.[36] More pertinent, however, is that the same court has considered the very point Mr. Martin raised, the judgment not having been reported in time for use by the House committee. In *Regina* v. *Sharpe*[37] the accused alleged that the onus placed upon him by the old section 4(4) and the presumption created by the old section 17(1) contravened section 2(f) of the Bill of Rights. In rejecting the allegation, the late Mr. Justice Morden stated the law simply and accurately as follows:

> The burden resting upon the Crown in a criminal case of proving the accused guilty of a reasonable doubt is a matter of substantive law and never shifts from the Crown. In contrast to this, the secondary burden—that of adducing evidence—may shift in the course of a trial depending upon the evidence adduced. The existence of these two burdens and the relation between them is well established in criminal law. . . .
>
> The statutory burdens or presumptions raised by s. 4(4) and s. 17 assist the prosecution by shifting the secondary burden, the burden of

[34]For an excellent discussion see Paul Brosman, "The Statutory Presumption" (1930), 5 *Tulane L.R.* 17, at p. 178. Prof. Edmond Cahn treats of the presumption of innocence generally in *The Moral Decision* (Bloomington, Ind., 1956), chap. 10.

[35][1961] O.W.N. 134. He also cited cases in which the Supreme Court of the United States held that a statute does not deny the equal protection of the law or otherwise fail in due process of law because it creates a presumption of liability, since its operation is only to supply an inference of liability in the absence of other evidence contradicting such inference. These references were made during debate on the "goofball" legislation, but the issue was identical to that referred to above in connection with the narcotic bill: *House of Commons Debates*, CV, Tuesday, June 6, 1961, p. 5952. The cases cited were *Mobile Jackson & Kansas City Railroad Co.* v. *J. A. Turnipseed* (1910), 219 U.S. 35 and *Yee Hem* v. *United States* (1925), 268 U.S. 178.

[36]This once again was during debate on the "goofball" rather than narcotic legislation: *House of Commons Debates*, *supra* note 35, p. 5942.

[37][1961] O.W.N. 261.

adducing evidence, to the accused after evidence is adduced by the prosecution of the basic facts which raise the presumption under s. 17 and a finding of possession is made under s. 4(4). An accused is not required to discharge the burden placed upon him beyond a reasonable doubt. He can do this upon a balance of probabilities: *Rex* v. *Carefoot*, [1948] O.W.N. 281, at pp. 285–6 and cases there cited. After all the evidence has been heard, if in the mind of the Court a reasonable doubt of guilt exists, the accused must be acquitted: *Reg.* v. *Capello*.... In my opinion, the impugned sections of the Opium and Narcotic Drug Act do not deprive an accused of the benefit of the presumption of innocence.

It is interesting to note that the U.S. Supreme Court has on many occasions held that statutory presumptions similar to those I have been considering are not a denial of due process of law guaranteed by the 5th and 14th amendments provided that there is a rational connection in common experience between the fact proved and the ultimate fact presumed: *Adams* v. *N.Y.* (1903), 192 U.S. 585, *Yee Hem* v. *U.S.* (1925), 268 U.S. 178, *W. & Atl. R.* v. *Henderson* (1929), 279 U.S. 639, *Tot* v. *U.S.* (1943), 319 U.S. 463, *Cooley*, Constitutional Limitations, 8th ed., pp. 639–642.[38]

It will be observed that in the passages quoted above the court merely denies without reasons that the application of the particular statute works a deprivation of the presumption of innocence. Reasons may have been unnecessary since it is certainly not obvious how rebuttable presumptions as they are applied in criminal cases today curtail the innocence referred to in the phrase "presumption of innocence." It will be seen too that a mere "note" was taken of the fact that the rational connection test has been used by the Supreme Court of the United States in relating presumption of innocence and due process. The Ontario judgment does not accept or reject that test. Since some measure of content has yet to be poured into the due process provision in the Canadian Bill[39] one cannot say how Canadian courts will consider the presumption in

[38]*Ibid.*, at pp. 262, 263. For periodical discussion of presumptions as they pertain to narcotics cases see J. C. Martin, "The Burden of Proof as Affected by Statutory Presumptions of Guilt" (1939), 17 *Can. Bar Rev.* 37; D. E. Jabour, "Onus of Proof in Narcotics Cases" (1961), 4 *Can. Bar. J.* 4. See too *Reg.* v. *Goldstein* (1961), 34 W.W.R. 236 (B.C. Mag. Court).

[39]Suggestive leads can be found in I. C. Rand, "Except by Due Process of Law" (1961), 2 *Osgoode Hall L.J.* 171; see too generally the symposium on the Bill of Rights in (1959), 37 *Can. Bar Rev.* 1–237, esp. remarks of Albert S. Abel at p. 147 ff.

the light of the constitutional provision. It is worth pointing out, however, that an eminent American authority disapproves of the rational connection test and advocates adoption of a different theory.[40]

Importation or Exportation of Narcotics

Section 5(1) establishes the new offence of illegal importation or exportation. It is well known that there is hardly any diversion of drugs from legal sources in Canada into the illicit traffic and that were it not for smuggled drugs there would be no trafficking problem in this country. The Senate committee recognized this and recommended establishing a special offence of illicit importation with an effective mandatory minimum penalty. Accordingly section 5(1) makes it an indictable offence to import into Canada or export from Canada any narcotic except as authorized by the Act or the regulations. Persons violating the provision are liable under section 5(2) to a maximum penalty of life imprisonment and a mandatory minimum of seven years. Exportation from Canada is penalized in the same way as importation because of the fact that narcotics often are smuggled into Canada for subsequent transhipment to the United States. This provision is in keeping with Canada's international obligations. The object of the new offence is deterrence and punishment. The penalties provided are heavy but, as with traffickers, of which they are only a particular class, illegal importers and exporters are subject to the principles of Part II.

Cultivation of Opium

The last offence enumerated in Part I is contained in section 6. It is there provided that no person shall cultivate opium poppy or marihuana except under licence issued under the regulations. Every person violating the provision is guilty of an indictable offence and is liable to imprisonment for seven years. Licences probably would be issued only for experimental scientific purposes. Though it is possible that a few people may be growing marihuana illegally on a small scale in parts of Canada, it is difficult to imagine this section generating much judicial activity. On the other hand, the addict's

[40]Charles T. McCormick, *Handbook of the Law of Evidence* (St. Paul, Minn., 1954), pp. 655–63 (an excellent discussion).

inventiveness is not to be underestimated: it was recently reported that a Greenwich Village resident eluded the police for months by choosing Washington Square Park to cultivate his personal plot of marihuana!

III

THE NEW SEARCH, seizure, and forfeiture provisions are somewhat more detailed than those which appeared in the Opium and Narcotic Drug Act. Under section 10, a peace officer may, at any time (*a*) without a warrant enter and search any place other than a dwelling house, and under the authority of a Writ of Assistance or a warrant issued under this section, enter and search any dwelling house in which he reasonably believes there is a narcotic in respect of which an offence under the Act has been committed; (*b*) search any person found in such place; and, (*c*) seize any narcotic found therein or anything in which he reasonably suspects a narcotic is contained. A magistrate who is satisfied that there are reasonable grounds for believing that there is a narcotic there present may issue a warrant authorizing a peace officer "at any time to enter the dwelling house and search for narcotics"; and upon the Minister's application a judge of the Exchequer Court of Canada must issue a Writ of Assistance empowering the person named "at any time to enter any dwelling house and search for narcotics." A peace officer may "break open any door, window, . . . floor, wall, ceiling, compartment, . . . or any other thing." And though, as will be mentioned, there is a provision on restoration of articles seized, there is no section on payment for damage caused by the Crown. Where this leaves the innocent householder whose house has been "searched" by a peace officer has not been decided by the courts. "Our policy is where it is the federal police carrying out the enforcement of a federal statute if the premises of the innocent person are injured or damaged in the course of executing a warrant, and if the damage is minor we make restitution at once; if the damage should be major, then the matter is referred to the minister or to the deputy minister of justice for a submission to treasury board with regard to restitution. That is the policy with respect to an innocent person."[41]

[41]*House of Commons Debates*, *supra* note 26, at p. 6219 (statement of Mr. Fulton).

The foregoing provisions touch upon basic problems which the courts probably will be invited to consider in detail in the years ahead, and which certainly are too complex to examine in a short paper such as this.[42] The writer would point out, however, that apart from the fact that the police power of search and seizure is not as precise in Canada as it might be[43] and that this new statute can be expected to produce its fair share of cases on illegally obtained evidence, resort to the aforementioned writ of assistance calls for careful scrutiny as well as raised eyebrows. This writ takes its name from the fact that it commanded all the king's subjects to aid in its enforcement when requested to do so by the person holding it.[44] Objectionable, however, is the fact that such writs were wholly general in character and did not relate to specific persons, places, or things to be searched or seized. Further, they were not returnable, but extended as continuing authority until six months following the death of the monarch in whose reign they were issued. It is generally conceded historical fact that use of these writs in colonial America prompted the Fourth Amendment.[45] In Canada provision has been made for the writ of assistance in narcotics

[42]Professor Paulsen of Columbia puts it this way: "Two points must be remembered. The rules restricting the police do not exist simply to protect against the inconvenience of police intrusion. The rules have a symbolic value of highest importance. They affirm the dignity of the human being. Even the meanest of us is of such worth that he ought to be treated not as a mere object but as a creation of God. The rules are part of the detail by which this moral insight is mirrored in reality. The second point is related. We must not see the problems of the administration of criminal justice as a battle between the legions of Crime and the armies of the Good. There can be no special exceptions for the bad from the regulations which protect the worthwhile. As surely as we fail to protect the worst in an even-handed manner, we will prove unable to safeguard the best. As Mr. Justice Frankfurter has written, 'The impact of a sordid little case is apt to obscure the implications of the generalization to which the case gives rise.' By recognizing through law the human worth of the law breaker we assert the dignity of all." M. G. Paulsen, "Safeguards in the Law of Search and Seizure" (1957), 52 *Northwestern U. L. Rev.* 65, at p. 67.

[43]See now the recent cases *Re a Search Warrant by Salteria, J.P.; Schumiatcher* v. *A.G. of Saskatchewan and Salterio, J.P.*, [1960] 33 W.W.R. 132 (Sask. Q.B.); *Re a Search Warrant by Bence, J.P.; Schumiatcher* v. *A.G. of Saskatchewan, Bence, J.P. and Mathews*, [1960] 33 W.W.R. 134 (Sask. Q.B.). For the U.K. see Patrick Devlin, *The Criminal Prosecution in England* (Oxford, 1960), pp. 53–6.

[44]Osmond K. Fraenkel, "Concerning Searches and Seizures" (1920–1), 34 *Harv. L.R.* 361 is a lucid exposition.

[45]See, for example, Charles A. Reynard, "The Right of Privacy," in A. L. Harding (ed.), *Fundamental Law in Criminal Prosecutions* (Dallas, Texas, 1959), p. 85.

legislation, the Excise Act, and the Customs Act. In the context of the present discussion, however, the question remains whether an authorization by the Exchequer Court amounts to a blank cheque. Once issued, will the writ enable the person named therein to examine the premises of anyone, anywhere, in any part of Canada, at any time?[46]

Where a narcotic or other thing has been seized under section 10(1) any person entitled to possession may apply to a magistrate for an order of restoration, which may be granted if certain conditions are satisfied. But where a person has been convicted of an offence under sections 3, 4, or 5, any narcotic, money, hypodermic needle, or other apparatus used in connection with the offence is forfeited automatically to the Crown. This is because those items form part of the commission of the actual offence. On the other hand, where a person has been convicted under section 4 or 5, the court may order that any conveyance seized under section 10(1) that has been used in connection with the offence be forfeited. It will be noted that the court has a discretion here, there being no automatic forfeiture as there was under section 21 of the Opium and Narcotic Drug Act. The old provision was designed to impede the mobility of traffickers, and though the new section would appear to have the same object it necessarily was toned down because of the Bill of ights. Since owners, mortgagees, lien-holders, and holders of other interests in the conveyance may be prejudiced by the forfeiture, section 11 now sets out a procedure whereby such innocent persons may obtain protection for their interests. As Mr. Fulton explained, this is another case where

> the government has been careful to revise such provisions and bring them into conformity with the bill of rights. The drafting of such legislation, motivated on the one hand by the proper desire to be severe with those who commit offences . . . or those who permit their property to be used and are careless whether or not their property or property in which they have an interest is used to facilitate the commission of an offence, presents a difficult problem from the point of view of being certain you do not go so far as to deprive an innocent party of his property without an opportunity to have a hearing before the courts.[47]

[46]A query raised by Hon. Paul Martin in *House of Commons Debates, supra* note 33, at p. 5626.

[47]*Ibid.*, June 7, 1961, p. 5988.

IV

IT IS in Part II of the statute that the sweep of the new policy reveals itself. Section 15 provides that where for the second time a person is convicted of trafficking, possession for the purpose of trafficking, or illegal importing or exporting, or where he has previously been sentenced to preventive detention under this section, the court must sentence him to preventive detention in a penitentiary for an indeterminate period, in lieu of any other sentence that might be imposed for the offence committed.

Section 16 provides that where a person is charged under sections 3, 4, or 5, the court may, upon application by the Crown or the person charged or his counsel, either before or after he is committed for trial and before any sentence is passed, remand him to custody for examination for not more than seven days. And, under section 17(1) where the person who has been so remanded is convicted, the court must, before sentencing him, consider the evidence from the examination, together with medical evidence, and if the court is satisfied that he is a narcotic addict, it must, despite section 15, sentence him to custody for treatment for an indeterminate period in lieu of any other sentence for the offence of which he was convicted. It is here that one sees, for the first time, that federal legislation recognizes addicts as patients, that it regards addiction as something more complex than criminal indulgence, and that it abandons the threadbare belief in the efficacy of punishment simpliciter. Sections 16 and 17 come to this: if those charged are not addicts they will be sentenced under sections 3, 4, and 5; if they are addicts they will be treated for their addiction, and this will be so whether the addict is a trafficker or not. If, for example, a trafficker is found to be an addict he should be sentenced to custody for treatment instead of being sentenced (possibly) to life imprisonment under section 4(3). The trafficker who peddles primarily to pay the cost of his own addiction is still considered to be no less a menace to society while at large than the trafficker who peddles for profit: both are involved in spreading the drug habit. But the addict peddler is a sick person—peddling is his particular method of meeting the demands of his illness—and one welcomes the fact that he is now officially regarded in terms of his addiction rather than of his peddling.[48]

Where a person is sentenced to custody for treatment for an indeterminate period, he will be placed, under section 18, in an institution operated under the Penitentiary Act and become subject to the Parole Act. If he has not previously been convicted under the narcotic statute, the length of his sentence for treatment is fixed by the Parole Board, but cannot exceed ten years from the time of his parole, unless before then his parole is forfeited or revoked. Parole, however, is only permitted when the board says that it is in the interest of society to release the inmate. The institutions to which persons will be committed to custody for treatment are not further menioned in the Act, but Mr. Fulton explained to the House that eventually they will be separate centres for treatment where it may be possible to treat non-criminal as well as criminal addicts.[49] In this regard, section 19 stipulates that where a provincial legislature provides for treatment for non-criminal addicts, the minister may enter into an agreement with the province for confining and treating such persons in federal institutions. This important provision reflects Parliament's concern that the gap be closed between what should be done and what federal legislation constitutionally can do. It will be recalled that Parliament's jurisdiction in the area is limited to criminal law, more particularly to the apprehension and treatment of criminals who happen to be addicts. Matters relating to health and welfare, and to juvenile delinquency,[50] a prime cause of addiction, as well as the treatment of addicts who are about to become criminals, are entirely within the provincial domain. It was

48The ambivalence of current views on how the addict-peddler should be treated is examined generally by R. R. Korn and L. W. McCorkle, *Criminology and Penology* (New York, 1960), at pp. 171–4.

49*House of Commons Debates*, June 7, 1961, p. 5987. The first centre will be about 20 minutes from downtown Vancouver to take advantage of the city's professional talents for treatment. Later, similar institutions will be built for Ontario and Quebec.

50During the Sept., 1961, meetings of the Canadian Bar Association in Winnipeg, Mr. Fulton announced that the Department of Justice was about to launch a full-scale study of juvenile delinquency. For a helpful resumé of recent literature on the subject see R. G. Andry, *Delinquency and Parental Pathology, A Study in Forensic and Clinical Psychology* (London, 1960), at pp. 135–50.

thus to encourage provincial co-operation, without which the Fulton plan cannot succeed, that section 19 was included.

To return for a moment to the federal centres for treatment. It must be appreciated that the institutions contemplated are not for entrants who can go voluntarily on terms arranged between themselves and the institutions. They are centres to which addicts will be committed as a result of the criminal procedure. The statute states that they will be operated under the authority of the Penitentiary Act, which means that they will have a definite element of custody though the purpose of the custody is treatment. The government has not overlooked the question of voluntary treatment for non-criminal addicts, however. Though it cannot act directly on the question, that once more being a local responsibility, it has in mind the possibility of assisting the provinces, perhaps under the health grants programme, to set up treatment centres to which persons might go voluntarily.[51] These centres would be quite separate, physically and administratively, from the federal institutions for the obvious reason that two different types of inmates are involved.

V

THE NARCOTIC CONTROL ACT is an enlightened response to the acknowledged fact that despite the best efforts of the R.C.M.P. the old policy of punishment *per se* has been a failure. The new statute, to be sure, retains strong punitive aspects, as evidenced by sections 4 and 5, but it provides additionally for committal to custody for treatment in (eventually) new institutions where addicts will be separated from non-addicts. It provides too for specific federal-provincial co-operation, without which any plan can have little hope of success.[52] These are wholly new departures from the old programme. How they will work out in practice remains to be seen. For some addicts the new plan will mean a life-time of medical care.

[51] *House of Commons Debates, supra* note 26, at p. 6208.

[52] The Ontario government among others is most anxious to co-operate with Mr. Fulton. Its research facilities for alcoholism have been expanded to include drug addiction, and personnel for treating female addicts are now being trained under a pilot project at the Don Jail. *Toronto Daily Star*, Wednesday, Jan. 25, 1961, p. 17, col. 4.

The government, however, has nowhere suggested that treatment facilities alone can beat the addiction problem. Its spokesmen have underscored the need for a positive attitude on the part of the addict himself, the importance of after-care, rehabilitation, job-opportunities, subsequent assimilation into society, and so forth.[53] The new scheme takes into account many more relevant factors than the old one did, and it is hard to resist the conclusion that all in all this is one of the most advanced statutes of its kind in the world today. Lest we be overly optimistic about its chances of success, however, it is well to remind ourselves of the perplexity involved in effecting cures of addiction: human personalities usually have to be made over, the difficulty being that large areas of the human personality, like the phenomenon of addiction itself, remain utterly and absolutely mysterious. Lonely, rootless, anxious men who are uncertain of the reliability of their alliances with their fellows, and who all too often regard themselves as little more than cosmic trivialities, are beyond the reach of current therapies. For them humane treatment as anciently prescribed is just as effective as current techniques.[54]

[53]This point was stressed during the debates in the Commons and, outside the House, especially by Mr. Monteith: see his Toronto speech, *supra* note 15, p. 9.

[54]A more specific warning has been sounded by Prof. Ploscowe, whose recent observation (*supra* note 4, at p. 373) on United States Policy seems especially timely for Canadians. He writes as follows:

One of the foundations of the present policy for dealing with narcotic addiction . . . is that [it] must be treated in an institutional setting . . . [This] led to the establishment of the Lexington, Kentucky and the Fort Worth, Texas, installations maintained by the Federal government. It also led to the foundation of the Riverside Hospital for adolescent narcotic addicts in New York City. Those who established these institutions were undoubtedly buoyed by the hope that the institutional treatment would result in the rehabilitation of a substantial percentage of addicts. The founders of Lexington, Fort Worth and Riverside must have held the opinion that the combination of medical and psychiatric treatment, and social work, educational and vocational treatment could eliminate the curse of addiction to narcotic drugs from the patients admitted to their institutions. We have already noted the limited facilities for drug addicts provided by the aforementioned hospitals. If sound statistical studies were available on the relapse of drug addiction and they showed considerable percentages of success secured by institutional treatment, then the conclusion might well be drawn that better and more extensive hospital facilities were necessary for any rational drug control program. Unfortunately, sound, carefully conceived studies on a broad scale of the success or failure of hospital treatment of drug addicts have simply not been made. Whatever studies have been made present a somewhat discouraging picture of the possibility of preventing narcotic drug use by chronic addicts through current methods of hospital treatment.

www.ingramcontent.com/pod-product-compliance
Lightning Source LLC
Chambersburg PA
CBHW070632100726
47907CB00007B/1956

* 9 7 8 1 4 8 7 5 7 6 8 5 1 *